antal dorati
1906-1988

discography
and concert
register

compiled by
john hunt

Acknowledgment

These publications have been made possible by contributions or advance subscriptions from

Richard Ames
Yoshihiro Asada
Marc Bridle
Brian Capon
Robert Dandois
John Derry
Henry Fogel*
Peter Fülop
Jean-Pierre Goossens
Alan Haine
Tadashi Hasegawa*
Bodo Igesz
Rodney Kempster
Detlef Kissmann
Douglas MacIntosh
Carlo Marinelli
Bruce Morrison
Alan Newcombe
Jim Parsons*
David Patmore*
James Pearson
Ingo Schwarz
John Shackleton
Michael Tanner
Nigel Wood*

Stefano Angeloni
J.M. Blyth*
J. Camps-Ros
Edward Chibas*
Dennis Davis
Hans-Peter Ebner*
Nobuo Fukumoto
Philip Goodman
Johann Gratz
Michael Harris*
Naoya Hirabayashi
Andrew Keener
Koji Kinoshita
Elisabeth Legge-Schwarzkopf*
John Mallinson*
Philip Moores
W. Moyle
Hugh Palmer*
Laurence Pateman
J.A. Payne
Tully Potter
Tom Scragg*
Yoshihiko Suzuki*
Urs Weber*
Graeme Wright*

*indicates life subscriber

Antal Dorati 1906-1988
Published by John Hunt.
© 2004 John Hunt
reprinted 2009
ISBN 978-1-901395-16-7

Sole distributors:
Travis & Emery,
17 Cecil Court,
London, WC2N 4EZ,
United Kingdom.
(+44) 20 7 459 2129.
sales@travis-and-emery.com

Antal Dorati: an introduction
The year 2006 will see the centenary of the birth of Antal Dorati, whose conducting work in the recording studios of both Europe and America was systematically preserved by a flourishing classical music industry. This discography is a revision of my 1997 effort, where Dorati appeared in tandem with eminent colleagues from his Hungarian homeland Fritz Reiner and George Szell. Although establishing his own early career in the United States and securing a high reputation for the orchestras he conducted there, Dorati also retained stronger links with Europe than either of those compatriots. And more than either of them, certainly more than the opportunistic Georg Solti, did he promote the music of his contemporaries Bartok and Kodaly, both in concert hall and recording studio.

This is a discography perhaps less strong in individuality as far as the German classics are concerned. However, special claim must be made for the pioneering Haydn cycle, starting with the symphonies (Decca) but going on to embrace concerti, oratorios and ultimately the little-known operas. Even in the case of the Haydn symphonies, though, I personally sense more point and character in earlier versions of individual works with orchestras like the London Symphony, Philharmonia Hungarica and Festival (Bath) Chamber Orchestra. Dorati's orchestral recordings of Wagner and Strauss contain such strong cogency that one must regret that he did not record more complete operas. Indeed, after the early operatic experience in Münster, he tended to prefer performing opera in the concert hall rather than in the opera house (did Dorati already have some premonition of the horrors which modern stage directors would soon be inflicting on the great stage works?). And those other peaks of his recording work, the trio of Tchaikovsky ballets, must be singled out, with earlier Minneapolis versions standing above remakes from London and Amsterdam for their sense of real spontaneous theatricality.

The discography follows the familiar pattern in its layout, aiming to list as many European and American incarnations as possible in the various formats of 78, 45, LP, CD, VHS video and DVD video. More precise recording dates are now included, although it must be remembered that when sessions for a work or group of works extend over several days or even weeks, then recording did not necessarily take place on every intervening day in the period.

As far as the concert register is concerned, now appearing for the very first time after my previous forays into the public appearances of Wilhelm Furtwängler, Herbert von Karajan, Leopold Stokowski and Carlo Maria Giulini, I would not yet claim this to be complete. Dorati's important Dallas years in the later 1940s, for example, have remained elusive to my research, and I look forward to hearing from any readers who can add to any of the concert data. I also suspect that more appearances were made in France and Italy than those listed here. And even earlier, the pre-war period remains somewhat blurred because of the nomadic existence forced upon young musicians in Central Europe by the prevailing political considerations. Dorati himself never kept any systematic diaries, although he does mention numerous isolated assignments in his memoirs "Notes of Seven Decades" (Hodder and Stoughton 1979). I have therefore divided the section up to 1945 into two groups with the titles "The Kapellmeister years" and "The Ballet years".

Work on this project was stimulated by the reminiscences of Bill Newman, who supervised EMI's Mercury sessions with the London Symphony Orchestra in the late 1950s and 1960s, and by many a helpful comment from Philips Stuart, compiler of discographies of various London orchestras. I also extend my thanks (whilst retaining responsibility for any errors that remain) to Leslie Austin, Rudolf Bruil, Colin Butler, Leslie Czechowski, Detroit Symphony Orchestra, Michael Gray, Syd Gray, Bill Holland, Roderick Krüsemann, Andreas Kuster, London Symphony Orchestra, Municipal Archive Den Haag (Corien Glaudemans), National Symphony Orchestra Washington, Ed Novitsky, James Pearson, Philharmonia Orchestra, Radio Filharmonisch Orkest Holland (Natasja Kardos), Residentie Otkest (Marjan Waaijer), Royal Philharmonic Orchestra, Michael Ruppli, Nico Steffen, Joy Tonks and Malcolm Walker.

John Hunt 2004

Contents
The discography *page 5*
The concert register *page 125*
Late additions to the concert register: Radio Filharmonisch Orkest Holland *page 303*
Late additions to the concert register: Residentie Orkest Den Haag *page 305*

Antal Dorati: discography and concert register
Published and copyright 2004 by John Hunt
ISBN 1 901395 16 2
Printed by Short Run Press Exeter

antal dorati
the discography

ISAAC ALBENIZ (1860-1909)
iberia, suite arranged by arbos

minneapolis	minneapolis	lp: mercury MG 50146/SR 90007
21 april	symphony	lp: emi mercury MMA 11081/AMS 16002
1957		lp: mercury wing MGW 14063/MGW 14085/ SRW 18063/SRW 18085
		lp: mercury golden imports SRI 75101
		lp: philips (france) 839 816GSY
		cd: philips mercury 434 3832

excerpts
45: emi mercury XEP 9052

PETER VAN ANROOY (1879-1954)
piet hein rhapsody

amsterdam	residentie	78: philips N 12060 G
1953	orchestra	lp: philips S 06036 R
		lp: philips fontana 6530 044
		cd: philips 432 3902
		cd: philips dutch masters 462 1042

ANTON ARENSKY (1861-1906)
variations on a theme of tchaikovsky

vienna	philharmonia	lp: mercury MG 50200/MG 50346/ SR 90200/SR 90346
8 june	hungarica	lp: emi mercury MMA 11091/AMS 16040
1958		lp: philips K71-BC 800
		cd: philips mercury 434 3912

GEORGES AURIC (1899-1983)
ouverture

watford	london	lp: mercury MG 50435/SR 90435
6 august	symphony	lp: philips SAL 3637/838 434LY
1965		lp: philips mercury (france) 121 047MGY/ 131 047MSY
		lp: philips sequenza 412 0281
		cd: philips mercury 434 3352

JOHANN SEBASTIAN BACH (1685-1750)
air from the third suite, arranged for violin and orchestra

los angeles	hollywood	cd: doremi DHR 7736-7737
15 july	bowl symphony	
1947	elman, violin	
new york	columbia	vhs video: emi MVD 491 4753
1947	symphony	dvd video: emi DVB 492 3639
	menuhin, violin	

BELA BARTOK (1881-1945)
concerto for orchestra

minneapolis 23-24 december 1953	minneapolis symphony	lp: mercury MG 50033 lp: mercury (france) MLP 7526 lp: nixa mercury MRL 2521 lp: emi mercury MMA 11082 lp: concert hall CM 2300
wembley 3 july 1962	london symphony	lp: mercury MG 50378/SR 90378 lp: mercury golden imports SRI 75105 lp: mercury (france) 121 019MSL/131 019MSY lp: philips fontana grandioso 894 020ZKY cd: philips mercury 432 0172/475 6255
budapest august 1969	hungarian state symphony	lp: hungaroton LPX 11437/SLPX 11437/ CALB 42-47 cd: hungaroton HCD 11437/HCD 41002
new york 20 april 1975	national symphony	cd: disco archivia 1062
amsterdam 27-29 june 1983	concertgebouw orchestra	lp: philips 411 1321 cd: philips 411 1322/468 1552 cd: philips eloquence 464 1252

music for strings, percussion and celesta

wembley 5-7 june 1960	london symphony	lp: mercury SR 90515 lp: philips 6500 931 lp: philips sequenza 6527 139 cd: philips 426 6612 cd: philips mercury 434 3572/475 6255
detroit 14-16 november 1983	detroit symphony	lp: decca 411 8941 cd: decca 411 8942/448 2762

dance suite

vienna 10-11 june 1958	philharmonia hungarica	lp: mercury MG 50183/SR 90183/SR 90533 lp: emi mercury MMA 11121/AMS 16068 lp: mercury (france) 121 026MSL/131 026MSY lp: philips 6500 931/6768 600 cd: philips 426 6612 cd: philips mercury 432 0172/475 6255

bartok/**violin concerto no 1**

london	new	lp: hmv ASD 2323
5-6	philharmonia	lp: electrola SME 91645/ASDW 2323
february	menuhin, violin	lp: emi 1C063 00333/2C065 00333/
1965		3C065 00333/1C053 02396/
		SXLP 30533
		lp: angel 36438
		cd: emi CDM 763 9852/CMS 763 9842/
		585 4872

recording completed on 24 february 1965

violin concerto no 2

dallas	dallas	78: hmv DB 6361-6365/DB 9291-9295
15-16	symphony	78: victor M 1120
january	menuhin, violin	cd: rca/bmg 09026 613952/74321 886902
1946		

new york	minneapolis	lp: mercury MG 50140/SR 90003
17 february	symphony	lp: mercury wing SRW 18104
1957	menuhin, violin	lp: mercury golden imports SRI 75002
		cd: philips mercury 434 3502/475 6255

london	new	lp: hmv ALP 2281/ASD 2281
5-6	philharmonia	lp: electrola SME 91491/ASDW 2281
february	menuhin, violin	lp: emi 1C053 02396/SXLP 30533
1965		lp: angel 36360
		cd: emi CMS 763 9852/585 4872/
		585 5622

recording completed on 24 february 1965

viola concerto

london	new	lp: hmv ASD 2323
28-29	philharmonia	lp: electrola SME 91645/ASDW 2323
september	menuhin, viola	lp: emi 1C063 00333/2C065 00333/
1966		3C065 00333
		lp: angel 36438
		cd: emi CDM 763 9852/CMS 763 9842/
		585 4872

bartok/**divertimento for strings**
minneapolis 1950	minneapolis symphony	45: victor WDM 1596/WDM 1750 lp: victor LM 1185/LM 1750 lp: victor (italy) A12R 0063
vienna june 1958	philharmonia hungarica	lp: philips fontana CFL 1022/698 004CL lp: epic (usa) LC 3513
watford 9 july 1964	bbc symphony	lp: mercury MG 50416/SR 90416 lp: philips AL 3569/SAL 3569/A04919L/ 838 419AY lp: philips (france) 837 882GY lp: mercury (france) 120 578MSL/130 578MSY lp: mercury golden imports SRI 75118 lp: philips sequenza 6527 139 cd: philips mercury 434 3622/475 6255
budapest august 1969	hungarian state orchestra	lp: hungaroton LPX 11437/SLPX 11437 cd: hungaroton HCD 11437/HCD 41002

two portraits op 5
vienna 10 june 1958	philharmonia hungarica	lp: mercury MG 50183/SR 90183 lp: emi mercury MMA 11121/AMS 16068 lp: mercury (france) 121 026MSL/131 026MSY cd: philips mercury 432 0172

two pictures op 10
detroit 7-10 april 1978	detroit symphony	lp: decca SXL 6897 lp: decca (germany) 642 460AW lp: london (usa) CS 7120 cd: decca 425 6252
amsterdam 27-29 june 1983	concertgebouw orchestra	lp: philips 411 1321 cd: philips 411 1322

bourrée and from the diary of a fly, arranged by serly from mikrokosmos
vienna 10-11 june 1958	philharmonia hungarica	lp: mercury MG 50183/MG 50338/ SR 90183/SR 90338 lp: emi mercury MMA 11121/AMS 16068 cd: philips mercury 432 0172

10

bartok/hungarian sketches
minneapolis	minneapolis	lp: mercury MG 50132/SR 90132
17 november	symphony	lp: nixa mercury MRL 2565
1956		lp: emi mercury MMA 11082/AMS 16025
		lp: mercury (france) 121 026MSL/ 131 026MSY/49 013
		cd: philips mercury 432 0052

two rumanian dances, arranged by weiner
vienna	philharmonia	lp: mercury MG 50179/SR 90179
5-7	hungarica	lp: nixa mercury MRL 2595
june		lp: emi mercury MMA 11077/AMS 16027
1958		

berkeley ca	string	lp: private issue by university of southern
13 august	orchestra	california
1970		

rumanian folk dances
minneapolis	minneapolis	lp: mercury MG 50151/MG 50132/SR 90132
17 november	symphony	lp: nixa mercury MRL 2565
1956		lp: emi mercury MMA 11077/AMS 16027
		lp: mercury (france) 121 026MSL/ 131 026MSY/49 013
		lp: mercury golden imports SRI 75105
		cd: philips mercury 432 0052

suite no 1
detroit	detroit	lp: decca SXL 6897
7-10	symphony	lp: decca (germany) 642 460AW
april		lp: london (usa) CS 7120
1978		cd: decca 448 2762

suite no 2
minneapolis	minneapolis	lp: mercury MG 50098/SR 90098/SR 90533
27 november	symphony	lp: nixa mercury MRL 2502
1955		lp: emi mercury MMA 11068
		cd: philips mercury 434 3502

duke bluebeard's castle
watford	london	lp: mercury MG 50311/SR 90311
19-21	symphony	lp: emi mercury MMA 11190/AMS 16140
july	szönyi	lp: philips A04903L/838 403AY/6768 600
1962	szekely	lp: mercury golden imports SR13 77012
		cd: philips mercury 434 3252/475 6255

stockholm	stockholm	cd: bis BISCD 421-424
23 february	philharmonic	*orchestra rehearsal extract only*
1982		

bartok/**the miraculous mandarin, ballet**
watford   bbc symphony   lp: mercury MG 50416/SR 90416
8 july   bbc chorus   lp: mercury golden imports SRI 75030
1964   lp: philips AL 3569/SAL 3569/A04919L/
                                      838 419AY/837 882GY/6768 600
                                  lp: mercury (france) 120 578MGL/130 578MGY
                                  cd: philips mercury 434 3622/475 6255
                                  excerpts
                                  lp: mercury MG 50531/SR 90531
                                  lp: philips universo 6582 011

detroit   detroit   lp: decca 411 8941
14-16   symphony   cd: decca 411 8942/448 2762
november
1983

the miraculous mandarin, ballet suite
chicago   chicago   lp: mercury MG 50038/MG 50151
8-9   symphony   lp: mercury (france) MLP 7525/49.013
january   lp: nixa mercury MRL 2541
1953   lp: emi mercury MMA 11068
                                  cd: philips mercury 434 3972

amsterdam   concertgebouw   cd: q-disc 97018
30 january   orchestra
1958

stockholm   stockholm   cd: bis BISCD 421-424
4 february   philharmonic
1970

the wooden prince, ballet
watford   london   lp: mercury MG 50426/SR 90426
24-25   symphony   lp: philips SAL 3670/838 451AY/6768 600
june   lp: mercury (france) 120 581MGL/130 581MGY
1964   lp: mercury golden imports SR13 77012
                                  cd: philips mercury 434 3572/475 6255

sonata for two pianos and percussion
watford   lso members   lp: mercury SR 90515
26-27   frid and ponse, cd: philips mercury 434 3622
july   pianos
1962

bartok/**cantata profana**
budapest	budapest	cd: hungaroton HCD 31503
1970	symphony	
	hungarian radio	
	and tv chorus	
	reti, gregor	

three village scenes
budapest	chamber	lp: hungaroton LPX 11510/SLPX 11510
1970	ensemble	cd: hungaroton HCD 31047/HCD 41002
	farago, adam	

hungarian folksongs, selection
budapest	budapest	lp: hungaroton LPX 11510/SLPX 11510
1970	symphony	
	liszt academy choir	

szekely songs for unaccompanied chorus
budapest	liszt academy	cd: hungaroton HCD 31047/HCD 41002
1970	choir	

LUDWIG VAN BEETHOVEN (1770-1827)
symphony no 1
watford	royal	lp: dg 2721 199/2535 334
20 september	philharmonic	lp: mercury golden imports SRI 75121
1976		lp: metronom (germany) 140.164

symphony no 2
barking	royal	lp: dg 2721 199/2535 334
4-5	philharmonic	lp: mercury golden imports SRI 75122
october		lp: metronom (germany) 140.187
1976		

symphony no 3 "eroica"
minneapolis	minneapolis	lp: mercury MG 50141/SR 90011
9 march	symphony	lp: mercury wing MGW 14047/SRW 18047/WL1046
1957		lp: mercury golden imports SRI 75067
		lp: mercury (france) 120 508MGL/130 508MGY
		lp: philips classical favourites GL 5805/642 236GL
		lp: philips festivo 839 534AY
		lp: philips fontana 6531 010

west ham	royal	lp: dg 2721 199/2535 335
24-25	philharmonic	lp: mercury golden imports SRI 75123
september		lp: metronom (germany) 140.163
1976		

beethoven/**symphony no 4**

minneapolis 26 november 1955	minneapolis symphony	lp: mercury MG 50100 lp: mercury wing MGW 14042/SRW 18042/WL1033 lp: emi mercury MMA 11016
london 8-12 may 1976	royal philharmonic	lp: dg 2721 199/2535 218 lp: mercury golden imports SRI 75124 lp: metronom (germany) 140.187

symphony no 5

minneapolis 5-7 february 1953	minneapolis symphony	lp: mercury MG 50017 lp: mercury wing MGW 14016/SRW 18016/WL1011 lp: nixa mercury MRL 2539 lp: philips pergola 832 026PGY
watford 24-26 july 1962	london symphony	lp: mercury MG 50317/SR 90317 lp: philips 838 502VY/SDAL 501 lp: philips diskothek der meister 610 902VL lp: philips festivo 839 530AY cd: philips mercury 434 3752
west ham 15-16 may 1975	royal philharmonic	lp: dg 2721 199/2535 216 lp: contour 2870 482 lp: mercury golden imports SRI 75125 lp: metronom (germany) 140.141

symphony no 6 "pastoral"

vienna 20-26 september 1958	vienna symphony	lp: philips fontana 698 018CL/SCFL 104/ 875 007CY lp: epic (usa) LC 3611/BC 1038
watford 15-26 july 1962	london symphony	lp: mercury MG 50415/SR 90415 lp: philips fontana 6531 009/6598 892 cd: philips mercury 434 3752
london 3-4 march 1976	royal philharmonic	lp: dg 2721 199/2535 219 lp: mercury golden imports SRI 75119 lp: metronom (germany) 140.142 lp: franklin mint FM 7011-7014

beethoven/**symphony no 7**

watford 9-10 july 1963	london symphony	lp: mercury SR 90523 cd: philips mercury 462 9582
barking 29-30 september 1976	royal philharmonic	lp: dg 2721 199/2535 336 lp: mercury golden imports SRI 75120 lp: metronom (germany) 140.142

symphony no 8

minneapolis 26 november 1955	minneapolis symphony	lp: mercury MG 50100 lp: mercury wing MGW 14042/SRW 18042/ WL 1033 lp: emi mercury MMA 11016
london 4-6 march 1976	royal philharmonic	lp: dg 2721 199/2726 073 lp: mercury golden imports SRI2-77013 lp: metronom (germany) 140.164
new york 15 october 1976	national symphony	cd: disco archivia 1066

symphony no 9 "**choral**"

walthamstow 22-24 july 1975	royal philharmonic brighton festival chorus farley hodgson burrows bailey	lp: dg 2721 199/2726 073 lp: mercury golden imports SRI2 77013 lp: metronom (germany) 140.143

two extracts from the final movement of the ninth symphony in performances conducted by dorati with the stockholm philharmonic orchestra (bars 92-163 on 15 september 1976 and bars 164-236 on 16 december 1967) are published on cd by bis BISCD 421-424: presumably these two recorded performances are stored in swedish radio archives in their entirety

beethoven/**missa solemnis**
london	bbc symphony	unpublished radio broadcast
15 august	orchestra	*recording stored in national sound archive*
1966	and chorus	
	harper	
	höffgen	
	young	
	wiemann	

berlin	european	cd: bis BISCD 406-407
3 july	symphony	laserdisc: japan LSZS 00196
1988	orchestra	*recorded at a public concert which was then*
	university of	*repeated in moscow, dresden and london: these*
	maryland chorus	*were dorati's final public conducting appearances;*
	kiberg	*the performance is prefaced by a spoken*
	lang	*introduction by christian brückner, and the*
	cochran	*cd edition also contains rehearsal extracts*
	krutikov	

piano concerto no 3
london	london	cd: arkadia CD 567/CDHP 567
7 december	philharmonic	
1967	rubinstein, piano	

piano concerto no 4
berlin	rias-orchester	cd: tahra TAH 409-412
24 may	gieseking, piano	
1950		

watford	london	lp: mercury MG 50381/SR 90381/SR2-9129
7-9	symphony	lp: philips 6547 005
july	bachauer, piano	lp: philips fontana grandioso 894 087ZKY
1963		lp: philips classical favourites GL 5823/SGL 5823/
		642 221GL/837 821GY
		cd: philips mercury 432 0182
		philips classical favourites editions incorrectly name
		conductor as stanislav skrowaczewski

london	london	cd: arkadia CD 567/CDHP 567
7 december	philharmonic	dvd video: emi DVA 492 8409
1967	rubinstein, piano	

new york	national	cd: disco archivia 1062
20 april	symphony	
1975	istomin, piano	

piano concerto no 5 "emperor"
london	london	cd: arkadia CD 567/CDHP 567
7 december	philharmonic	
1967	rubinstein, piano	

beethoven/**violin concerto**

watford 17-22 june 1961	london symphony szigeti, violin	lp: mercury MG 50358/SR 90358 lp: philips fontana grandioso 894 021ZKY *issued on cd in japan by seven seas*
paris 4 february 1965	orchestre national grumiaux, violin	dvd video: emi DVB 490 4459

coriolan overture

minneapolis 5-7 february 1953	minneapolis symphony	lp: mercury MG 50017 lp: mercury wing MGW 14016/MGW 14032/ SRW 18016/SRW 18032/WL 1011/ WL 1019 lp: nixa mercury MRL 2539
west ham 16 may 1975	royal philharmonic	dg unpublished

egmont overture

minneapolis 5-7 february 1953	minneapolis symphony	lp: mercury MG 50017 lp: mercury wing MGW 14016/SRW 18016/ WL 1011 lp: nixa mercury MRL 2539
watford 23 july 1962	london symphony	lp: mercury MG 50317/SR 90317/SR2-9134 lp: mercury wing MFW 14037/SRW 18037 lp: mercury golden imports SRI 75124 lp: philips festivo 839 530VGY/88 188DY cd: philips mercury 462 9582
west ham 16 may 1975	royal philharmonic	dg unpublished

die geschöpfe des prometheus overture

wembley 12 june 1960	london symphony	lp: mercury LPC 5000/LPS 9000/GL 90/ GLS 90 lp: mercury golden imports SRI 75122 lp: emi mercury MMA 11143/AMS 16091 cd: philips mercury 434 3752

beethoven/**leonore** **no 3 overture**
minneapolis	minneapolis	lp: mercury MG 50017
5-7	symphony	lp: mercury wing MGW 14016/SRW 18016/
february		WL 1011
1953		lp: nixa mercury MRL 2539

wembley	london	lp: mercury LPS 5000/LPS 9000/GL 90/GLS 90
7-12	symphony	lp: mercury wing MGW 14037/SRW 18037
june		lp: mercury golden imports SRI 75121
1960		lp: emi mercury MMA 11143/AMS 16091
		cd: philips mercury 462 9582

west ham	royal	dg unpublished
16 may	philharmonic	
1975		

die weihe des hauses overture
watford	london	lp: mercury MG 50317/SR 90317
16 july	symphony	lp: mercury golden imports SRI 75125
1962		lp: philips festivo 839 530VGY
		cd: philips mercury 462 9582

wellingtons sieg
wembley	london	lp: mercury MGD 19/SRD 19/LPS 5000/
9 june	symphony	LPS 9000/GL 90/GLS 90
1960		lp: mercury golden imports SRI 75142
		lp: mercury (france) 120 514ML/
		130 514MGY
		lp: emi mercury MMA 11143/AMS 16091
		lp: philips AL 3461/SAL 3461/A04908L/
		838 408AY
		lp: philips fontana grandioso 894 028ZKY
		cd: philips 416 4482
		cd: philips mercury 434 3602
		some issues contained a commentary by deems taylor; sound effects added at a later date

ROBERT RUSSELL BENNETT (1894-1981)
the fun and faith of william billings american
washington	national	lp: london (usa) OS 26442
23-30	symphony	
april	university of	
1975	maryland chorus	

ALBAN BERG (1885-1935)
three pieces for orchestra

watford	london	lp: mercury MG 50316/SR 90316
14 april	symphony	lp: philips AL 3539/SAL 3539/A04909L/
1962		838 409AY/6539 061
		lp: philips (france) 6555 078
		lp: philips festivo 839 264VGY
		cd: philips mercury 432 0062
		recording completed on 21 july 1962

lulu, symphonic suite; three wozzeck fragments

watford	london	lp: mercury MG 50278/SR 90278
19-24	symphony	lp: mercury golden imports SRI 75065
june	pilarczyk	lp: mercury (france) 120 501MGL/130 501MGY
		lp: emi mercury MMA 11167/AMS 16117
		lp: philips festivo 839 263DSY
		cd: philips mercury 432 0062 (lulu)/
		434 3252 (wozzeck)
		cd: philips 470 5312

HECTOR BERLIOZ (1803-1869)
symphonie fantastique

minneapolis	minneapolis	lp: mercury MG 50034
23-24	symphony	lp: mercury wing MGW 14005/WL 1004
december		lp: mercury (france) MLP 7522
1953		lp: nixa mercury MRL 2532
		lp: philips fontana special 200 046WGY/700 046WGY
		lp: pickwick PC 4040/SPP 4040

new york	national	cd: disco archivia 1064
2 february	symphony	
1975		

benvenuto cellini

london	bbc symphony	cd: music and arts CD 618
23 january	bbc chorus	
1963	carlyle	
	veasey	
	lewis	
	cameron	
	garrard	
	ward	
	sung in english	

berlioz/**le carnaval romain overture**

minneapolis	minneapolis	lp: mercury MG 50005
19-20	symphony	lp: mercury wing MGW 14009/WL 1045
february		lp: nixa mercury MRL 2516
1952		lp: philips classical favourites 642 216GL/ 837 816GY
		also issued by mercury in usa on 45rpm format

la damnation de faust, suite: ballet des sylphes; menuet des follets; marche hongroise

amsterdam	concertgebouw	lp: philips 835 062AY
25 september	orchestra	lp: philips festivo 6530 020
1959		lp: epic (usa) LC 3723/BC 1094
		cd: decca collection classique 464 0922
		excerpts
		45: philips SBF 275/313 123SF
		lp: philips 6833 173/6882 100/6999 013
		lp: philips festivo 839 817VGY

amsterdam	concertgebouw	lp: philips 6514 219/6769 089
18 january	orchestra	
1982		

roméo et juliette, suite: roméo seul; grande fete chez capulets; scene d'amour; scherzo la reine mab

walthamstow	royal	lp: readers digest RD3-15/RDS 3-15/
16-17	philharmonic	RDM 1027/RDS 9633/GROM 8A
october		lp: quintessence (usa) PMC 7045
1962		

roméo et juliette, scene d'amour

amsterdam	concertgebouw	lp: philips 835 062AY/6585 026
25 september	orchestra	lp: philips festivo 6530 026
1959		lp: epic (usa) LC 3723/BC 1094
		cd: decca collection classique 464 0922

FRANZ BERWALD (1796-1868)
symphony no 2 "sinfonia capricieuse"

stockholm	stockholm	lp: victor VIC 1319/VICS 1319
31 october	philharmonic	lp: emi (sweden) SP 141/RIKSLP 13
1967		cd: swedish society SCD 1046

WILLIAM BILLINGS (1746-1800)
three hymns: be glad then america!; where jesus wept; chester

washington	university of	lp: london (usa) OS 26442
23-30	maryland chorus	
april		
1975		

GEORGES BIZET (1838-1875)
l'arlésienne, suites nos 1 and 2

paris	lamoureux	lp: philips fontana CFL 1061/SCFL 117/ 698 030CL/875 024CY
31 may-	orchestra	lp: philips fontana weltserie 695 029KL
1 june		lp: philips diskothek der meister 663 020ER
1959		lp: philips fontana special 200 008WGL/ 700 008WGY
		lp: epic (usa) LC 3646/BC 1063
		cd: philips 442 2722

carmen, suites nos 1 and 2

paris	lamoureux	lp: philips fontana CFL 1061/SCFL 117/ 698 030CL/875 024CY
31 may-	orchestra	lp: philips fontana weltserie 695 029KL
1 june		lp: philips fontana special 200 008WGL/ 700 008WGY
1959		lp: epic (usa) LC 3646/BC 1063
		cd: philips 442 2722

jeux d'enfants, suite

london	london	78: hmv C 2940-2941
17 september	philharmonic	78: electrola EH 1091-1092
1937		78: victor M 510
		lp: victor CAL 365
		cd: dutton CDAX 8005
		cd: avid AMSC 601
		cd: dante LYS 261
		recording completed on 27 september 1937

ERNEST BLOCH (1880-1959)
sinfonia breve

minneapolis	minneapolis	lp: mercury MG 50288/SR 90288
17april	symphony	lp: emi mercury MMA 11177/AMS 16127
1960		lp: mercury golden imports SRI 75116
		lp: composers' recordings CRIS 248
		cd: philips mercury 434 3292

KARL BLOMDAHL (1916-1968)
symphony no 2

stockholm	stockholm	lp: emi 4E061 35142/7C061 35142
13-15	philharmonic	*orchestra described as swedish radio orchestra*
january		
1971		

sisyphos, ballet suite

stockholm	stockholm	lp: victor VIC 1319/VICS 1319
16 october	philharmonic	lp: caprice CAP 1016
1967		cd: caprice CAP 21365

LUIGI BOCCHERINI (1743-1805)
scuola di ballo, ballet arranged by francaix
london	london	78: columbia DX 944-945
27 july	philharmonic	78: columbia (france) LFX 714-715
1939		78: columbia (italy) GQX 11033-11034
		78: columbia (argentina) C266233-266234
		78: columbia (usa) X 157
		lp: columbia (usa) RL 3043
		cd: pearl GEMM 0036

ALEXANDER BORODIN (1833-1887)
symphony no 2
minneapolis	minneapolis	lp: mercury MG 50004
19-20	symphony	lp: mercury wing MGW 14010/SRW 18010
february		lp: nixa mercury MRL 2550
1952		lp: philips A04902L
		lp: mercury (france) 121 042MSL/131 042MSY
		lp: philips fontana special SFL 14026/700 427WGY

prince igor, overture
walthamstow	london	lp: mercury MG 50265/MG 50324/MG 50346/
6 june	symphony	SR 90265/SR 90324/SR 90346
1959		lp: mercury golden imports SRI 75016
		lp: emi mercury MMA 11154/AMS 16102
		lp: philips 6511 017
		lp: philips universo 6582 012
		lp: franklin mint FM 7011-7014
		cd: philips mercury 434 3732

prince igor, polovtsian dances
walthamstow	london	45: mercury (france) 48.006
4 july	symphony	45: emi mercury XEP 9046/SEX 15003
1956	orchestra	lp: mercury MG 50122/MG 50265/
	and chorus	MG 50327/SR 90122/SR 90265/
		SR 90327/SR2-9130
		lp: mercury wing MGW 14070/SRW 18070
		lp: mercury golden imports SRI 75016
		lp: nixa mercury MRL 2537
		lp: emi mercury MMA 11058/MMA 11154/
		AMS 16008/AMS 16102
		lp: philips S06403R/836 603VZ/
		6511 017/6567 003
		lp: philips diskothek der meister 610 901VL/
		838 501VY
		lp: philips fontana special SFL 14024/700 425WGY
		lp: philips universo 6582 012
		lp: metronom (germany) 140.170
		lp: franklin mint FM 7011-7014
		cd: philips mercury 434 3082

borodin/**in the steppes of central asia**
walthamstow	london	mercury unpublished
6 june	symphony	*recording probably not completed*
1959		

JOHANNES BRAHMS (1833-1897)
symphony no 1
watford	london	lp: mercury MG 50268/SR 90268
16-18	symphony	lp: emi mercury MMA 11135/AMS 16082
june		lp: philips fontana special SFL 14080/
1959		700 136WGY/200 136 WGL
		cd: philips fontana 434 3802

symphony no 2
minneapolis	minneapolis	lp: mercury MG 50171/SR 90171
17 december	symphony	lp: mercury wing MGW 14052/SRW 18052/
1957		WL 1047
		lp: emi mercury MMA 11049
		lp: philips fontana special SFL 14011/
		700 424WGY/200 424WGL
		lp: pickwick S 4046
		cd: philips mercury 434 3802

symphony no 3
minneapolis	minneapolis	lp: mercury MG 50072
6 april	symphony	lp: mercury wing MGW 14032/SRW 18032/
1955		WL 1019
		lp: emi mercury MMA 11138

watford	london	lp: mercury SR 90502
13-14	symphony	cd: philips mercury 434 3802
july		
1963		

symphony no 4
watford	london	lp: mercury SR 90503
11-13	symphony	cd: philips mercury 434 3802
july		
1963		

piano concerto no 2
walthamstow	london	lp: readers digest RD4 603-604
30-31	symphony	cd: chesky CD 36
may	bachauer	cd: readers digest RDCD 741-743
1967		

brahms/**violin concerto**
den haag   residentie   cd: music and arts CD 837/CD 4837
10 june   orchestra
1949   neveu

watford   london   lp: mercury MG 50308/SR 90308
18-22   symphony   lp: emi mercury MMA 11184/AMS 16134
july   szeryng   lp: philips AL 3558/SAL 3558/A04900L/
1962   838 400AY
                                     lp: philips festivo SFM 23021/839 545VGY
                                     lp: philips fontana 6531 001/6531 050
                                     lp: mercury (france) 120 528MGL/130 528MGY
                                     lp: metronom (germany) 140.129
                                     lp: contour classics CC 7523
                                     lp: quintessence PMC 7095
                                     cd: philips mercury 434 3182
                                     also issued on lp in germany by orbis record club

haydn variations
watford   london   lp: mercury MG 50154/MG 50336/MG 50502/
9 july   symphony   SR 90154/SR 90336/SR 90502
1957   lp: mercury (france) 49.017
                                     lp: emi mercury MMA 11051/AMS 16006
                                     lp: philips classical favourites GL 5824/
                                         SGL 5824/642 226GL/837 826GY
                                     cd: philips mercury 434 3262

academic festival overture
minneapolis   minneapolis   lp: mercury MG 50072/MG 50336/MG 50503/
27 november   symphony   SR 90336/SR 90503
1955   lp: emi mercury MMA 11138
                                     lp: philips classical favourites GL 5824/
                                         SGL 5824/642 226GL/837 826GY

tragic overture
minneapolis   minneapolis   lp: mercury MG 50072/MG 50336/SR 90336/
27 november   symphony   SR2-9134
1955   lp: philips classical favourites GL 5824/
                                         SGL 5824/642 226GL/837 826GY

24
brahms/**hungarian dance no 1**
watford	london	45: mercury XEP 9028/SEX 15004
5 july	symphony	lp: mercury MG 50154/MG 50336/MG 50437/
1957		SR 90154/SR 90336/SR 90437/SR 6003
		lp: mercury golden imports SRI 75024
		lp: mercury wing MGW 14084/SRW 18084
		lp: emi mercury MMA 11051/AMS 16006
		lp: philips classical favourites GL 5824/
		SGL 5824/642 226GL/837 826GY
		lp: philips universo 6582 017
		lp: philips sequenza 6527 032
		lp: franklin mint FM 7011-7014
		cd: philips mercury 434 3262

hungarian dance no 2, arranged by hallen
watford	london	45: mercury XEP 9028/SEX 15004/
6 july	symphony	lp: mercury MG 50154/MG 50336/MG 50437/
1957		SR 90154/SR 90336/SR 90437/SR 6003
		lp: mercury golden imports SRI 75024
		lp: emi mercury MMA 11051/AMS 16006
		lp: philips classical favourites GL 5824/
		SGL 5824/642 226GL/837 826GY
		lp: philips universo 6582 017
		lp: philips sequenza 6527 032
		cd: philips mercury 434 3262

hungarian dance no 3
watford	london	lp: mercury MG 50437/SR 90437/SR 6003
31 july	symphony	lp: mercury wing MGW 14084/SRW 18084
1965		lp: mercury golden imports SRI 75024
		lp: philips fontana 6531 003
		lp: philips universo 6582 017
		lp: franklin mint FM 7011-7014
		cd: philips mercury 434 3262

hungarian dance no 4, arranged by hallen
watford	london	lp: mercury MG 50437/SR 90437/SR 6003
2 august	symphony	lp: mercury golden imports SRI 75024
1965		lp: philips fontana 6531 003
		lp: philips universo 6582 017
		lp: franklin mint FM 7011-7014
		cd: philips mercury 434 3262

brahms/**hungarian dance no 5, arranged by parlow**
watford   london   45: emi mercury XEP 9028/SEX 15004
6 july   symphony   lp: mercury MG 50154/MG 50336/MG 50437/
1957   SR 90154/SR 90336/SR 90437/SR 6003
                                lp: mercury golden imports SRI 75024
                                lp: emi mercury MMA 11051/AMS 16006
                                lp: philips classical favourites GL 5824/
                                    SGL 5824/642 226GL/837 826GY
                                lp: philips fontana 6531 003
                                lp: philips universo 6582 017
                                lp: philips sequenza 6527 032
                                lp: franklin mint FM 7011-7014
                                cd: philips mercury 434 3262

hungarian dance no 6, arranged by parlow
watford   london   lp: mercury MG 50154/MG 50336/MG 50437/
6 july   symphony   SR 90154/SR 90336/SR 90437/SR 6003
1957   lp: mercury golden imports SRI 75024
                                lp: emi mercury MMA 11051/AMS 16006
                                lp: philips classical favourites GL 5824/
                                    SGL 5824/642 226GL/837 826GY
                                lp: philips fontana 6531 003
                                lp: philips universo 6582 017
                                lp: philips sequenza 6527 032
                                lp: franklin mint FM 7011-7014
                                cd: philips mercury 434 3262

hungarian dance no 7, arranged by hallen
watford   london   45: emi mercury XEP 9028/SEX 15004/
6 july   symphony   lp: mercury MG 50154/MG 50336/MG 50437/
1957   SR 90154/SR 90336/SR 90437/SR 6003
                                lp: mercury golden imports SRI 75024
                                lp: emi mercury MMA 11051/AMS 16006
                                lp: philips classical favourites GL 5824/
                                    SGL 5824/642 226GL/837 826GY
                                lp: philips fontana 6531 003
                                lp: philips universo 6582 017
                                lp: philips sequenza 6527 032
                                lp: franklin mint FM 7011-7014
                                cd: philips mercury 434 3262

hungarian dance no 10
watford   london   lp: mercury MG 50437/SR 90437/SR 6003
31 july   symphony   lp: mercury wing MGW 14084/SRW 18084
1965   lp: mercury golden imports SRI 75024
                                lp: philips fontana 6531 003
                                lp: philips universo 6582 017
                                cd: philips mercury 434 3262

brahms/**hungarian dance no 11, arranged by parlow**
watford	london	45: emi mercury XEP 9028/SEX 15004
6 july	symphony	lp: mercury MG 50154/MG 50336/MG 50437/
1957		SR 90154/SR 90336/SR 90437/SR 6003
		lp: mercury golden imports SRI 75024
		lp: emi mercury MMA 11051/AMS 16006
		lp: philips classical favourites GL 5824/SGL 5824/
		642 226GL/837 826GY
		lp: philips fontana 6531 003
		lp: philips universo 6582 017
		lp: philips sequenza 6527 032
		lp: franklin mint FM 7011-7014
		cd: philips mercury 434 3262

hungarian dance no 12, arranged by parlow
watford	london	lp: mercury MG 50437/SR 90437/SR 6003
2 august	symphony	lp: mercury golden imports SRI 75024
1965		lp: philips fontana 6531 003
		lp: philips universo 6582 017
		cd: philips mercury 434 3262

hungarian dance no 15, arranged by parlow
watford	london	lp: mercury MG 50437/SR 90437/SR 6003
2 august	symphony	lp: mercury golden imports SRI 75024
1965		lp: philips fontana 6531 003
		lp: philips universo 6582 017
		cd: philips mercury 434 3262

hungarian dance no 17, arranged by dvorak
watford	london	lp: mercury MG 50437/SR 90437/SR 6003
2 august	symphony	lp: mercury golden imports SRI 75024
1965		lp: mercury wing MGW 14084/SRW 18084
		lp: philips fontana 6531 003
		lp: philips universo 6582 017
		lp: franklin mint FM 7011-7014
		cd: philips mercury 434 3262

hungarian dance no 18, arranged by dvorak
watford	london	lp: mercury MG 50437/SR 90437/SR 6003
2 august	symphony	lp: mercury wing MGW 14084/SRW 18084
1965		lp: mercury golden imports SRI 75024
		lp: philips fontana 6531 003
		lp: philips universo 6582 017
		cd: philips mercury 434 3262

brahms/**hungarian dance no 19, arranged by dvorak**
watford	london	lp: mercury MG 50437/SR 90437/SR 6003
2 august	symphony	lp: mercury wing MGW 14084/SRW 18084
1965		lp: mercury golden imports SRI 75024
		lp: philips fontana 6531 003
		lp: philips universo 6582 017
		cd: philips mercury 434 3262

hungarian dance no 20, arranged by dvorak
watford	london	lp: mercury MG 50437/SR 90437/SR 6003
2 august	symphony	lp: mercury wing MGW 14084/SRW 18084
1965		lp: mercury golden imports SRI 75024
		lp: philips fontana 6531 003
		lp: philips universo 6582 017
		lp: franklin mint FM 7011-7014
		cd: philips mercury 434 3262

hungarian dance no 21
watford	london	45: mercury XEP 9028/SEX 15004
5 july	symphony	lp: mercury MG 50154/MG 50336/MG 50437/
1957		SR 90154/SR 90336/SR 90437/SR 6003
		lp: mercury wing MGW 14084/SRW 18084
		lp: mercury golden imports SRI 75024
		lp: emi mercury MMA 11051/AMS 16006
		lp: philips classical favourites GL 5824/SGL 5824/
		642 226GL/837 826GY
		lp: philips fontana 6531 003
		lp: philips universo 6582 017
		lp: philips sequenza 6527 032
		cd: philips mercury 434 3262

BENJAMIN BRITTEN (1913-1976)
young person's guide to the orchestra
minneapolis	minneapolis	lp: mercury MG 50047/MG 50055
20 november	symphony	lp: mercury wing MGW 14033/SRW 18033
1954	deems taylor,	lp: nixa mercury MRL 2533
	narrator	lp: emi mercury MMA 11023
		lp: philips wing WL 1036
		lp: philips fontana special SFL 14010/700 423WGY
		MG 50047 does not contain the narration

london	royal	lp: decca LK 4801/PFS 4104/SPA 520/VIV 40
9 march	philharmonic	lp: london (usa) PM 55005/SPC 21007
1966	connery,	cd: pickwick IMPX 9009
	narrator	cd: decca 444 1042
		cd: decca belart 450 0242

MAX BRUCH (1838-1920)
concerto for two pianos and orchestra

london	london	lp: emi 1C063 02493
23 november	symphony	lp: angel 36997
1973	berkovsky and twining, pianos	

kol nidrei for cello and orchestra

watford	london	lp: mercury MG 50303/SR 90303
10 july	symphony	lp: mercury golden imports SRI 75045
1962	starker, cello	lp: mercury (france) 120 531MGL/130 531MGY
		lp: emi mercury MMA 11183/AMS 16133
		lp: philips festivo SFM 23020/839 544VGY
		lp: philips fontana 6531 013
		lp: philips fontana grandioso 894 024ZKY
		lp: metronom (germany) 140.169
		lp: contour classics CC 7585
		cd: philips 420 8732
		cd: philips mercury 432 0012

ALFREDO CASELLA (1883-1947)
suite from la giara

minneapolis	minneapolis	cd: minnesota orchestra centenary set
10 february	symphony	
1956		

EMMANUEL CHABRIER (1841-1894)
cotillon, ballet music arranged by rieti

london	london	78: columbia DX 877-878
9 august	philharmonic	78: columbia (france) LFX 701-702
1938		78: columbia (argentina) DOX 585-586
		78: columbia (usa) X 113
		cd: pearl GEM 0036

FREDERIC CHOPIN (1810-1849)
piano concerto no 1

watford	london	lp: mercury MG 50368/SR 90368
8-9	symphony	cd: philips mercury 434 3742
july	bachauer, piano	
1963		

chopin/**piano concerto no 2**
watford	london	lp: mercury MG 50432/SR 90432
22-23	symphony	cd: philips mercury 434 3742
june	bachauer, piano	
1964		

amsterdam	concertgebouw	lp: decca 411 9421
29 june-	orchestra	cd: decca 411 9422
1 july	schiff, piano	
1983		

FRANCESCO CILEA (1866-1950)
l'arlesiana, excerpt (e la solita storia)
new york	victor	78: victor MO 1191/VO 13
24 september	orchestra	78: hmv DB 6869
1947	tagliavini	lp: victor LM 20062
		cd: myto MCD 93382
		cd: grandi voci GVS 15

AARON COPLAND (1900-1990)
symphony no 3
minneapolis	minneapolis	lp: mercury MG 50018/MG 50421/
5-7	symphony	SR 90421
february		lp: emi mercury MMA 11050
1953		*recorded under auspices of the koussevitzky music foundation*

dance symphony
detroit	detroit	lp: decca SXDL 7547
11-13	symphony	lp: london (usa) LDR 71047
may		cd: decca 414 2732/430 7052/448 2612
1981		

appalachian spring, ballet suite
watford	london	lp: mercury MG 50246/SR 90246
15-16	symphony	lp: emi mercury MMA 11172/AMS 16122
june		cd: philips mercury 434 3012
1961		*excerpts*
		cd: philips mercury 442 5412

detroit	detroit	lp: decca/london 414 4571
30 october-	symphony	cd: decca 414 4572/430 7052/444 4512
1 november		*excerpts*
1984		cd: decca 460 6562/473 1462

copland/**billy the kid, ballet**
watford   london   lp: mercury MG 50246/SR 90246
15-16   symphony   lp: emi mercury MMA 11172/AMS 16122
june   cd: philips mercury 434 3012
1961   *recording completed on 24 june 1961*

billy the kid, waltz from the ballet
dallas   dallas   78: victor M 1214
february   symphony   45: victor WDM 1214
1947

danzon cubano
minneapolis   minneapolis   45: emi mercury XEP 9004
20 december   symphony   lp: mercury MG 50172/MG 50326/
1957   SR 90172/SR 90326
                                   lp: emi mercury MMA 11005/AMS 16021
                                   cd: philips mercury 434 3012

fanfare for the common man
detroit   detroit   lp: decca SXDL 7547
11-13   symphony   lp: london (usa) LDR 71047
may   cd: decca 414 2732/430 7052/460 6562
1981

rodeo, four dance episodes
dallas   dallas   78: victor M 1214
february   symphony   45: victor WDM 1214
1947   lp: victor LM 32

minneapolis   minneapolis   lp: mercury MG 50172/SR 90172
20 december   symphony   lp: emi mercury MMA 11005/AMS 16021
1957   cd: philips mercury 434 3292
                                   excerpts
                                   45: emi mercury XEP 9004
                                   lp: mercury MG 50494/SR 90494
                                   lp: philips 6999 013

detroit   detroit   lp: decca SXDL 7547
11-13   symphony   lp: london (usa) LDR 71047
may   cd: decca 414 2732/430 7052/448 2612
1981   *excerpts*
                                   cd: decca 444 4512

copland/**el salon mexico**
minneapolis	minneapolis	lp: mercury MG 50172/SR 90172
20 december	symphony	lp: emi mercury MMA 11005/AMS 16021
1957		*excerpts*
		lp: mercury MB 1001
detroit	detroit	lp: decca SXDL 7547
11-13	symphony	lp: london (usa) LDR 71047
may		cd: decca 414 2732/430 7052/448 2612
1981		

LUIGI DALLAPICCOLA (1904-1975)
il prigionero
washington	national	lp: decca HEAD 10
6-7	symphony	lp: london (usa) OSA 1166
april	university of	
1974	maryland chorus	
	barrera	
	mazzieri	
	emile	

ALEXANDER DARGOMIZHSKY (1813-1869)
russalka, ballet music
london	london	78: columbia DX 804
27 september	philharmonic	78: columbia (germany) DWX 1603
1937		78: columbia (usa) 69126D

CLAUDE DEBUSSY (1862-1918)
ibéria/images
washington	national	lp: decca SXL 6742
23-30	symphony	lp: london (usa) CS 6968
april		*issued on cd by polygram in japan*
1975		

jeux
washington	national	decca/london unpublished
23-30	symphony	*recording may not have been completed*
april		
1975		

la mer
minneapolis	minneapolis	cd: minnesota orchestra centenary set
3 february	symphony	
1956		

debussy/**trois nocturnes**

minneapolis	minneapolis	lp: mercury MG 50005/MG 50025
19-20	symphony	lp: mercury wing MGW 14029/SRW 18029
february	cecilian	lp: nixa mercury MRL 2516
1952	singers	

washington	national	lp: decca SXL 6742
23-30	symphony	lp: london (usa) CS 6968
april	oratorio	*issued on cd by polygram in japan*
1975	society choir	

LEO DELIBES (1836-1891)
coppélia, ballet

minneapolis   minneapolis
21-22   symphony
december
1957

lp: mercury MG 50185-50186/
    SR 90185-90186/OL2-105/SR2-9005
lp: mercury golden imports SRI-2 77004
lp: emi mercury MMA 11000-11001/
    AMS 16018-16019
lp: mercury (france) 120 511-120 512MGL/
    130 511-130 512MGY
lp: philips 6747 228/6780 253
lp: philips classical favourites GL 5780-5781/
    642 208-642 209GL
lp: philips fontana special SFL 14100-14101/
    700 460-700 461WGY
cd: philips mercury 434 3132
excerpts
45: emi mercury XEP 9018/XEP 9026
lp: mercury MG 50328/MG 50494/
    SR 90328/SR 90494
lp: mercury wing MGW 14087/SRW 18087
lp: philips diskothek der meister 610 905VL/
    838 505VY
lp: philips (france) 77 519
lp: philips festivo 839 536VGY
lp: philips fontana special 700 008WGY
philips (france) 77 519 includes a french narration

ERNO DOHNANYI (1877-1960)
wedding waltz/the veil of pierrette

vienna   philharmonia
5 june   hungarica
1958

45: emi mercury XEP 9076/SEX 15020
lp: mercury MG 50190/MG 50444/
    SR 90190/SR 90444
lp: emi mercury MMA 11116/AMS 16063
lp: mercury golden imports SRI 75098
lp: philips wing WL 1208
lp: philips argento (italy) 6599 900
cd: philips mercury 434 3382

GAETONO DONIZETTI (1797-1848)
l'elisir d'amore, excerpt (una furtiva lagrima)

new york	victor	78: victor MO 1191/VO 13
24 september	orchestra	78: hmv DB 6856
1947	tagliavini	lp: victor LM 1202
		lp: emi EX 769 7411
		cd: emi CHS 769 7412
		cd: myto MCD 93382
		cd: opera 54508
		cd: grandi voci GVS 15
		opera 54508 incorrectly dated 1940-1943

ANTAL DORATI (1906-1988)
symphony no 1

minneapolis	minneapolis	lp: mercury MG 50248/MG 50499/
16-17	symphony	SR 90248/SR 90499
april		
1960		
stockholm	stockholm	cd: bis BISCD 408
12-13	philharmonic	
january		
1972		

symphony no 2 "querala pacis"

stockholm	stockholm	cd: bis BISCD 408
26-29	philharmonic	
may		
1988		

piano concerto

washington	national	lp: vox turnabout TV 34669
3 april	symphony	
1976	alpenheim, piano	

trittico for oboe and orchestra

basel	basel symphony	lp: philips 416 9871
16 january	holliger, oboe	
1986		

die stimmen, for bass soloist and orchestra

stockholm	stockholm	lp: bachtele verlag SBV 003
11 october	philharmonic	
1978	lagger	

ANTONIN DVORAK (1841-1904)
symphony no 6

stockholm 5 december 1973	stockholm philharmonic	cd: royal stockholm philharmonic archive recordings

symphony no 7

watford 17-18 july 1963	london symphony	lp: mercury SR 90516 cd: philips mercury 434 3122

symphony no 8

minneapolis 21 march 1958	minneapolis symphony	unpublished radio broadcast *copy of recording stored in national sound archive*
watford 19-20 june 1959	london symphony	lp: mercury MG 50236/SR 90236 lp: mercury wing MGW 14080/SRW 18080 lp: emi mercury MMA 11128/AMS 16075 lp: concert hall CMS 2445/SMSC 2445 cd: philips mercury 434 3122

symphony no 9 "from the new world"

amsterdam 17 october 1952	residentie orchestra	lp: philips ABL 3021/A00154L lp: philips classical favourites G03135L lp: epic (usa) LC 3001
amsterdam 21-22 september 1959	concertgebouw orchestra	lp: philips ABL 3309/SABL 161/ A00545L/835 032AY/6500 218/ 6701 006 lp: philips classical favourites GL 5848/ SGL 5848/G03247L/837 075GY lp: philips fontana special SFL 14030 lp: philips fontana grandioso 894 007ZKY lp: philips diskothek der meister 610 113VR/ 836 237VZ lp: philips festivo 839 502VGY lp: philips universo 6582 014/6582 072/ 6582 502 cd: philips 442 4012/454 5382
london 8-9 december 1965	new philharmonia	lp: decca LK 4880/PFS 4128/JB 37 lp: london (usa) SPC 21025/STS 15567 lp: contour classics CC 7579 cd: decca 443 7652/448 9472
london 31 january 1977	royal philharmonic	lp: vox (france) 35087 lp: vox turnabout TV 34702 *also issued in a french lp club edition by hachette*

dvorak/**violin concerto**
minneapolis	minneapolis	78: victor M 1537
march	symphony	45: victor WDM 1537
1951	milstein, violin	lp: victor LM 1147
		lp: hmv (france) FALP 158/FALP 241
		cd: naxos 811.0975

cello concerto
watford	london	lp: mercury MG 50303/SR 90303
6-10	symphony	lp: mercury golden imports SRI 75045
july	starker, cello	lp: emi mercury MMA 11183/AMS 16133
1962		lp: philips festivo SFM 23020/839 544VGY
		lp: philips fontana 6531 013
		lp: philips fontana grandioso 894 024ZKY
		lp: contour classics CC 7585
		cd: philips 420 8732
		cd: philips mercury 432 0012

carnival overture
watford	london	lp: mercury MG 50236/MG 50323/SR 90236/
20 june	symphony	SR 90323/SR 90516
1959		lp: mercury wing MGW 14080/SRW 18080
		lp: emi mercury MMA 11128/AMS 16075
		lp: concert hall CMS 2445/SMSC 2445

in nature's realm, overture
amsterdam	concertgebouw	lp: philips 420 6071
6-10	orchestra	cd: philips 420 6072
october		
1986		

slavonic rhapsody no 1
amsterdam	concertgebouw	lp: philips L 09003-09004 L/6701 008
15 september	orchestra	lp: epic (usa) SC 6026
1956		

slavonic rhapsody no 2
amsterdam	concertgebouw	lp: philips L 09003-09004 L/6701 008
22 october	orchestra	lp: epic (usa) SC 6026
1957		

slavonic rhapsody no 3
amsterdam	residentie	lp: philips NBR 6010/N00620R/S06053R
1953	orchestra	lp: philips fontana special 200 039WGL
		700 039WGY
		lp: epic (usa) LC 3015

detroit	detroit	lp: decca SXL 6896
7-10	symphony	lp: decca (germany) 642 452AS
april		lp: london (usa) CS 7119
1978		cd: decca 425 0872/460 2932

dvorak/**slavonic dance no 1**

teheran 16 september 1957	minneapolis symphony	cd: minnesota orchestra centenary set

minneapolis
5 april
1958
	minneapolis
	symphony
		45: emi mercury XEP 9030
		lp: mercury OL2-107/MG 50335/
		    SR2-9007/SR 90335
		lp: mercury wing MGW 14082/SRW 18082
		lp: mercury golden imports SRI 77001
		lp: emi mercury MMA 11029-11030/
		    AMS 16046-16047
		lp: philips classical favourites GL 5832/
		    SGL 5832/642 267GL
		lp: philips sequenza 6527 032
		cd: philips mercury 434 3842

bamberg march 1974	bamberg symphony	lp: vox (france) FSM 73001 lp: vox turnabout TV 34582/QTV 34582 cd: cantus classics CACD 800043/ CACD 500031
london 31 january 1983	royal philharmonic	lp: decca 411 7351 cd: decca 411 7352/417 7492/430 7352/ 436 4762/460 2932/467 4232 *recordings completed in september and october 1983*

slavonic dance no 2

minneapolis
5 april
1958
	minneapolis
	symphony
		45: mercury EP 40041
		45: emi mercury XEP 9039
		lp: mercury OL2-107/MG 50335/
		    SR2-9007/SR 90335
		lp: mercury wing MGW 14082/SRW 18082
		lp: mercury golden imports SRI 77001
		lp: emi mercury MMA 11029-11030/
		    AMS 16046-16047
		lp: philips classical favourites GL 5832/
		    SGL 5832/642 267GL
		cd: philips mercury 434 3842

bamberg march 1974	bamberg symphony	lp: vox (france) FSM 73001 lp: vox turnabout TV 34582/QTV 34582 cd: cantus classics CACD 800043/ CACD 500031
london 31 january 1983	royal philharmonic	lp: decca 411 7351 cd: decca 411 7352/417 7492/430 7352/ 436 4762/460 2932 *recordings completed in september and october 1983*

dvorak/**slavonic dance no 3**

minneapolis
5 april
1958
	minneapolis
	symphony
		45: emi mercury XEP 9030
		lp: mercury OL2-107/MG 50335/
		     SR2-9007/SR 90335/SR 90526
		lp: mercury wing MGW 14082/SRW 18082
		lp: mercury golden imports SRI 77001
		lp: emi mercury MMA 11029-11030/
		     AMS 16046-16047
		lp: philips classical favourites GL5832/
		     SGL 5832/642 267GL
		lp: philips sequenza 6527 032
		cd: philips mercury 434 3842

bamberg march 1974	bamberg symphony	lp: vox (france) FSM 73001 lp: vox turnabout TV 34582/QTV 34582 cd: cantus classics CACD 800043/ CACD 500031
london 31 january 1983	royal philharmonic	lp: decca 411 7351 cd: decca 411 7352/417 7492/430 7352/ 436 4762/460 2932 *recordimgs completed in september and october 1983*

slavonic dance no 4

minneapolis
5 april
1958
	minneapolis
	symphony
		45: emi mercury XEP 9063/SEX 15014
		lp: mercury OL2-107/MG 50335/
		     SR2-9007/SR 90335
		lp: mercury wing MGW 14082/SRW 18082
		lp: mercury golden imports SRI 77001
		lp: emi mercury MMA 11029-11030/
		     AMS 16046-16047
		lp: philips classical favourites GL 5832/
		     SGL 5832/642 267GL
		lp: philips sequenza 6527 032
		cd: philips mercury 434 3842

bamberg march 1974	bamberg symphony	lp: vox (france) FSM 73001 lp: vox turnabout TV 34582/QTV 34582 cd: cantus classics CACD 800043/ CACD 500031
london 31 january 1983	royal philharmonic	lp: decca 411 7351 cd: decca 411 7352/417 7492/430 7352/ 436 4762/460 2932 *recordings completed in september and october 1983*

dvorak/**slavonic dance no 5**

minneapolis
5 april
1958
	minneapolis
	symphony
		45: mercury EP 40041
		45: emi mercury XEP 9039
		lp: mercury OL2-107/MG 50335/
		    SR2-9007/SR 90335
		lp: mercury wing MGW 14082/SRW 18082
		lp: mercury golden imports SRI 77001
		lp: emi mercury MMA 11029-11030/
		    AMS 16046-16047
		lp: philips classical favourites GL 5832/
		    SGL 5832/642 267GL
		lp: philips sequenza 6527 032
		cd: philips mercury 434 3842

bamberg march 1974	bamberg symphony	lp: vox (france) FSM 73001 lp: vox turnabout TV 34582/QTV 34582 cd: cantus classics CACD 800043/ CACD 500031
london 31 january 1983	royal philharmonic	lp: decca 411 7351 cd: decca 411 7352/417 7492/430 7352/ 436 4762/460 2932 *recordings completed in september and october 1983*

slavonic dance no 6

minneapolis
5 april
1958
	minneapolis
	symphony
		lp: mercury OL2-107/MG 50335/
		    SR2-9007/SR 90335
		lp: mercury wing MGW 14082/SRW 18082
		lp: mercury golden imports SRI 77001
		lp: emi mercury MMA 11029-11030/
		    AMS 16046-16047
		lp: philips classical favourites GL 5832/
		    SGL 5832/642 267GL
		lp: philips sequenza 6527 032
		cd: philips mercury 434 3842

bamberg march 1974	bamberg symphony	lp: vox (france) FSM 73001 lp: vox turnabout TV 34582/QTV 34582 cd: cantus classics CACD 800043/ CACD 500031
london 31 january 1983	royal philharmonic	lp: decca 411 7351 cd: decca 411 7352/417 7492/430 7352/ 436 4762/460 2932 *recordings completed in september and october 1983*

dvorak/**slavonic dance no 7**

minneapolis
5 april
1958
	minneapolis
	symphony
		45: emi mercury XEP 9030
		lp: mercury OL2-107/MG 50335/
		    SR2-9007/SR 90335
		lp: mercury wing MGW 14082/SRW 18082
		lp: mercury golden imports SRI 77001
		lp: emi mercury MMA 11029-11030/
		    AMS 16046-16047
		lp: philips classical favoutites GL 5832/
		    SGL 5832/642 267GL
		lp: philips sequenza 6527 032
		cd: philips mercury 434 3842

bamberg march 1974	bamberg symphony	lp: vox (france) FSM 73001 lp: vox turnabout TV 34582/QTV 34582 cd: cantus classics CACD 800043/ CACD 500031
london 31 january 1983	royal philharmonic	lp: decca 411 7351 cd: decca 411 7352/417 7492/430 7352/ 436 4762/460 2932

recordings completed in september and october 1983

slavonic dance no 8

minneapolis
5 april
1958
	minneapolis
	symphony
		45: emi mercury XEP 9030
		lp: mercury OL2-107/MG 50335/
		    SR2-9007/SR 90335
		lp: mercury wing MGW 14082/SRW 18082
		lp: mercury golden imports SRI 77001
		lp: emi mercury MMA 11029-11030/
		    AMS 16046-16047
		lp: philips classical favourites GL 5832/
		    SGL 5832/642 267GL
		lp: philips sequenza 6527 032
		cd: philips mercury 434 3842

bamberg march 1974	bamberg symphony	lp: vox (france) FSM 73001 lp: vox turnabout TV 34582/QTV 34582 cd: cantus classics CACD 800043/ CACD 500031
london 31 january 1983	royal philharmonic	lp: decca 411 7351 cd: decca 411 7352/417 7492/430 7352/ 436 4762/460 2932

slavonic dance no 9

minneapolis
5 april
1958
	minneapolis
	symphony
		lp: mercury OL2-107/MG 50335/
		    SR2-9007/SR 90335
		lp: mercury wing MGW 14082/SRW 18082
		lp: mercury golden imports SRI 77001
		lp: emi mercury MMA 11029-11030/
		    AMS 16046-16047
		lp: philips classical favourites GL 5832/
		    SGL 5832/642 267GL
		cd: philips mercury 434 3842

bamberg march 1974	bamberg symphony	lp: vox (france) FSM 73001 lp: vox turnabout TV 34582/QTV 34583 cd: cantus classics CACD 800043/ CACD 500031
london 31 january 1983	royal philharmonic	lp: decca 411 7351 cd: decca 411 7352/417 7492/430 7352/ 436 4762/448 9912/460 2932 *recordings completed in september and october 1983*

slavonic dance no 10

minneapolis
6 april
1958
	minneapolis
	symphony
		45: mercury EP 40041
		45: emi mercury XEP 9039
		lp: mercury OL2-107/MG 50335/
		    SR2-9007/SR 90335
		lp: mercury wing MGW 14082/SRW 18082
		lp: mercury golden imports SRI 77001
		lp: emi mercury MMA 11029-11030/
		    AMS 16046-16047
		lp: philips classical favourites GL 5832/
		    SGL 5832/642 267GL
		cd: philips mercury 434 3842

bamberg march 1974	bamberg symphony	lp: vox (france) FSM 73001 lp: vox turnabout TV 34582/QTV 34583 cd: cantus classics CACD 800043/ CACD 500031
london 31 january 1983	royal philharmonic	lp: decca 411 7351 cd: decca 411 7352/417 7492/430 7352/ 436 4762/448 9912/460 2932 *recordings completed in september and october 1983*

dvorak/**slavonic dance no 11**
minneapolis 5 april 1958	minneapolis symphony	lp: mercury OL2-107/MG 50335/ 　　SR2-9007/SR 90335 lp: mercury wing MGW 14082/SRW 18082 lp: mercury golden imports SRI 77001 lp: emi mercury MMA 11029-11030/ 　　AMS 16046-16047 lp: philips classical favourites GL 5832/ 　　SGL 5832/642 267GL cd: philips mercury 434 3842
bamberg march 1974	bamberg symphony	lp: vox (france) FSM 73001 lp: vox turnabout TV 34582/QTV 34583 cd: cantus classics CACD 800043/ 　　CACD 500031
london 31 january 1983	royal philharmonic	lp: decca 411 7351 cd: decca 411 7352/417 7492/430 7352/ 　　436 4762/448 9912/460 2932 *recordings completed in september and october 1983*

slavonic dance no 12
minneapolis 6 april 1958	minneapolis symphony	lp: mercury OL2-107/MG 50335/ 　　SR2-9007/SR 90335 lp: mercury wing MGW 14082/SRW 18082 lp: mercury golden imports SRI 77001 lp: emi mercury MMA 11029-11030/ 　　AMS 16046-16047 lp: philips classical favourites GL 5832/ 　　SGL 5832/642 267GL cd: philips mercury 434 3842
bamberg march 1974	bamberg symphony	lp: vox (france) FSM 73001 lp: vox turnabout TV 34582/QTV 34583 cd: cantus classics CACD 800043/ 　　CACD 500031
london 31 january 1983	royal philharmonic	lp: decca 411 7351 cd: decca 411 7352/417 7492/430 7352/ 　　436 4762/448 9912/460 2932 *recordings completed in september and october 1983*

dvorak/**slavonic dance no 13**

minneapolis
5 april
1958
	minneapolis
	symphony
		45: mercury EP 40041
		45: emi mercury XEP 9039
		lp: mercury OL2-107/MG 50335/
		    SR2-9007/SR 90335
		lp: mercury wing MGW 14082/SRW 18082
		lp: mercury golden imports SRI 77001
		lp: emi mercury MMA 11029-11030/
		    AMS 16046-16047
		lp: philips classical favourites GL 5832/
		    SGL 5832/642 267GL
		cd: philips mercury 434 3842

bamberg march 1974	bamberg symphony	lp: vox (france) FSM 73001 lp: vox turnabout TV 34582/QTV 34583 cd: cantus classics CACD 800043/ CACD 500031
london 31 january 1983	royal philharmonic	lp: decca 411 7351 cd: decca 411 7352/417 7492/430 7352/ 436 4762/448 9912/460 2932

recordings completed in september and october 1983

slavonic dance no 14

minneapolis
6 april
1958
	minneapolis
	symphony
		lp: mercury OL2-107/MG 50335/
		    SR2-9007/SR 90335
		lp: mercury wing MGW 14082/SRW 18082
		lp: mercury golden imports SRI 77001
		lp: emi mercury MMA 11029-11030/
		    AMS 16046-16047
		lp: philips classical favourites GL 5832/
		    SGL 5832/642 267GL
		cd: philips mercury 434 3842

bamberg march 1974	bamberg symphony	lp: vox (france) FSM 73001 lp: vox turnabout 34582/QTV 34583 cd: cantus classics CACD 800043/ CACD 500031
london 31 january 1983	royal philharmonic	lp: decca 411 7351 cd: decca 411 7352/417 7492/430 7352/ 436 4762/448 9912/460 2932

recordings completed in september and october 1983

dvorak/**slavonic dance no 15**

minneapolis
5 april
1958
	minneapolis
	symphony
		45: emi mercury XEP 9063/SEX 15014
		lp: mercury OL2-107/MG 50335/
		  SR2-9007/SR 90335
		lp: mercury wing MGW 14082/SRW 18082
		lp: mercury golden imports SRI 77001
		lp: emi mercury MMA 11029-11030/
		  AMS 16046-16047
		lp: philips classical favourites GL 5832/
		  SGL 5832/642 267GL
		cd: philips mercury 434 3842

bamberg march 1974	bamberg symphony	lp: vox (france) FSM 73001 lp: vox turnabout TV 34582/QTV 34583 cd: cantus classics CACD 800043/ CACD 500031
london 31 january 1983	royal philharmonic	lp: decca 411 7351 cd: decca 411 7352/417 7492/430 7352/ 436 4762/448 9912/460 2932 *recordings completed in september and october 1983*

slavonic dance no 16

minneapolis
6 april
1958
	minneapolis
	symphony
		lp: mercury OL2-107/MG 50335/
		  SE2-9007/SR 90335
		lp: mercury wing MGW 14082/SRW 18082
		lp: mercury golden imports SRI 77001
		lp: emi mercury MMA 11029-11030/
		  AMS 16046-16047
		lp: philips classical favourites GL 5832/
		  SGL 5832/642 267GL
		cd: philips mercury 434 3842

bamberg march 1974	bamberg symphony	lp: vox (france) FSM 73001 lp: vox turnabout TV 34582/QTV 34583 cd: cantus classics CACD 800043/ CACD 500031
london 31 january 1983	royal philharmonic	lp: decca 411 7351 cd: decca 411 7352/417 7492/430 7352/ 436 4762/448 9912/460 2932 *recordings completed in september and october 1983*

american suite

london 5-6 october 1983	royal philharmonic	lp: decca 411 7351 cd: decca 411 7352/430 7022/ 448 9812/460 2932

dvorak/**czech suite**
detroit	detroit	lp: decca SXDL 7522
30 may-	symphony	lp: london (usa) LDR 71024
3 june		cd: decca 414 3702/436 4762/443 0152/
1980		448 2452/460 2932

nocturne for strings
detroit	detroit	lp: decca SXDL 7522
30 may-	symphony	lp: london (usa) LDR 71024
3 june		cd: decca 414 3702/436 4762/460 2932
1980		

polka in b flat
detroit	detroit	lp: decca SXDL 7522
30 may-	symphony	lp: london (usa) LDR 71024
3 june		cd: decca 414 3702/436 4762/460 2932
1980		

polonaise in e flat
detroit	detroit	lp: decca SXDL 7522
30 may-	symphony	lp: london (usa) LDR 71024
3 june		cd: decca 414 3702/436 4762/460 2932
1980		

prague waltzes
detroit	detroit	lp: decca SXDL 7522
30 may-	symphony	lp: london (usa) LDR 71024
3 june		cd: decca 436 4762/443 0152/
1980		448 2452/460 2932

requiem
new york	national	cd: disco archivia 1066
10 november	symphony	
1974	westminster choir	
	gibbs	
	finnilä	
	vaas	
	shirley-quirk	

EDWARD ELGAR (1857-1934)
pomp and circumstance, march no 1
amsterdam	concertgebouw	45: philips ABE 10245/SABE 2010/
25 september	orchestra	SBF 275/313 123SF
1959		lp: philips 6747 327/6780 753
		lp: readers digest RDS 6997
		cd: philips 438 4342

GEORGE ENESCU (1881-1955)
rumanian rhapsody no 1
watford	london	lp: mercury MG 50235/SR 90235
14 june	symphony	lp: mercury golden imports SRI 75018
1960		lp: mercury (france) 120 513MGL/130 513MGY
		lp: emi mercury MMA 11153/AMS 16101
		lp: philips 6747 394
		cd: philips mercury 432 0152
detroit	detroit	lp: decca SXL 6896
7-10	symphony	lp: decca (germany) 642 452AS
april		lp: london (usa) CS 7119
1978		cd: decca 425 0872

rumanian rhapsody no 2
watford	london	lp: mercury MG 50235/SR 90235
14 june	symphony	lp: mercury golden imports SRI 75018
1960		lp: mercury (france) 120 513MGL/130 513MGY
		lp: emi mercury MMA 11153/AMS 16101
		cd: philips mercury 434 3262

FERENC ERKEL (1810-1893)
hungarian national hymn
vienna	philharmonia	unpublished video recording
15 october	hungarica	*austrian television*
1957		

FREDERIC D'ERLANGER (1868-1943)
les cent baisers, ballet
london	london	78: hmv C 3098-3099
27 september	philharmonic	78: victor M 511
1937		cd: pearl GEM 0036

CESAR ESPEJO
airs tziganes for violin and orchestra
los angeles	hollywood	cd: eklipse EKRCD 1404
15 july	bowl symphony	cd: doremi DHR 7736-7737
1947	elman, violin	

MANUEL DE FALLA (1876-1946)
harpsichord concerto
watford	london	mercury unpublished
11 july	symphony	*puyana later recorded this concerto on lp for*
1964	puyana,	*philips conducted by charles mackerras*
	harpsichord	

el amor brujo
new york	ballet theatre	78: decca (usa) DA 390
june	orchestra	cd: sonifolk (spain) 20090
1944	l'argentinita	*dorati's first recording with an american orchestra*

falla/**el sombrero de 3 picos, suite no 2**
minneapolis	minneapolis	cd: minnesota orchestra centenary set
28 march	symphony	
1958		

la vida breve, interlude and dance no 1
minneapolis	minneapolis	45: emi mercury XEP 9052
21 april	symphony	lp: mercury MG 50146/SR 90007
1957		lp: mercury wing MGW 14063/MGW 14085/ SRW 18063/SRW 18085
		lp: mercury golden imports SRI 75101
		lp: mercury (france) 839 816GSY
		lp: emi mercury MMA 11081/AMS 16002
		cd: philips mercury 432 8292
		dance only
		lp: mercury SR2-9130

PAUL FETLER (born 1920)
contrasts for orchestra
minneapolis	minneapolis	lp: mercury MG 50282/SR 90282
17 april	symphony	lp: emi mercury MMA 11151/AMS 16099
1960		lp: philips (france) 839 275DY
		cd: philips mercury 434 3352

CAROLUS FODOR (1786-1846)
symphony no 4
den haag	residentie	lp: residentie orchestra 6812 901-6812 906
1978	orchestra	cd: olympia OCD 501
		cd: residentie orchestra 6812 841

JEAN FRANCAIX (1912-1997)
concertino for piano and orchestra
watford	london	lp: mercury MG 50435/SR 90435
5-6	symphony	lp: mercury (france) 121 047MSL/131 047MSY
august	c.francaix,	lp: philips SAL 3637/838 434LY
1965	piano	lp: philips sequenza 412 0281
		cd: philips mercury 434 3352

CESAR FRANCK (1822-1890)
symphony in d minor
london	royal	lp: vox turnabout TV 34663
5-6	philharmonic	
february		
1976		

variations symphoniques pour piano et orchestre
london	royal	lp: vox turnabout TV 34663
5-6	philharmonic	
february	alpenheim, piano	
1976		

ROBERTO GERHARD (1896-1970)
symphony no 1

london	bbc symphony	lp: hmv ALP 2063/ASD 613
march		lp: decca argo ZRG 752
1964		lp: angel seraphim 60071

dances from don quixote

london	bbc symphony	lp: hmv ALP 2063/ASD 613
march		lp: decca argo ZRG 752
1964		lp: angel seraphim 60071

the plague

london	bbc symphony	unpublished radio broadcast of premiere
1 april	bbc chorus	*recording stored in national sound archive*
1964	murray, narrator	

washington	national	lp: decca HEAD 6
11 may	symphony	*also published in usa under same catalogue number*
1973	orchestra	
	and chorus	
	mccowen,	
	narrator	

GEORGE GERSHWIN (1898-1937)
an american in paris

minneapolis	minneapolis	lp: mercury MG 50290/MG 50431/
20 december	symphony	SR 90290/SR 90431
1957		lp: emi mercury MMA 11004/MMA 11185/
		AMS 16135
		lp: mercury (france) 120 532MSL/
		130 532MSY/134 303WGY
		lp: philips 6513 003/6531 008
		lp: philips wing WL 1206
		lp: philips classical favourites GL 5820/
		SGL 5820/642 228GL/837 828GY
		lp: philips universo 6582 019
		cd: philips mercury 434 3292/434 3652
		excerpts
		lp: philips 6999 013
		lp: philips universo 6582 104

gershwin/**porgy and bess, symphonic suite arranged by bennett**

minneapolis	minneapolis	lp: mercury MG 50016/MG 50394/SR 90394
14 december	symphony	lp: nixa mercury MRL 2506
1952		lp: emi mercury MMA 11004
		lp: mercury (france) 121 017MSL/131 017MSY
		lp: philips (france) 6538 011
detroit	detroit	lp: decca 410 1101
24-26	symphony	cd: decca 410 1102/430 7122/458 6512
october		
1982		

ALBERTO GINASTERA (1916-1983)
variaciones concertantes

minneapolis	minneapolis	lp: mercury MG 50047
20 november	symphony	lp: nixa mercury MRL 2533
1954		

ALEXANDER GLAZUNOV (1865-1936)
the seasons, ballet

dallas	dallas	78: victor M 1072
15-18	symphony	
january		
1946		

MORTON GOULD (1913-1996)
spirituals for string orchestra

minneapolis	minneapolis	45: mercury EP 15028
5-7	symphony	lp: mercury MG 50016
february		lp: mercury wing MGW 14034/SRW 18034
1953		lp: nixa mercury MRL 2506

EDVARD GRIEG (1843-1907)
piano concerto

new york	victor orchestra	78: victor M 1343
22 august	rubinstein, piano	45: victor WDM 1343/ERB 16
1949		lp: victor LM 1018
		lp: hmv ALP 1065
		cd: dante HPC 148
		cd: history 2045691.308
		cd: rca/bmg 09026 630002/09026 630222

grieg/**peer gynt, suite no 1**
vienna   vienna
september   symphony
1958

45: philips fontana CFE 15037/495 017CE
lp: philips fontana CFL 1043/SCFL 102/EFR 2009/
    697 012EL/875 010CY/663 010ER
lp: philips fontana special SFL 14043/700 126WGY
lp: epic (usa) LC 3606
cd: decca collection classique 464 0962
excerpts
45: philips fontana EFF 545/270 613EF

peer gynt, suite no 2
vienna   vienna
september   symphony
1958

lp: philips fontana EFR 2009/663 010ER
lp: philips fontana special SFL 14043/700 126WGY
lp: epic (usa) LC 3606
cd: decca collection classique 464 0962
excerpts
lp: philips fontana CFL 1043/SCFL 102/
    697 012EL/875 010CY

FERDE GROFE (1892-1972)
grand canyon suite
detroit   detroit
24-26   symphony
october
1982

lp: decca 410 1101
cd: decca 410 1102/430 7122
excerpts
cd: decca 444 4512

GEORGE FRIDERIC HANDEL (1685-1759)
messiah
washington   smithsonian
9-10   orchestra
november   university of
1982   maryland and
                   cathedral choirs
                   mathis, bowman,
                   ahnsjö, krause

lp: intersound DMM 232
cd: intersound CDD 232/CDD 3546
excerpts
cd: pro arte CDM 810/CDS 527

music for the royal fireworks, arranged by harty
watford   london
6-8   symphony
july
1957

lp: mercury MG 50158/SR 90158
lp: mercury (france) 120 507MSL/
    130 507MSY/48 015
lp: mercury golden imports SRI 75005
lp: emi mercury MMA 11017/AMS 16031
cd: philips mercury 434 3982
also issued in germany by electrola on a 45 rpm disc

water music, arranged by harty
watford   london
6-8   symphony
july
1957

lp: mercury MG 50158/SR 90158
lp: mercury (france) 120 507MSL/
    130 507MSY/190 158/49 016
lp: mercury golden imports SRI 75005
lp: emi mercury MMA 11017/AMS 16031
cd: philips mercury 434 3982

FRANZ JOSEF HAYDN (1732-1809)

symphonies "a" in b flat and "b" in b flat
marl	philharmonia	lp: decca HDNK 47-48
1-6	hungarica	lp: decca (germany) 648 293DM/
september		SHD 25126/635 244GK
1972		lp: london (usa) STS 15316-15317
		cd: decca 425 9352/430 1002/448 5312

symphony no 1
marl	philharmonia	lp: decca HDNA 1-6
23-31	hungarica	lp: decca (germany) SHD 25111/635 241FK
may		lp: london (usa) STS 15310-15315
1972		cd: decca 425 9002/430 1002/448 5312

recordings completed in june 1972

symphony no 2
marl	philharmonia	lp: decca HDNA 1-6
23-31	hungarica	lp: decca (germany) SHD 25111/635 241FK
may		lp: london (usa) STS 15310-15315
1972		cd: decca 425 9002/430 1002/448 5312

recordings completed in june 1972

symphony no 3
marl	philharmonia	lp: decca HDNA 1-6
23-31	hungarica	lp: decca (germany) SHD 25111/635 241FK
may		lp: london (usa) STS 15310-15315
1972		cd: decca 425 9002/430 1002/448 5312

recordings completed in june 1972

symphony no 4
marl	philharmonia	lp: decca HDNA 1-6
23-31	hungarica	lp: decca (germany) SHD 25111/635 241FK
may		lp: london (usa) STS 15310-15315
1972		cd: decca 425 9002/430 1002/448 5312

recordings completed in june 1972

symphony no 5
marl	philharmonia	lp: decca HDNA 1-6
21-31	hungarica	lp: decca (germany) SHD 25111/635 241FK
august		lp: london (usa) STS 15310-15315
1972		cd: decca 425 9002/430 1002/448 5312

haydn/**symphony no 6 "le matin"**
marl philharmonia lp: decca HDNA 1-6
23-31 hungarica lp: decca (germany) SHD 25111/635 241FK
may lp: london (usa) STS 15310-15315
1972 cd: decca 421 6272/425 9002/
430 1002/448 5312
recordings completed in june 1972

symphony no 7 "le midi"
marl philharmonia lp: decca HDNA 1-6
23-31 hungarica lp: decca (germany) SHD 25111/635 241FK
may lp: london (usa) STS 15310-15315
1972 cd: decca 421 6272/425 9002/
430 1002/448 5312
recordings completed in june 1972

symphony no 8 "le soir"
marl philharmonia lp: decca HDNA 1-6
23-31 hungarica lp: decca (germany) SHD 25111/635 241FK
may lp: london (usa) STS 15310-15315
1972 cd: decca 421 6272/425 9002/
430 1002/448 5312
recordings completed in june 1972

symphony no 9
marl philharmonia lp: decca HDNA 1-6
23-31 hungarica lp: decca (germany) SHD 25111/635 241FK
may lp: london (usa) STS 15310-15315
1972 cd: decca 425 9002/430 1002/448 5312
recordings completed in june 1972

symphony no 10
marl philharmonia lp: decca HDNA 1-6
21-31 hungarica lp: decca (germany) SHD 25111/635 241FK
august lp: london (usa) STS 15310-15315
1972 cd: decca 425 9002/430 1002/448 5312

symphony no 11
marl philharmonia lp: decca HDNA 1-6
21-31 hungarica lp: decca (germany) SHD 25111/635 241FK
august lp: london (usa) STS 15310-15315
1972 cd: decca 425 9002/430 1002/448 5312

symphony no 12
marl philharmonia lp: decca HDNA 1-6
21-31 hungarica lp: decca (germany) SHD 25111/635 241FK
august lp: london (usa) STS 15310-15315
1972 cd: decca 425 9002/430 1002/448 5312

haydn/**symphony no 13**

marl	philharmonia	lp: decca HDNA 1-6
21-31	hungarica	lp: decca (germany) SHD 25111/635 241FK
august		lp: london (usa) STS 15310-15315
1972		cd: decca 425 9002/430 1002/448 5312

symphony no 14

marl	philharmonia	lp: decca HDNA 1-6
21-31	hungarica	lp: decca (germany) SHD 25111/635 241FK
august		lp: london (usa) STS 15310-15315
1972		cd: decca 425 9002/430 1002/448 5312

symphony no 15

marl	philharmonia	lp: decca HDNA 1-6
21-31	hungarica	lp: decca (germany) SHD 25111/635 241FK
august		lp: london (usa) STS 15310-15315
1972		cd: decca 425 9002/430 1002/448 5312

symphony no 16

marl	philharmonia	lp: decca HDNA 1-6
1-6	hungarica	lp: decca (germany) SHD 25111/635 241FK
september		lp: london (usa) STS 15310-15315
1972		cd: decca 425 9002/430 1002/448 5312

symphony no 17

marl	philharmonia	lp: decca HDNA 1-6
1-6	hungarica	lp: decca (germany) SHD 25111/635 241FK
september		lp: london (usa) STS 15310-15315
1972		cd: decca 425 9052/430 1002/448 5312

symphony no 18

marl	philharmonia	lp: decca HDNA 1-6
1-6	hungarica	lp: decca (germany) SHD 25111/635 241FK
september		lp: london (usa) STS 15310-15315
1972		cd: decca 425 9052/430 1002/448 5312

symphony no 19

marl	philharmonia	lp: decca HDNA 1-6
1-6	hungarica	lp: decca (germany) SHD 25111/635 241FK
september		lp: london (usa) STS 15310-15315
1972		cd: decca 425 9052/430 1002/448 5312

symphony no 20

marl	philharmonia	lp: decca HDNB 7-12/SDD 468
27 november-	hungarica	lp: decca (germany) SHD 25077/635 240FK
9 december		lp: london (usa) STS 15257-15262
1971		cd: decca 425 9052/430 1002/448 5312

haydn/**symphony no 21**
marl philharmonia lp: decca HDNB 7-12/SDD 468
27 november- hungarica lp: decca (germany) SHD 25077/635 240FK
9 december lp: london (usa) STS 15257-15262
1971 cd: decca 425 9052/430 1002/448 5312

symphony no 22 "philosopher"
marl philharmonia lp: decca HDNB 7-12/SDD 468
27 november- hungarica lp: decca (germany) SHD 25077/635 240FK
9 december lp: london (usa) STS 15257-15262
1971 cd: decca 425 9052/430 1002/448 5312

symphony no 22 "philosopher", second version
marl philharmonia lp: decca HDNK 47-48
27 november- hungarica lp: decca (germany) 648 293DM/
9 december SHD 25126/635 244GK
1971 lp: london (usa) STS 15316-15317
 cd: decca 425 9352/430 1002/448 5312

symphony no 23
marl philharmonia lp: decca HDNB 7-12
27 november- hungarica lp: decca (germany) SHD 25077/635 240FK
9 december lp: london (usa) STS 15257-15262
1971 cd: decca 425 9052/430 1002/448 5312

symphony no 24
marl philharmonia lp: decca HDNB 7-12
27 november- hungarica lp: decca (germany) SHD 25077/635 240FK
9 december lp: london (usa) STS 15257-15262
1971 cd: decca 425 9052/430 1002/448 5312

symphony no 25
marl philharmonia lp: decca HDNB 7-12/SDD 457
27 november- hungarica lp: decca (germany) SHD 25077/635 240FK
9 december lp: london (usa) STS 15257-15262
1971 cd: decca 425 9052/430 1002/448 5312

symphony no 26 "lamentatione"
marl philharmonia lp: decca HDNB 7-12/SDD 457
27 november- hungarica lp: decca (germany) SHD 25077/635 240FK
9 december lp: london (usa) STS 15257-15262
1971 cd: decca 425 9052/430 1002/448 5312

symphony no 27
marl philharmonia lp: decca HDNB 7-12/SDD 457
27 november hungarica lp: decca (germany) SHD 25077/635 240FK
9 december lp: london (usa) STS 15257-15262
1971 cd: decca 425 9052/430 1002/448 5312

haydn/**symphony no 28**
marl philharmonia lp: decca HDNB 7-12/SDD 457
27 november- hungarica lp: decca (germany) SHD 25077/635 240FK
9 december   lp: london (usa) STS 15257-15262
1971   cd: decca 425 9052/430 1002/448 5312

symphony no 29
marl philharmonia lp: decca HDNB 7-12/SDD 458
27 november- hungarica lp: decca (germany) SHD 25077/635 240FK
9 december   lp: london (usa) STS 15257-15262
1971   cd: decca 425 9052/430 1002/448 5312

symphony no 30 "**allelujah**"
marl philharmonia lp: decca HDNB 7-12/SDD 458
27 november- hungarica lp: decca (germany) SHD 25077/635 240FK
9 december   lp: london (usa) STS 15257-15262
1971   cd: decca 425 9052/430 1002/448 5312

symphony no 31 "**horn signal**"
marl philharmonia lp: decca HDNB 7-12/SDD 458
7-17 hungarica lp: decca (germany) SHD 25077/635 240FK
july   lp: london (usa) STS 15257-15262
1971   cd: decca 425 9052/430 1002/448 5312

symphony no 32
marl philharmonia lp: decca HDNB 7-12
15-26 hungarica lp: decca (germany) SHD 25077/635 240FK
june   lp: london (usa) STS 15257-15262
1971   cd: decca 425 9052/430 1002/448 5312

symphony no 33
marl philharmonia lp: decca HDNB 7-12
7-17 hungarica lp: decca (germany) SHD 25077/635 240FK
july   lp: london (usa) STS 15257-15262
1971   cd: decca 425 9052/430 1002/448 5312

haydn/**symphony no 34**
marl philharmoonia lp: decca HDNB 7-12
27 november- hungarica lp: decca (germany) SHD 25077/635 240FK
9 december lp: london (usa) STS 15257-15262
1971 cd: decca 425 9102/430 1002/448 5312

symphony no 35
marl philharmonia lp: decca HDNB 7-12
7-17 hungarica lp: decca (germany) SHD 25077/635 240FK
july lp: london (usa) STS 15257-15262
1971 cd: decca 425 9102/430 1002/448 5312

symphony no 36
marl philharmonia lp: decca HDNC 13-18
15-26 hungarica lp: decca (germany) SHD 25076/635 239FK
june lp: london (usa) STS 15249-15254
1971 cd: decca 425 9102/430 1002/448 5312

symphony no 37
marl philharmonia lp: decca HDNC 13-18
7-17 hungarica lp: decca (germany) SHD 25076/635 239FK
july lp: london (usa) STS 15249-15254
1971 cd: decca 425 9102/430 1002/448 5312

symphony no 38
marl philharmonia lp: decca HDNC 13-18
7-17 hungarica lp: decca (germany) SHD 25076/635 239FK
july lp: london (usa) STS 15249-15254
1971 cd: decca 425 9102/430 1002/448 5312

symphony no 39
marl philharmonia lp: decca HDNC 13-18
7-17 hungarica lp: decca (germany) SHD 25076/635 239FK
july lp: london (usa) STS 15249-15254
1971 cd: decca 425 9102/430 1002/448 5312

symphony no 40
marl philharmonia lp: decca HDNC 13-18
15-26 hungarica lp: decca (germany) SHD 25076/635 239FK
june lp: london (usa) STS 15249-15254
1971 cd: decca 425 9102/430 1002/448 5312

symphony no 41
marl philharmonia lp: decca HDNC 13-18
7-17 hungarica lp: decca (germany) SHD 25076/635 239FK
july lp: london (usa) STS 15249-15254
1971 cd: decca 425 9102/430 1002/448 5312

haydn/**symphony no 42**

marl	philharmonia	lp: decca HDNC 13-18/SDD 414
15-26	hungarica	lp: decca (germany) SHD 25076/635 239FK
june		lp: london (usa) STS 15249-15254
1971		cd: decca 425 9102/430 1002/448 5312

symphony no 43 "mercury"

marl	philharmonia	lp: decca HDNC 13-18/SDD 546
11-18	hungarica	lp: decca (germany) SHD 25076/635 239FK
november		lp: london (usa) STS 15249-15254
1970		cd: decca 425 9102/430 1002/448 5312

symphony no 44 "trauer"

marl	philharmonia	lp: decca HDNC 13-18/SDD 546
11-18	hungarica	lp: decca (germany) SHD 25076/635 239FK
november		lp: london (usa) STS 15249-15254
1970		cd: decca 425 9102/430 1002/448 5312

symphony no 45 "farewell"

watford	london	lp: mercury MG 50280/SR 90280
22 june	symphony	lp: philips classical favourites GL 5819/
1961		SGL 5819/642 229GL/837 829GY
marl	philharmonia	lp: decca HDNC 13-18/SDD 414
11-18	hungarica	lp: decca (germany) SHD 25076/635 239FK
november		lp: london (usa) STS 15249-15254
1970		cd: decca 425 9102/430 1002/448 5312/
		467 4492

symphony no 46

marl	philharmonia	lp: decca HDNC 13-18
7-25	hungarica	lp: decca (germany) SHD 25076/635 239FK
july		lp: london (usa) STS 15249-15254
1970		cd: decca 425 9102/430 1002/448 5312

symphony no 47

marl	philharmonia	lp: decca HDNC 13-18
7-25	hungarica	lp: decca (germany) SHD 25076/635 239FK
july		lp: london (usa) STS 15249-15254
1970		cd: decca 425 9102/430 1002/448 5312/
		467 4492

symphony no 48 "maria theresia"

marl	philharmonia	lp: decca HDNC 13-18/SDD 547
7-25	hungarica	lp: decca (germany) SHD 25076/635 239FK
july		lp: london (usa) STS 15249-15254
1970		cd: decca 425 9152/430 1002/448 5312/
		467 4492

symphony no 49 "la passione"
bielefeld philharmonia lp: decca HDND 19-22/SDD 359/SDD 547
30 june- hungarica lp: decca (germany) SHD 25053/635 242GK
19 july lp: london (usa) STS 15127-15130
1969 cd: decca 425 9152/430 1002/448 5312

symphony no 50
bielefeld philharmonia lp: decca HDND 19-22
30 june- hungarica lp: decca (germany) SHD 25053/635 242GK
19 july lp: london (usa) STS 15127-15130
1969 cd: decca 425 9152/430 1002/448 5312

symphony no 51
bielefeld philharmonia lp: decca HDND 19-22/SDD 359/SDD 415
30 june- hungarica lp: decca (germany) SHD 25053/635 242GK
19 july lp: london (usa) STS 15127-15130
1969 cd: decca 425 9152/430 1002/448 5312

symphony no 52
bielefeld philharmonia lp: decca HDND 19-22
30 june- hungarica lp: decca (germany) SHD 25053/635 242GK
19 july lp: london (usa) STS 15127-15130
1969 cd: decca 425 9152/430 1002/448 5312

symphony no 53 "l'impériale"
bielefeld philharmonia lp: decca HDND 19-22
30 june- hungarica lp: decca (germany) SHD 25053/635 242GK
19 july lp: london (usa) STS 15127-15130
1969 cd: decca 425 9152/430 1002/448 5312

symphony no 53 "l'impériale", three alternative versions of the final movement *the third of these versions is also known as overture in d*
marl philharmonia lp: decca HDNK 47-48
27 november- hungarica lp: decca (germany) 648 293DM
2 december   SHD 25126/635 244GK
1972 lp: london (usa) STS 15316-15317
 cd: decca 425 9352/430 1002/448 5312

symphony no 54
bielefeld philharmonia lp: decca HDND 19-22
30 june- hungarica lp: decca (germany) SHD 25053/635 242GK
19 july lp: london (usa) STS 15127-15130
1969 cd: decca 425 9152/430 1002/448 5312

haydn/**symphony no 55 "schoolmaster"**
bielefeld	philharmonia	lp: decca HDND 19-22/SDD 415
30 june-	hungarica	lp: decca (germany) SHD 25053/635 242GK
19 july		lp: london (usa) STS 15127-15130
1969		cd: decca 425 9152/430 1002/448 5312

symphony no 56
bielefeld	philharmonia	lp: decca HDND 19-22
30 june-	hungarica	lp: decca (germany) SHD 25053/635 242GK
19 july		lp: london (usa) STS 15127-15130
1969		cd: decca 425 9152/430 1002/448 5312

symphony no 57
bielefeld	philharmonia	lp: decca HDNE 23-26
30 june-	hungarica	lp: decca (germany) SHD 25053/635 242GK
19 july		lp: london (usa) STS 15131-15134
1969		cd: decca 425 9152/430 1002/448 5312

symphony no 58
bielefeld	philharmonia	lp: decca HDNE 23-26
30 june-	hungarica	lp: decca (germany) SHD 25053/635 242GK
19 july		lp: london (usa) STS 15131-15134
1969		cd: decca 425 9152/430 1002/448 5312

symphony no 59 "fire"
watford	bath festival	lp: mercury MG 50436/SR 90436
6-7	orchestra	lp: mercury (france) 121 037MGL/131 037MGY
august		lp: philips 838 431AY
1965		*orchestra described for this recording as festival chamber orchestra*

bielefeld	philharmonia	lp: decca HDNE 23-26
30 june-	hungarica	lp: decca (germany) SHD 25053/635 242GK
19 july		lp: london (usa) STS 15131-15134
1969		cd: decca 425 9152/430 1002/448 5312

symphony no 60 "il distratto"
bielefeld	philharmonia	lp: decca HDNE 23-26/SDD 358
30 june-	hungarica	lp: decca (germany) SHD 25053/635 242GK
19 july		lp: london (usa) STS 15131-15134
1969		cd: decca 425 9202/430 1002/448 5312

symphony no 61
bielefeld	philharmonia	lp: decca HDNE 23-26
30 june-	hungarica	lp: decca (germany) SHD 25053/635 242GK
19 july		lp: london (usa) STS 15131-15134
1969		cd: decca 425 9202/430 1002/448 5312

haydn/**symphony no 62**
bielefeld philharmonia lp: decca HDNE 23-26
30 june- hungarica lp: decca (germany) SHD 25053/635 242GK
19 july lp: london (usa) STS 15131-15134
1969 cd: decca 425 9202/430 1002/448 5312

symphony no 63 "la roxolane"
bielefeld philharmonia lp: decca HDNE 23-26
30 june- hungarica lp: decca (germany) SHD 25053/635 242GK
19 july lp: london (usa) STS 15131-15134
1969 cd: decca 425 9202/430 1002/448 5312

symphony no 63 "la roxolane", earlier version
marl philharmonia lp: decca HDNK 47-48
1-6 hungarica lp: decca (germany) 648 293DM/
september SHD 25126/635 244GK
1972 lp: london (usa) STS 15316-15317
cd: decca 425 9352/430 1002/448 5312

symphony no 64 "tempora mutantur"
bielefeld philharmonia lp: decca HDNE 23-26
30 june- hungarica lp: decca (germany) SHD 25053/635 242GK
19 july lp: london (usa) STS 15131-15134
1969 cd: decca 425 9202/430 1002/448 5312

symphony no 65
bielefeld philharmonia lp: decca HDNF 27-30
30 june- hungarica lp: decca (germany) SHD 25054/635 243GK
19 july lp: london (usa) STS 15135-15138
1969 cd: decca 425 9202/430 1002/448 5312

symphony no 66
bielefeld philharmonia lp: decca HDNF 27-30
30 june- hungarica lp: decca (germany) SHD 25054/635 243GK
19 july lp: london (usa) STS 15135-15138
1969 cd: decca 425 9202/430 1002/448 5312

symphony no 67
bielefeld philharmonia lp: decca HDNF 27-30/SDD 358
30 june- hungarica lp: decca (germany) SHD 25054/635 243GK
19 july lp: london (usa) STS 15135-15138
1969 cd: decca 425 9202/430 1002/448 5312

symphony no 68
bielefeld philharmonia lp: decca HDNF 27-30
30 june- hungarica lp: decca (germany) SHD 25054/635 243GK
19 july lp: london (usa) STS 15135-15138
1969 cd: decca 425 9202/430 1002/448 5312

haydn/**symphony no 69**
bielefeld	philharmonia	lp: decca HDNF 27-30
30 june-	hungarica	lp: decca (germany) SHD 25054/635 243GK
19 july		lp: london (usa) STS 15135-15138
1969		cd: decca 425 9202/430 1002/448 5312

symphony no 70
bielefeld	philharmonia	lp: decca HDNF 27-30
30 june-	hungarica	lp: decca (germany) SHD 25054/635 243GK
19 july		lp: london (usa) STS 15135-15138
1969		cd: decca 425 9202/430 1002/448 5312

symphony no 71
bielefeld	philharmonia	lp: decca HDNF 27-30
30 june-	hungarica	lp: decca (germany) SHD 25054/635 243GK
19 july		lp: london (usa) STS 15135-15138
1969		cd: decca 425 9202/430 1002/448 5312

symphony no 72
bielefeld	philharmonia	lp: decca HDNF 27-30
30 june-	hungarica	lp: decca (germany) SHD 25054/635 243GK
19 july		lp: london (usa) STS 15135-15138
1969		cd: decca 425 9252/430 1002/448 5312

symphony no 73 "la chasse"
marl	philharmonia	lp: decca HDNG 31-34/SDD 413
7-25	hungarica	lp: decca (germany) SHD 25054/635 243GK
july		lp: london (usa) STS 15182-15185
1970		cd: decca 425 9252/430 1002/448 5312

symphony no 74
marl	philharmonia	lp: decca HDNG 31-34/SDD 413
7-25	hungarica	lp: decca (germany) SHD 25054/635 243GK
july		lp: london (usa) STS 15182-15185
1970		cd: decca 425 9252/430 1002/448 5312

symphony no 75
marl	philharmonia	lp: decca HDNG 31-34
7-25	hungarica	lp: decca (germany) SHD 25054/635 243GK
july		lp: london (usa) STS 15182-15185
1970		cd: decca 425 9252/430 1002/448 5312

symphony no 76
marl	philharmonia	lp: decca HDNG 31-34
7-25	hungarica	lp: decca (germany) SHD 25054/635 243GK
july		lp: london (usa) STS 15182-15185
1970		cd: decca 425 9252/430 1002/448 5312

haydn/**symphony no 77**
marl	philharmonia	lp: decca HDNG 31-34
7-25	hungarica	lp: decca (germany) SHD 25054/635 243GK
july		lp: london (usa) STS 15182-15185
1970		cd: decca 425 9252/430 1002/448 5312

symphony no 78
marl	philharmonia	lp: decca HDNG 31-34
7-25	hungarica	lp: decca (germany) SHD 25054/635 243GK
july		lp: london (usa) STS 15182-15185
1970		cd: decca 425 9252/430 1002/448 5312

symphony no 79
marl	philharmonia	lp: decca HDNG 31-34
7-25	hungarica	lp: decca (germany) SHD 25054/635 243GK
july		lp: london (usa) STS 15182-15185
1970		cd: decca 425 9252/430 1002/448 5312

symphony no 80
marl	philharmonia	lp: decca HDNG 31-34
7-25	hungarica	lp: decca (germany) SHD 25054/635 243GK
july		lp: london (usa) STS 15182-15185
1970		cd: decca 425 9252/430 1002/448 5312

symphony no 81
watford	bath festival	lp: mercury MG 50436/SR 90436
7 august	orchestra	lp: mercury (france) 121 037MGL/
1965		131 037MGY
		lp: philips 838 431AY
		orchestra described for this recording as festival chamber orchestra

marl	philharmonia	lp: decca HDNG 31-34
7-25	hungarica	lp: decca (germany) SHD 25054/635 243GK
july		lp: london (usa) STS 15182-15185
1970		cd: decca 425 9252/430 1002/448 5312

symphony no 82 "l'ours"
marl	philharmonia	lp: decca HDNH 35-40/SDD 482
11-28	hungarica	lp: decca (germany) SHD 25062/635 238FK
november		lp: london (usa) STS 15229-15234
1970		cd: decca 425 9252/430 1002/448 1942/ 448 5312/473 8012

symphony no 83 "la poule"
marl	philharmonia	lp: decca HDNH 35-40/SDD 482
11-28	hungarica	lp: decca (germany) SHD 25062/635 238FK
november		lp: london (usa) STS 15229-15234
1970		cd: decca 425 9252/430 1002/448 1942/ 448 5312/473 8012

haydn/**symphony no 84**

marl	philharmonia	lp: decca HDNH 35-40/SDD 483
11-28	hungarica	lp: decca (germany) SHD 25062/635 238FK
november		lp: london (usa) STS 15229-15234
1970		cd: decca 425 9302/430 1002/448 1942/
		448 5312/473 8012

symphony no 85 "la reine"

marl	philharmonia	lp: decca HDNH 35-40/SDD 483
11-28	hungarica	lp: decca (germany) SHD 25062/635 238FK
november		lp: london (usa) STS 15229-15234
1970		cd: decca 425 9302/430 1002/448 1942/
		448 5312/473 8012

symphony no 86

marl	philharmonia	lp: decca HDNH 35-40/SDD 484
11-28	hungarica	lp: decca (germany) SHD 25062/635 238FK
november		lp: london (usa) STS 15229-15234
1970		cd: decca 425 9302/430 1002/448 1942/
		448 5312/473 8012

symphony no 87

marl	philharmonia	lp: decca HDNH 35-40/SDD 484
15-26	hungarica	lp: decca (germany) SHD 25062/635 238FK
june		lp: london (usa) STS 15229-15234
1971		cd: decca 425 9302/430 1002/448 1942/
		448 5312/473 8012

symphony no 88

marl	philharmonia	lp: decca HDNH 35-40/SDD 431
15-26	hungarica	lp: decca (germany) SHD 25062/635 238FK
june		lp: london (usa) STS 15229-15234
1971		cd: decca 425 9302/430 1002/448 5312

symphony no 89

marl	philharmonia	lp: decca HDNH 35-40/SDD 431
15-26	hungarica	lp: decca (germany) SHD 25062/635 238FK
june		lp: london (usa) STS 15229-15234
1971		cd: decca 425 9302/430 1002/448 5312

symphony no 90

marl	philharmonia	lp: decca HDNH 35-40/SDD 412
15-26	hungarica	lp: decca (germany) SHD 25062/635 238FK
june		lp: london (usa) STS 15229-15234
1971		cd: decca 425 9302/430 1002/448 5312

haydn/**symphony no 91**
marl   philharmonia   lp: decca HDNH 35-40
15-26   hungarica   lp: decca (germany) SHD 25062/635 238FK
june   lp: london (usa) STS 15229-15234
1971   cd: decca 425 9302/430 1002/448 5312

symphony no 92 "oxford"
marl   philharmonia   lp: decca HDNH 35-40/SDD 412
15-26   hungarica   lp: decca (germany) SHD 25062/635 238FK
june   lp: london (usa) STS 15229-15234
1971   cd: decca 425 9302/430 1002/448 5312

symphony no 93
marl   philharmonia   lp: decca HDNJ 41-46/SDD 500
23-31   hungarica   lp: decca (germany) SHD 25126/635 244GK
may   lp: london (usa) STS 15319-15324
1972   cd: decca 425 9302/430 1002/
                                          448 5312/452 2562
                                     recordings completed in june 1972

symphony no 94 "surprise"
vienna   philharmonia   lp: mercury MG 50208/SR 90208/SR2-9128
2-3   hungarica   lp: mercury wing MGW 14077/SRW 18077
june   lp: mercury (france) 121 022MSL/131 022MSY
1958   lp: emi mercury MMA 11139/AMS 16085
                                     lp: philips fontana grandioso 894 089ZKY
                                     lp: metronom (germany) 140.132

marl   philharmonia   lp: decca HDNJ 41-46/SDD 500/SPA 494
23-31   hungarica   lp: decca (germany) SHD 25126/635 244GK/
may   642 215AF/648 293DM
1972   lp: london (usa) STS 15319-15324
                                     cd: decca 417 7182/425 9302/430 1002/
                                          448 5312/452 2562/467 4052
                                     recordings completed in june 1972

symphony no 95
marl   philharmonia   lp: decca HDNJ 41-46/SDD 501
23-31   hungarica   lp: decca (germany) SHD 25126/635 244GK
may   lp: london (usa) STS 15319-15324
1972   cd: decca 425 9302/430 1002/
                                          448 5312/452 2562
                                     recordings completed in june 1972

haydn/**symphony no 96 "miracle"**

marl	philharmonia	lp: decca HDNJ 41-46/SDD 501
23-31	hungarica	lp: decca (germany) SHD 25126/635 244GK/
may		648 293DM
1972		lp: london (usa) STS 15319-15324
		cd: decca 417 7182/425 9352/430 1002/
		448 5312/452 2562
		recordings completed in june 1972

symphony no 97

marl	philharmonia	lp: decca HDNJ 41-46/SDD 502
23-31	hungarica	lp: decca (germany) SHD 25126/635 244GK
may		lp: london (usa) STS 15319-15324
1972		cd: decca 425 9352/430 1002/
		448 5312/452 2562
		recordings completed in june 1972

symphony no 98

marl	philharmonia	decca unpublished
1-5	hungarica	
july		
1972		

marl	philharmonia	lp: decca HDNJ 41-46/SDD 502
21-31	hungarica	lp: decca (germany) SHD 25126/635 244GK
august		lp: london (usa) STS 15319-15324
1972		cd: decca 425 9352/430 1002/
		448 5312/452 2562

symphony no 99

marl	philharmonia	lp: decca HDNJ 41-46/SDD 503
23-31	hungarica	lp: decca (germany) SHD 25126/635 244GK
may		lp: london (usa) STS 15319-15324
1972		cd: decca 425 9352/430 1002/
		448 5312/452 2592
		recordings completed in june 1972

haydn/**symphony no 100 "military"**

watford	london	lp: mercury MG 50155/MG 50415/SR 90155/
7-9	symphony	SR 90415
july		lp: mercury wing MGW 14064/SRW 18064
1957		lp: mercury (france) 121 021MSL/131 021MSY
		lp: nixa mercury MRL 2592
		lp: emi mercury MMA 11055
		lp: philips fontana special 6547 009

marl	philharmonia	lp: decca HDNJ 41-46/SDD 503
23-31	hungarica	lp: decca (germany) SHD 25126/635 244GK
may		lp: london (usa) STS 15319-15324
1972		cd: decca 417 7182/425 9352/430 1002/
		448 5312/452 2592/460 6282/467 4052
		recordings completed in june 1972

symphony no 101 "clock"

watford	london	lp: mercury MG 50155/SR 90155
7-10	symphony	lp: mercury wing MGW 14064/SRW 18064
july		lp: mercury (france) 121 021MSL/131 021MSY
1957		lp: nixa mercury MRL 2592
		lp: emi mercury MMA 11055
		lp: philips fontana special 6547 009

marl	philharmonia	lp: decca HDNJ 41-46/SDD 504/SPA 494
1-5	hungarica	lp: decca (germany) SHD 25126/635 244GK/
july		642 215AF/648 293DM
1972		lp: london (usa) STS 15319-15324
		cd: decca 425 9352/430 1002/
		448 5312/452 2592/467 4052

symphony no 102

marl	philharmonia	lp: decca HDNJ 41-46/SDD 504
27 november-	hungarica	lp: decca (germany) SHD 25126/635 244GK
2 december		lp: london (usa) STS 15319-15324
1972		cd: decca 425 9352/430 1002/
		448 5312/452 2592

symphony no 103 "drum roll"

vienna	philharmonia	lp: mercury MG 50208/SR 90208
3 june	hungarica	lp: mercury (france) 121 022MSL/131 022MSY
1958		lp: mercury wing MGW 14077/SRW 18077
		lp: emi mercury MMA 11139/AMS 16085
		lp: philips fontana grandioso 894 089ZKY
		lp: metronom (germany) 140.132
		lp: franklin mint FM 7011-7014

marl	philharmonia	lp: decca HDNJ 41-46/SDD 505
27 november-	hungarica	lp: decca (germany) SHD 25126/635 244GK/
2 december		648 293DM
1972		lp: london (usa) STS 15319-15324
		cd: decca 425 9352/430 1002/448 5312/452 2592

haydn/**symphony no 103 "drum roll", alternative version of final movement**
marl	philharmonia	lp: decca HDNK 47-48
1-6	hungarica	lp: decca (germany) SHD 25126/635 244GK/
september		648 293DM
1972		lp: london (usa) STS 15316-15317
		cd: decca 425 9352/430 1002/448 5312

symphony no 104 "london"
marl	philharmonia	lp: decca HDNJ 41-46/SDD 505
27 november-	hungarica	lp: decca (germany) SHD 25126/635 244GK
2 december		648 293DM/642 210AN
1972		lp: london (usa) STS 15319-15324
		cd: decca 425 9352/430 1002/
		448 5312/452 2592/460 6282

sinfonia concertante for violin, cello, oboe, bassoon and orchestra
numbered as symphony no 105
marl	philharmonia	lp: decca HDNH 35-40/SDD 445
7-17	hungarica	lp: decca (germany) SHD 25062/635 238FK/
july	ozim, violin	642 566AH
1971	racz, cello	lp: london (usa) STS 15229-15234
	engle, oboe	cd: decca 425 9352/430 1002/448 5312
	baranyai,	
	bassoon	

24 minuets with trios
marl	philharmonia	lp: decca HDNW 90-91
9-11	hungarica	lp: london (usa) STS 15359-15360
september		cd: decca 436 2202
1975		

cello concerti nos 1 and 2
bamberg	bamberg	lp: vox (france) FSM 43019
march	symphony	lp: vox turnabout TV 34695
1974	varga, cello	*concerto no 2 appears on cd vox masters MMD 8508*

haydn/5 keyboard concerti: no 2 in d; no 3 in f; no 4 in g; no 11 in d
bamberg   bamberg   lp: vox SVBX 5136
march   symphony   lp: vox (france) FSM 43031-43033
1974   alpenheim, piano   lp: vox turnabout TV 37090-37092
                                            cd: vox 11.54992/CDX 5-17
                                            cd: panthéon D 19157
                                            recordings completed in may 1975; concerti nos 4 and 9 also appear on cd concerto royale 206230.360

die schöpfung
london   royal   lp: decca D50 D2
17-21   philharmonic   lp: decca (germany) 635 426EK
december   brighton   lp: london (usa) OSA 12108
1976   festival chorus   cd: decca 421 6052/443 0272/458 3252
                       popp   *excerpts*
                       doese   cd: decca 411 9572
                       hollweg   cd: decca belart 461 0592
                       luxon
                       moll

die jahreszeiten
london   royal   lp: decca D88 D3
13-21   philharmonic   lp: decca (germany) 635 425FK
june   brighton   lp: london (usa) OSA 13128
1977   festival chorus   cd: decca 425 7082/448 1012/458 3252
                       cotrubas   *excerpts*
                       krenn   cd: decca belart 460 5882
                       sotin   *recording completed on 21 october 1977*

il ritorno di tobia, oratorio
london   royal   lp: decca D216 D4
14-21   philharmonic   lp: decca (germany) 635 523GK
december   brighton   lp: london (usa) OSA 1445
1979   festival chorus   cd: decca 440 0382/458 3252
                       hendricks
                       zoghby
                       d.jones
                       langridge
                       luxon

armida
épilanges   lausanne   lp: philips 6769 021
september   chamber   cd: philips 432 4382/473 4762
1978   orchestra   *excerpts*
                       norman   lp: philips 6529 060
                       burrowes   lp: philips sequenza 6527 147
                       ahnsjö   cd: philips 426 6412/434 9872
                       leggate   cd: bbc music MM 10
                       rolfe-johnson
                       ramey

haydn/**la fedelta premiata**
épilanges	lausanne	lp: philips 6707 028
june	chamber	cd: philips 432 4302/473 4762
1975	orchestra	*excerpts*
	cotrubas	lp: philips sequenza 6527 147/6527 218
	landy	lp: franklin mint FM 7011-7014
	valentini-terrani	cd: philips 420 0842/434 9872
	von stade	cd: bbc music MM 10
	alva	
	titus	

l'incontro improvviso
épilanges	lausanne	lp: philips 6769 040
june	chamber	cd: philips 432 4162/473 8512
1979	orchestra	*excerpts*
	zoghby	lp: philips sequenza 6527 147/6527 218
	marshall	cd: philips 434 9872
	d.jones	cd: bbc music MM 10
	ahnsjö	*recording completed in june 1980*
	trimarchi	
	luxon	

l'infedelta delusa
épilanges	lausanne	lp: philips 6769 061
june	chamber	cd: philips 432 4132/473 8512
1980	orchestra	*excerpts*
	mathis	lp: philips sequenza 6527 147/6527 218
	hendricks	
	ahnsjö	
	baldin	
	devlin	

il mondo della luna
épilanges	lausanne	lp: philips 6769 003
september	chamber	cd: philips 432 4202/473 8512
1977	orchestra	*excerpts*
	auger	lp: philips sequenza 6527 147/6527 218
	mathis	lp: franklin mint FM 7011-7014
	von stade	cd: philips 420 0842/434 9872
	alva	cd: bbc music MM 10
	rolfe-johnson	
	trimarchi	

haydn/**l'isola disabitata**
épilanges	lausanne	lp: philips 6700 119
may	chamber	cd: philips 432 4272/473 8512
1977	orchestra	*excerpts*
	zoghby	lp: philips sequenza 6527 147/6527 218
	lerer	lp: franklin mint FM 7011-7014
	alva	cd: philips 438 8972
	bruson	cd: bbc music MM 10

orlando paladino
épilanges	lausanne	lp: philips 6707 029
june	chamber	cd: philips 432 4342/473 4762
1976	orchestra	*excerpts*
	auger	lp: philips sequenza 6527 218
	ameling	lp: franklin mint FM 7011-7014
	killebrew	cd: philips 434 9872
	ahnsjö	cd: bbc music MM 10
	shirley	
	luxon	
	trimarchi	

la vera costanza
épilanges	lausanne	lp: philips 6703 077
may	chamber	cd: philips 432 4242/473 4762
1976	orchestra	*excerpts*
	norman	lp: philips sequenza 6527 060/6527 147/ 6527 218
	donath	
	ahnsjö	cd: philips 426 6412/434 9872/454 6932
	trimarchi	cd: bbc music MM 10
	ganzarolli	

AKE HERMANSON (born 1923)
symphony no 1
stockholm	stockholm	lp: caprice CAP 1206
7 december	philharmonic	
1973		

ALAN HOVHANESS (1911-2000)
prelude and quadruple fugue
minneapolis	minneapolis	unpublished radio broadcast
21 march	symphony	*recording stored in national sound archive*
1958		

EMMERICH KALMAN (1882-1953)
die czardasfürstin, waltz

vienna	philharmonia	45: emi mercury XEP 9076/SEX 15020
7 june	hungarica	lp: mercury MG 50190/MG 50444/
1958		SR 90190/SR 90444
		lp: mercury (france) 120 505MGL/130 505MGY
		lp: mercury wing MGW 14087/SRW 18087
		lp: emi mercury MMA 11116/AMS 16063
		cd: philips mercury 434 3382
		mercury wing issues incorrectly described orchestra as minneapolis symphony

ARAM KHACHATURIAN (1903-1978)
violin concerto

watford	london	lp: mercury MG 50393/SR 90393
4 july	symphony	lp: mercury (france) 120 557MGL/130 557MGY
1964	szeryng, violin	lp: philips AL 3503/SAL 3503/
		A04924L/838 424AY
		cd: philips mercury 434 3182
		cd: philips 462 8562

gayaneh, suite

wembley	london	lp: mercury MG 50209/SR 90209
15-17	symphony	lp: mercury wing MGW 14095/SRW 18095
june		lp: emi mercury MMA 11166/AMS 16116
1960		lp: philips diskothek der meister 836 603VZ
		lp: philips wing WL 1210
		lp: philips sequenza 6527 187
		cd: philips mercury 434 3232
		excerpts
		lp: mercury MG 50293/SR 90293/SR2-9127
		lp: philips 6768 292/6882 102/6999 013
		cd: philips mercury 442 5412

ZOLTAN KODALY (1882-1967)
ballet music

marl	philharmonia	lp: decca SXLM 6665-6667/SXL 6714
26 november	hungarica	lp: london (usa) CSA 2313/CS 6862-6864
1973		*recordings completed in december 1973*

concerto for orchestra

marl	philharmonia	lp: decca SXLM 6665-6667/SXL 6712
25-29	hungarica	lp: decca (france) 592.133
september		lp: london (usa) CSA 2313/CS 6862-6864
1973		cd: decca 443 0062/443 0422

kodaly/**dances of galanta**

vienna 2 june 1958	philharmonia hungarica	lp: mercury MG 50179/SR 90179 lp: mercury (france) 121 018MGL/131 018MGY lp: emi mercury MMA 11077/AMS 16027 cd: philips mercury 432 0052
marl 26 november 1973	philharmonia hungarica	lp: decca SXLM 6665-6667/SXL 6712/JB 138 lp: decca (france) 592.133 lp: decca (germany) 642 269AS lp: london (usa) CSA 2313/CS 6863-6864 cd: decca 425 0342/443 0062/443 0422 *recordings completed in december 1973*

dances of marosszek

vienna 2 june 1958	philharmonia hungarica	lp: mercury MG 50179/SR 90179 lp: mercury (france) 121 018MGL/131 018MGY lp: emi mercury MMA 11077/AMS 16027 cd: philips mercury 432 0052
marl 26 november 1973	philharmonia hungarica	lp: decca SXLM 6665-6667/SXL 6712/414 0761 lp: decca (france) 592.133 lp: decca (germany) 642 269AS lp: london (usa) CSA 2313/CS 6862-6864 cd: decca 425 0342/443 0062/443 0422 *recordings completed in december 1973*

hary janos, suite from the incidental music

minneapolis 1950	minneapolis symphony	45: victor WDM 1750 lp: victor LM 1750 lp: victor (italy) A12R 0063

minneapolis
17 november
1956
	minneapolis
	symphony
		lp: mercury MG 50132/SR 90132
		lp: mercury (france) 121 018MGL/
		    131 018MGY/53.005
		lp: nixa mercury MRL 2565
		lp: emi mercury MMA 11072/AMS 16025
		cd: philips mercury 432 0052
		excerpts
		lp: mercury MG 50398/MG 50526/
		    SR 90398/SR 90526/MB 1001
		lp: philips 6882 100/6999 013

hilversum 4 june 1973	netherlanda radio philharmonic	lp: decca PFS 4355/414 0761 lp: london (usa) SPC 21146 cd: decca 448 9472 *intermezzo only* cd: rca/bmg 74321 308892
marl 25-29 september 1973	philharmonia hungarica	lp: decca SXLM 6665-6667/SXL 6713/JB 138 lp: decca (germany) 642 269AS lp: london (usa) CSA 2313/CS 6862-6864 cd: decca 425 0342/443 0062/443 0422

kodaly/**hungarian rondo**
marl philharmonia lp: decca SXLM 6665-6667/SXL 6714/414 0761
26 november hungarica lp: london (usa) CSA 2313/CS 6862-6864
1973 *recordings completed in december 1973*

hungarian tunes
marl philharmonia lp: decca SXLM 6665-6667/SXL 6714
26 november hungarica lp: london (usa) CSA 2313/CS 6862-6864
1973 *recordings completed in december 1973*

jesus and the traders, for unaccompanied chorus
dallas north texas 78: victor M 1331
january college choir
1949

minuetto serio
marl philharmonia lp: decca SXLM 6665-6667/SXL 6713
26 november hungarica lp: london (usa) CSA 2313/CS 6862-6864
1973 *recordings completed in december 1973*

peacock variations
chicago chicago lp: mercury MG 50038
8-9 symphony lp: mercury (france) 53.005
january lp: nixa mercury MRL 2541
1954 lp: emi mercury MMA 11072
  cd: philips mercury 434 3972

budapest hungarian lp: hungaroton SLPX 11392
24-28 state orchestra cd: hungaroton HCD 11392
september
1968

marl philharmonia lp: decca SXLM 6665-6667/SXL 6714/JB 138
25-29 hungarica lp: london (usa) CSA 2313/CS 6862-6864
september cd: decca 425 0342/443 0062/443 0422
1973

kodaly/**psalmus hungaricus**
dallas	dallas	78: victor M 1331
january	symphony	
1949	north texas	
	college choir	
	carelli	

stockholm	stockholm	cd: bis BISCD 421-424
16 december	philharmonic	
1967	orchestra	
	and chorus	
	szimandy	

budapest	hungarian	lp: hungaroton SLPX 11392
24-27	state orchestra	cd: hungaroton HCD 11392/HCD 31503
september	and chorus	
1968	szimandy	

summer evening
marl	philharmonia	lp: decca SXLM 6665-6667/SXL 6714
26 november	hungarica	lp: london (usa) CSA 2313/CS 6862-6864
1973		cd: decca 443 0062
		recordings completed in december 1973

symphony in c
marl	philharmonia	lp: decca SXLM 6665-6667/SXL 6713
26 november	hungarica	lp: london (usa) CSA 2313/CS 6862-6864
1973		*recordings completed in december 1973*

theatre overture
marl	philharmonia	lp: decca SXLM 6665-6667/SXL 6712
26 november	hungarica	lp: decca (france) 592.133
1973		lp: london (usa) CSA 2313/CS 6862-6864
		recordings completed in december 1973

CHARLES KOECHLIN (1867-1950)
les bandar-log, symphonic poem
london	bbc symphony	lp: hmv ALP 2092/ASD 639
27 september		lp: electrola E 91457/SME 91457
1964		lp: angel 36295
		lp: decca argo ZRG 756
		cd: emi CDM 763 9482
		recording completed on 11-16 october 1964

JOHN LA MONTAINE (born 1920)
wilderness journal
washington	national	cd: fredonia FDCD 12
10 october	symphony	
1972	gramm	

JOSEF LANNER (1801-1843)
die schönbrunner, waltz

vienna	philharmonia	lp: mercury MG 50190/MG 50289/
8 june	hungarica	SR 90190/SR 90289
1958		lp: mercury wing MGW 14087/SRW 18087
		lp: mercury (france) 120 505MGL/130 505MGY
		lp: mercury golden imports SRI 75098
		lp: emi mercury MMA 11116/AMS 16063
		cd: philips mercury 434 3382

mercury wing editions incorrectly described orchestra as minneapolis symphony

BENJAMIN LEES (born 1924)
concerto grosso for string quartet and orchestra

new york	national	cd: disco archivia 1063
20 april	symphony	
1975		

FRANZ LEHAR (1870-1948)
die lustige witwe, waltz
also known as ballsirenen

vienna	philharmonia	45: emi mercury XEP 9076/SEX 15020
7 june	hungarica	lp: mercury MG 50190/MG 50289/
1958		MG 50444/SR 90190/SR 90289/
		SR 90444
		lp: mercury wing MGW 14087/SRW 18087
		lp: mercury golden imports SRI 75098
		lp: philips wing WL 1208
		lp: emi mercury MMA 11116/AMS 16063
		cd: philips mercury 434 3382
		cd: philips 456 4982

mercury wing editions incorrectly described orcheatra as minneapolis symphony

FRANZ LISZT (1811-1886)
a faust symphony

amsterdam	concertgebouw	lp: philips 6769 089
13-15	orchestra	cd: philips 442 6422
january	and chorus	
1982	kozma	

liszt/**piano concerto no 1**
dallas   dallas   78: victor M 1144
11 february   symphony   78: hmv DB 9487-9488
1947   rubinstein, piano   45: victor WDM 1144
                                     lp: victor LM 1018
                                     lp: hmv (france) FALP 162
                                     cd: rca/bmg GD 60046/09026 630222
                                     cd: dante HPC 148

christus, oratorio
budapest   hungarian state   lp: hungaroton SLPD 12831-12834
1985   orchestra   cd: hungaroton HCD 12831-12833
                 and chorus
                 kincses
                 takacs
                 nagy
                 solyom-nagy
                 polgar

mephisto waltz
vienna   philharmonia   philips fontana unpublished
15-17   hungarica   *recording probably planned but not completed*
october
1957

les préludes
vienna   philharmonia   philips fontana unpublished
15-17   hungarica   *recording probably planned but not completed*
october
1957

wembley   london   lp: mercury MG 50214/SR 90214
6-7   symphony   lp: mercury wing MGW 14084/SRW 18084
june   lp: emi mercury MMA 11159/AMS 16105
1960   lp: metronom (germany) 140.170
                                     cd: philips mercury 462 9532

tasso
vienna   philharmonia   philips fontana unpublished
15-17   hungarica   *recording probably planned but not completed*
october
1957

liszt/hungarian rhapsody no 1 in f minor

watford	london	lp: mercury MG 50371/SR 90371
21 july	symphony	lp: mercury golden imports SRI 75089
1963		lp: philips classical favourites GL 5789/ SGL 5789/642 234GL/837 834GY
		lp: philips fontana grandioso 894 080ZKY
		lp: philips festivo 6570 140
		lp: philips sequenza 6527 202
		cd: philips mercury 432 0152

hungarian rhapsody no 2 in d minor

vienna	philharmonia	philips fontana unpublished
15-17	hungarica	*recording probably planned but not completed*
october		
1957		

wembley	london	lp: mercury MG 50235/SR 90235/SR 90526
14 june	symphony	lp: mercury wing MGW 14084/SRW 18084
1960		lp: mercury golden imports SRI 75018/ SRI 75089
		lp: mercury (france) 120 513MGL/130 513MGY
		lp: emi mercury MMA 11153/AMS 16101
		lp: philips 6882 100/6999 013
		lp: philips festivo 839 821GY/6570 140
		lp: philips sequenza 6527 202
		cd: philips mercury 432 0152

detroit	detroit	lp: decca SXL 6896
7-10	symphony	lp: decca (germany) 642 452AS
april		lp: london (usa) CS 7119
1978		

liszt/**hungarian rhapsody no 3 in d**
wembley   london   lp: mercury MG 50235/SR 90235
13 june   symphony   lp: mercury golden imports SRI 75018/
1960   SRI 75089
                                  lp: mercury (france) 120 513MGL/130 513MGY
                                  lp: emi mercury MMA 11153/AMS 16101
                                  lp: philips festivo 6570 140
                                  lp: philips sequenza 6527 202
                                  cd: philips mercury 432 0152

hungarian rhapsody no 4 in d minor
watford   london   lp: mercury MG 50371/SR 90371
20 july   symphony   lp: mercury golden imports SRI 75089
1963   lp: philips 6599 428
                                  lp: philips classical favourites GL 5789/
                                      SGL 5789/642 234GL/837 834GY
                                  lp: philips fontana grandioso 894 080ZKY
                                  lp: philips festivo 839 821GY/6570 140
                                  lp: philips sequenza 6527 202
                                  cd: philips mercury 432 0152
                                  cd: delta 33102

hungarian rhapsody no 5 in e minor
watford   london   lp: mercury MG 50371/SR 90371
19 july   symphony   lp: mercury golden imports SRI 75089
1963   lp: philips 6718 012
                                  lp: philips classical favourites GL 5789/
                                      SGL 5789/642 234GL/837 834GY
                                  lp: philips fontana grandioso 894 080ZKY
                                  lp: philips festivo 6570 140
                                  lp: philips sequenza 6527 202
                                  cd: philips mercury 432 0152

hungarian rhapsody no 6 in d
watford   london   lp: mercury MG 50371/SR 90371
21 july   symphony   lp: mercury golden imports SRI 75089
1963   lp: philips classical favourites GL 5789/
                                      SGL 5789/642 234GL/837 834GY
                                  lp: philips fontana grandioso 894 080ZKY
                                  lp: philips festivo 6570 140
                                  lp: philips sequenza 6527 202
                                  cd: philips mercury 432 0152

GUSTAV MAHLER (1860-1911)
symphony no 5

stockholm 14-15 september 1973	stockholm philharmonic	lp: lyssna LY 74.4

symphony no 6

new york 27 october 1974	national symphony	cd: disco archivia 1063
london 24 september 1978	royal philharmonic	unpublished radio broadcast *recording stored in national sound archive*

lieder eines fahrenden gesellen

london 24 september 1978	royal philharmonic luxon	unpublished radio broadcast *recording stored in national sound archive*

FELIX MENDELSSOHN-BARTHOLDY (1809-1847)
symphony no 3 "scotch"

walthamstow 3-4 july 1956	london symphony	lp: mercury MG 50123/SR 90123 lp: mercury wing MGW 14056/SRW 18056 lp: emi mercury MMA 11048 lp: philips SDAL 502 lp: concert hall M 2465/SM 2465 cd: philips mercury 434 3632

symphony no 4 "italian"

minneapolis 27-29 april 1952	minneapolis symphony	lp: mercury MG 50010 lp: mercury wing MGW 14006/SRW 18006 lp: nixa mercury MRL 2540 lp: philips 6747 239 lp: philips wing WL 1038 lp: philips fontana special SFL 14067/700 176WGY/ 200 061WGL/700 061WGY lp: philips pergola 832 096PGY lp: metronom (germany) 140.137

mendelssohn/**violin concerto**
los angeles	hollywood bowl	cd: eklipse EKR 1404
15 july	symphony	cd: doremi DHR 7736-7737
1947	elman, violin	

watford	london	lp: mercury MG 50406/SR 90406
3 july	symphony	lp: mercury (france) 120 557MGL/130 557MGY
1964	szeryng, violin	lp: philips AL 3504/SAL 3504/L04917L/ 838 417LY
		lp: philips sequenza 6527 061
		lp: quintessence PMC 7194
		cd: philips mercury 434 3392

first movement cadenza from a 1947 new york performance with menuhin and the columbia symphony orchestra appears on warner/nvc arts vhs video 8573 858013 and dvd video 8573 858012

hebrides overture
walthamstow	london	lp: mercury MG 50123/MG 50323/ SR 90123/SR 90323
5 july	symphony	
1956		lp: mercury wing MGW 14056/SRW 18056
		lp: emi mercury MMA 11048
		lp: philips SDAL 502
		lp: concert hall M 2465/SM 2465
		cd: philips mercury 434 3632
		cd: decca collection classique 464 0962

a version of the overture published on philips classical favourites GBL 5581/G03066L/G05398R with concertgebouw orchestra conducted by bernard haitink incorrectly described the conductor as dorati

meeresstille und glückliche fahrt, overture
amsterdam	concertgebouw	lp: philips classical favourites GBL 5581/ G03066L/G05398R
23-25	orchestra	
september		lp: epic (usa) LC 3723/BC 1094
1959		

a midsummer night's dream, overture
vienna	vienna	lp: philips fontana CFL 1043/SCFL 102/ 695 009CL/875 010CY/697 012EL
3-6	symphony	
may		lp: philips 6747 239
1958		lp: philips fontana special SFL 14043/ 700 126WGY/200 049WGL
		lp: philips pergola 832 096PGY
		lp: epic (usa) LC 3606
		cd: decca collection classique 464 0962

a midsummer night's dream, scherzo
vienna	vienna	45: philips fontana CFE 15037/495 016CE
5-6	symphony	lp: philips fontana CFL 1043/695 009CL/ 697 012EL
may		
1958		lp: philips 6747 239
		lp: philips fontana special SFL 14043/ 700 126WGY/200 049WGL
		lp: philips pergola 832 096PGY
		lp: epic (usa) LC 3606
		cd: decca collection classique 464 0962

mendelssohn/**a midsummer night's dream, nocturne**

vienna	vienna	lp: philips fontana CFL 1043/SCFL 102/
5-6	symphony	695 009CL/875 010CY/697 012EL
may		lp: philips 6747 239
1958		lp: philips fontana special SFL 14043/
		700 126WGY/200 049WGL
		lp: philips pergola 832 096PGY
		lp: epic (usa) LC 3606
		cd: decca collection classique 464 0962

a midsummer night's dream, wedding march

vienna	vienna	45: philips fontana CFE 15037/495 016CE
5-6	symphony	lp: philips fontana CFL 1043/SCFL 102/
may		695 009CL/875 010CY/697 012EL/
1958		K71-BX 200
		lp: philips 6718 012/6747 050/6747 239
		lp: philips fontana special SFL 14043/
		700 126WGY/200 049WGL
		lp: philips pergola 832 096PGY
		lp: epic (usa) LC 3606
		cd: decca collection classique 464 0962

unspecified items from this midsummer night's dream suite also published on lp by philips 6545 042

OLIVIER MESSIAEN (1908-1992)
la transfiguration de notre seigneur

washington	national	lp: decca HEAD 1-2
28-29	symphony	cd: decca 425 6162
april	westminster	
1972	choir	

chronochromie

london	bbc symphony	lp: hmv ALP 2092/ASD 639
27 october		lp: electrola E 91457/SME 91457
1964		lp: decca argo ZRG 756
		lp: angel 36295
		cd: emi CDM 763 9482

GIACOMO MEYERBEER (1791-1864)
l'africaine, excerpt (o paradis!)

new york	victor	78: victor MO 1191/VO 13
24 september	orchestra	78: hmv DB 6869
1947	tagliavini	lp: victor LM 20062
	sung in italian	cd: myto MCD 93382
		cd: preiser 89163
		cd: grandi voci GVS 15

DARIUS MILHAUD (1892-1974)
le boeuf sur le toit

watford	london	lp: mercury MG 50435/SR 90435
4-5 august	symphony	lp: mercury (france) 121 047MSL/131 047MSY
1965		lp: philips SAL 3637/838 434LY/6747 228
		lp: philips sequenza 412 0281
		cd: philips mercury 434 3352

WOLFGANG AMADEUS MOZART (1756-1791)
symphony no 31 "paris"

minneapolis	minneapolis	45: victor WDM 1595
1951	symphony	lp: victor LM 1185

symphony no 36 "linz"

walthamstow	london	lp: mercury MG 50121/SR 90121
6 july	symphony	lp: mercury wing MGW 14064/SRW 18064
1956		lp: mercury (france) MLP 7507
		lp: nixa mercury MRL 2562
		lp: emi mercury MMA 11087

symphony no 40

minneapolis	minneapolis	lp: mercury MG 50010
27-29	symphony	lp: mercury wing MGW 14006/SRW 18006
april		lp: nixa mercury MRL 2540
1952		lp: philips wing WL 1038
		lp: philips fontana special SFL 14067/ 700 176WGY

watford	london	lp: mercury MG 50280/SR 90280/SR 90511
23 june	symphony	lp: philips classical favourites GL 5819/ SGL 5819/642 229GL/837 829GY
1961		lp: philips fontana 6531 006
		lp: metronom (germany) 140.135
		6531 006 incorrectly describes orchestra as minneapolis symphony

piano concerto no 25

minneapolis	minneapolis	cd: minnesota orchestra centenary set
15 november	symphony	
1957	e.dohnanyi, piano	

mozart/**serenade no 13 "eine kleine nachtmusik"**
walthamstow	london	lp: mercury MG 50121/MG 50412/
6 july	symphony	SR 90121/SR 90412
1956		lp: mercury (france) 49.006
		lp: nixa mercury MRL 2562
		lp: emi mercury MMA 11087
		cd: philips mercury 434 3982

le nozze di figaro, overture
watford	london	lp: mercury SR2-9134
26 july	symphony	
1962		

lucio silla, overture
watford	bath festival	lp: mercury MG 50438/SR 90438
1 august	orchestra	*orchestra described for this recording as festival chamber*
1965		*orchestra*

three german dances k605
watford	bath festival	lp: mercury MG 50438/SR 90438
5 august	orchestra	cd: philips mercury 434 3982
1965		*orchestra described for this recording as festival chamber orchestra*

allegro in d k121
watford	bath festival	lp: mercury MG 50438/SR 90438
5 august	orchestra	cd: philips mercury 434 3982
1965		*orchestra described for this recording as festival chamber orchestra*

march k249; 2 marches k335; minuet k409
watford	bath festival	lp: mercury MG 50438/SR 90438
1 august	orchestra	cd: philips mercury 434 3982
1965		*orchestra described for this recording as festival chamber orchestra*

ave verum corpus; kyrie k341
london	bbc symphony	unpublished radio broadcast
15 august	bbc chorus	*recordings stored in national sound archive*
1966		

MODEST MUSSORGSKY (1839-1881)
pictures from an exhibition, arranged by ravel

amsterdam 21-22 february 1952	concertgebouw orchestra	lp: philips A00437L/ABR 4013/A00607R S06165R
		lp: philips classical favourites GBR 6521/ G05309R
		lp: epic (usa) LC 3015
minneapolis 21 april 1959	minneapolis symphony	lp: mercury MG 50217/MG 50293/ MG 50342/SR 90217/SR 90293/ SR 90342
		lp: mercury (france) 120 515MGL/ 121 039MGL/130 515MGY/ 131 039MGY
		lp: mercury golden imports SRI 75025
		lp: emi mercury MMA 11100/AMS 16051
		lp: philips 6538 012/6545 027/6598 402
		lp: philips fontana grandioso 894 090ZKY
		lp: readers digest RDS 6999/RDES 2591
		cd: philips mercury 434 3462

night on bare mountain, arranged by rimsky-korsakov

wembley 8 june 1960	london symphony	45: mercury EP 41101/EPS 41101
		45: emi mercury XEP 9103/SEX 15042
		lp: mercury MG 50214/MG 50342/ SR 90214/SR 90342
		lp: mercury (france) 121 039MGL/131 039MGY
		lp: mercury golden imports SRI 75025
		lp: emi mercury MMA 11159/AMS 16105
		lp: philips 6538 012
		lp: columbia record club (usa) GB 8
		lp: metronom (germany) 140.170
		cd: philips mercury 432 0042

khovantschina, entr'acte and dance of the persian slaves

minneapolis 21 april 1959	minneapolis symphony	45: emi mercury XEP 9071/SEX 15018
		45: mercury (france) 48.010
		lp: mercury MG 50217/MG 50293/MG 50342/ SR 90217/SR 90293/SR 90342/SR2-9130
		lp: mercury (france) 120 515MGL/121 039MGL/ 130 515MGY/131 039MGY
		lp: mercury golden imports SRI 75025
		lp: emi mercury MMA 11100/AMS 16051
		lp: philips fontana grandioso 894 090ZKY
		cd: philips mercury 434 3882
		entr'acte only
		lp: mercury MG 50324/SR 90324
		lp: philips classical favourites 642 216GL/ 837 816GY

JACQUES OFFENBACH (1819-1880)
gaité parisienne, ballet arranged by rosenthal

minneapolis	minneapolis	lp: mercury MG 50152/MG 50431/SR 90016/
20 april	symphony	SR 90152/SR 90431
1957		lp: mercury wing MGW 14086/SRW 18086
		lp: mercury (france) 120 519MGL/130 519MGY
		lp: mercury golden imports SRI 75014
		lp: emi mercury MMA 11038/AMS 16005
		lp: philips 6747 228/6768 241
		lp: philips festivo 839 809GY
		cd: philips mercury 434 3652

excerpts

lp: mercury MG 50493/SR 90493
lp: philips 6882 104

la belle hélene, suite arranged by dorati

minneapolis	minneapolis	78: victor M 1381
april	symphony	45: victor WDM 1381
1950		lp: victor LM 22/LM 9033
		lp: victor (italy) A12R 0007

JULIAN ORBON (1925-1991)
cantigas del rey

watford	london	lp: philips 6505 001
10 july	symphony	*unpublished mercury lp recording*
1964	harper	
	puyana,	
	harpsichord	

CARL ORFF (1895-1982)
carmina burana

london	royal	lp: decca PFS 4368/JB 78/417 7141
2-3	philharmonic	lp: decca (germany) 642 175AS
february	brighton	lp: london (usa) SPC 21153
1976	festival chorus	cd: decca 417 7142/444 1052/444 1172/
	southend	445 5242/458 1782/458 6432/
	boys choir	466 5262
	burrowes	cd: decca belart 460 6462
	devos	*excerpts*
	shirley-quirk	lp: decca SPA 555
		cd: decca 457 3862
		cd: decca belart 450 0152

WAYNE PETERSON (born 1927)
free variations for orchestra

minneapolis	minneapolis	lp: mercury MG 50288/SR 90288
21 april	symphony	lp: emi mercury MMA 11177/AMS 16127
1959		

ALLAN PETTERSON (1911-1980)
symphony no 7

stockholm	stockholm	lp: decca SXL 6538
18-20	philharmonic	lp: london (usa) CS 6740
september		lp: swedish society SLT 33194
1969		cd: swedish society SCD 1002

symphony no 10

stockholm	swedish radio	lp: emi 4E061 35142/7C061 35142
13-14	orchestra	
june		
1974		

songs for baritone and orchestra, arranged by dorati

stockholm	stockholm	lp: lyssna LY 74.4
14-15	philharmonic	
september	saeden	
1973		

SERGE PROKOFIEV (1891-1953)
symphony no 5

minneapolis	minneapolis	lp: mercury MG 50258/MG 50343/
14-15	symphony	SR 90258/SR 90343
november		lp: mercury wing MGW 14081/SRW 18081
1959		lp: mercury (france) 121 023MGL/131 023MGY
		lp: emi mercury MMA 11126/AMS 16073
		cd: philips mercury 432 7532

piano concerto no 3

dallas	dallas	78: victor M 1326
7 january	symphony	lp: victor LM 1058/VIC 1420/GL 85266
1949	kapell, piano	cd: rca/bmg GD 60921/09026 684422/
		09026 689932

lieutenant kije, suite

hilversum	netherlands	lp: decca PFS 4355/414 0761
3 june	radio	lp: london (usa) SPC 21146
1973	philharmonic	cd: decca 444 1042/448 2732

prokofiev/**the love of three oranges, suite**

watford 4 july 1957	london symphony	lp: mercury MG 50157/MG 50342/SR 90006/ SR 90342/SR 90531 lp: mercury golden imports SRI 75030 lp: emi mercury MMA 11028/AMS 16009 lp: philips universo 6582 011 cd: philips mercury 432 7532 *excerpts* lp: mercury MB 1001 lp: philips 6882 102/6999 013 cd: philips mercury 442 5412

peter and the wolf

london 8-9 march 1966	royal philharmonic connery, narrator	lp: decca LK 4801/PFS 4104/VIV 40/SPA 520 lp: london (usa) SPC 21007 lp: contour classics CC 7519 cd: pickwick IMPX 9002 cd: decca 444 1042 cd: decca belart 450 0242

scythian suite

watford 4 july 1957	london symphony	lp: mercury MG 50157/MG 50342/SR 90006/ SR 90342/SR 90531 lp: mercury golden imports SRI 75030 lp: mercury (france) 121 023MSL/131 023MSY lp: emi mercury MMA 11028/AMS 16009 lp: philips universo 6582 011 cd: philips mercury 432 7532

SERGEI RACHMANINOV (1873-1943)
piano concerto no 2

minneapolis 18 april 1960	minneapolis symphony janis, piano	lp: mercury MG 50260/MG 50448/ SR 90260/SR 90448 lp: mercury golden imports SRI 75032 lp: mercury (france) 120 502MGL/ 120 529MGL/130 502MGY/ 130 529MGY lp: emi mercury MMA 11124/AMS 16071 lp: philips AL 3496/SAL 3496/A04912L/ 838 412AY/6780 251 cd: philips mercury 432 7592 cd: philips 462 1762 sacd: mercury 470 6432 *special lp edition also published by observer newspaper*

rachmaninov/**piano concerto no 3**
watford london   lp: mercury MG 50283/SR 90283
18   symphony   lp: mercury golden imports SRI 75068
june   janis, piano lp: mercury (france) 120 512MGL/130 512MGY
1961   lp: emi mercury MMA 11162/AMS 16109
                     lp: philips 6780 251
                     lp: philips universo 6582 006
                     cd: philips mercury 432 7592
                     sacd: mercury 470 6432

MAURICE RAVEL (1875-1937)
piano concerto in g
new york   national   cd: disco archivia 1064
2 february symphony
1975   béroff, piano

introduction and allegro for harp and orchestra
new york   national   cd: disco archivia 1065
2 february symphony
1975

alborada del gracioso
minneapolis minneapolis 45: mercury EP 15000
19-20   symphony   45: emi mercury XEP 9012
february   lp: mercury MG 50005
1952   lp: mercury wing MGW 14030/SRW 18030
                          lp: nixa mercury MRL 2516

daphnis et chloé, complete ballet
minneapolis minneapolis lp: mercury MG 50040/MG 50048
2-4   symphony   lp: emi mercury MMA 11015
december   macalester   lp: philips 6572 011/6747 228
1954   choir   *excerpts*
                          lp: mercury OLD 6

daphnis et chloé, second suite
stockholm   stockholm   cd: bis BISCD 421-424
2 may   philharmonic
1966

pavane pour une infante défunte
minneapolis minneapolis 45: mercury EP 15000
19-20   symphony   45: emi mercury XEP 9012
february   lp: mercury MG 50005
1952   lp: mercury wing MGW 14029/SRW 18029
                          lp: nixa mercury MRL 2516

rapsodie espagnole
detroit   detroit   lp: decca SXL 6896
7-10   lp: decca (germany) 642 452AS
april   lp: london (usa) CS 7119
1975

OTTORINO RESPIGHI (1879-1936)

antiche arie e danzi per liuta, suites nos 1, 2 and 3

vienna	philharmonia	lp: mercury MG 50199/SR 90199
9-11	hungarica	lp: mercury golden imports SRI 75009
june		lp: mercury (france) 121 009MSL/131 009MSY
1958		lp: emi mercury MMA 11078/AMS 16028
		lp: philips 6538 010
		lp: philips universo 6582 010
		cd: philips 416 4962
		cd: philips mercury 434 3042
		sacd: mercury 470 6432

excerpts
lp: mercury SR2-9132
lp: philips 6747 329
cd: philips mercury 442 5412

feste romane

minneapolis	minneapolis	lp: mercury MG 50046
20 november	symphony	lp: mercury wing MGW 14039/SRW 18039
1954		lp: mercury golden imports SRI 75113
		lp: nixa mercury MRL 2002
		lp: emi mercury MMA 11095

fontane di roma

minneapolis	minneapolis	lp: mercury MG 50011
12-14	symphony	lp: mercury wing MGW 14035/SRW 18035
december		lp: nixa mercury MRL 2007
1952		lp: emi mercury MMA 11083

minneapolis	minneapolis	lp: mercury MG 50298/SR 90298
19 april	symphony	lp: mercury (france) 120 551MGL/130 551MGY
1960		lp: philips 6538 021/6780 756
		lp: philips fontana special 6547 039
		lp: philips universo 6582 015
		cd: philips mercury 432 0072

gli uccelli

watford	london	lp: mercury MG 50153/SR 90153
7-10	symphony	lp: mercury golden imports SRI 75023
july		lp: mercury (france) 121 012MGL/131 012MGY
1957		lp: emi mercury MMA 11053/AMS 16036
		lp: philips fontana special 6547 043
		cd: philips mercury 432 0072

impressioni brasiliane

watford	london	lp: mercury MG 50153/SR 90153
5 july	symphony	lp: mercury golden imports SRI 75023
1957		lp: mercury (france) 121 012MGL/131 012MGY
		lp: emi mercury MMA 11053/AMS 16036
		lp: philips fontana special 6547 043
		cd: philips mercury 432 0072
		cd: dg panorama 469 1812

respighi/**pini di roma**

minneapolis 12-14 december 1952	minneapolis symphony	lp: mercury MG 50011 lp: mercury wing MGW 14035/SRW 18035 lp: nixa mercury MRL 2007 lp: emi mercury MMA 11083
minneapolis 19 april 1960	minneapolis symphony	lp: mercury MG 50298/SR 90298 lp: mercury (france) 120 551MGL/130 551MGY lp: philips 6538 021 lp: philips fontana special 6547 039 lp: philips universo 6582 015 cd: philips mercury 432 0072

vetrate di chiesa

minneapolis 20 november 1954	minneapolis symphony	lp: mercury MG 50046 lp: mercury wing MGW 14039/SRW 18039 lp: mercury golden imports SRI 75113 lp: nixa mercury MRL 2002 lp: emi mercury MMA 11095

NIKOLAI RIMSKY-KORSAKOV (1844-1908)
scheherazade, symphonic suite

london 13 september 1937	london philharmonic	78: hmv C 2968-2972/C7495-7499 auto 78: victor M 509 45: victor bluebird WBC 1006 lp: victor bluebird LBC 1006 cd: dante LYS 261 cd: history 204569.308
minneapolis 27-29 april 1952	minneapolis symphony	lp: mercury MG 50009 lp: mercury wing MGW 14008/SRW 18008 lp: nixa mercury MRL 2503 lp: emi mercury MMA 11022 lp: philips wing WL 1006

minneapolis
22 december
1958
	minneapolis
	symphony
		lp: mercury MG 50195/MG 50332
		    SR 90195/SR 90332
		lp: mercury (france) 120 510NGL/130 510MGY
		lp: mercury golden imports SRI 75008
		lp: emi mercury AMS 16057
		lp: philips classical favourites GL 5835/
		    SGL 5835/642 226GL/837 866GY
		lp: philips diskothek der meister 610 901VL/
		    838 501VY
		lp: philips fontana special 6547 028
		lp: philips fontana grandioso 894 027ZKY
		cd: philips mercury 462 9532
		excerpts
		lp: mercury SR 90532
		lp: philips 6882 102
		philips mono versions GL 5835/642 226GL and 610
		901VL may have contained the 1952 mono recording

rimsky-korsakov/**capriccio espagnol**
walthamstow	london	lp: mercury MG 50265/SR 90265
6 june	symphony	lp: mercury golden imports SRI 75101
1959		lp: emi mercury MMA 11154/AMS 16102
		lp: philips fontana K71-BX 800
		cd: philips mercury 434 3082
		sacd: mercury 470 6432

le coq d'or, suite
walthamstow	london	lp: mercury MG 50122/MG 50344/
5 july	symphony	SR 90122/SR 90344
1956		lp: mercury (france) 121 003MGL/131 003MGY
		lp: mercury wing MGW 14070/SRW 18070
		lp: mercury golden imports SRI 75016
		lp: nixa mercury MRL 2537
		lp: emi mercury MMA 11058/AMS 16008
		lp: philips classical favourites GL 5822/642 225GL
		lp: philips fontana special SFL 14024/
		700 425WGY
		lp: philips universo 6582 012
		lp: franklin mint FM 7011-7014
		cd: philips mercury 434 3082
		sacd: mercury 470 6432

excerpts
lp: mercury SR2-9130

russian easter festival overture
walthamstow	london	lp: mercury MG 50265/MG 50332/
6 june	symphony	SR 90265/SR 90332/MB 1001
1959		lp: emi mercury MMA 11154/AMS 16102
		lp: philips 6567 003
		lp: philips classical favoutites GL 5835/
		SGL 5835/642 266GL/837 866GY
		cd: philips mercury 434 3082
		sacd: mercury 470 6432

HILDING ROSENBERG (1892-1985)

intermezzo and railway fugue/voyage to america
stockholm	stockholm	lp: victor VIC 1319/VICS 1319
19 october	philharmonic	lp: victor (sweden) RIKSLP 13
1967		

GIOACCHINO ROSSINI (1792-1868)
il barbiere di siviglia, overture

minneapolis	minneapolis	45: mercury EP 40015
10 march	symphony	45: emi mercury XEP 9015
1957		lp: mercury MG 50139/MG 50323/SR 90139/SR 90323/SR2-9130
		lp: mercury wing MGW 14055/SRW 18055
		lp: mercury (france) 48.004
		lp: emi mercury MMA 11006/AMS 16090
		lp: philips SDAL 502/6538 015/6591 102
		lp: philips wing WL 1086
		lp: philips pergola 832 035PGY
		cd: philips mercury 434 3452

la boutique fantasque, ballet arranged by respighi

london	royal	lp: decca PFS 4407/JB 79
11-12	philharmonic	lp: london (usa) SPC 21172
december		cd: decca 452 4932
1976		

la cenerentola, overture

minneapolis	minneapolis	45: mercury EP 40015
10 march	symphony	45: emi mercury XEP 9015
1957		lp: mercury MG 50139/MG 50324/SR 90139/SR 90324
		lp: mercury wing MGW 14055/SRW 18055
		lp: emi mercury MMA 11006/AMS 16090
		lp: philips 6538 015/6591 102
		lp: philips wing WL 1086
		lp: philips pergola 832 035PGY
		cd: philips mercury 434 3452

la gazza ladra, overture

minneapolis	minneapolis	lp: mercury MG 50139/SR 90139
10 march	symphony	lp: mercury wing MGW 14055/SRW 18055
1957		lp: emi mercury MMA 11006/AMS 16090
		lp: philips 6538 015/6591 102
		lp: philips wing WL 1086
		lp: philips pergola 832 035PGY
		cd: philips mercury 434 3452

l'italiana in algeri, overture

minneapolis	minneapolis	45: emi mercury XEP 9001
10 march	symphony	lp: mercury MG 50139/SR 90139
1957		lp: mercury wing MGW 14055/SRW 18055
		lp: emi mercury MMA 11006/AMS 16090
		lp: philips 6538 015/6591 102
		lp: philips wing WL 1086
		lp: philips pergola 832 035PGY
		cd: philips mercury 434 3452

rossini/**rossiniana, suite arranged by respighi**
london	royal	lp: decca PFS 4407/JB 79
11-12	philharmonic	lp: london (usa) SPC 21172
december		cd: decca 444 1062
1976		

la scala di seta, overture
minneapolis	minneapolis	45: emi mercury XEP 9001
10 march	symphony	lp: mercury MG 50139/SR 90139
1957		lp: mercury wing MGW 14055/SRW 18055
		lp: emi mercury MMA 11006/AMS 16090
		lp: philips 6538 015/6591 102
		lp: philips wing WL 1086
		lp: philips pergola 832 035PGY
		cd: philips mercury 434 3452

il signor bruschino, overture
minneapolis	minneapolis	lp: mercury MG 50139/SR 90139
10 march	symphony	lp: mercury wing MGW 14055/SRW 18055
1957		lp: emi mercury MMA 11006/AMS 16090
		lp: philips 6538 015/6591 102
		lp: philips wing WL 1086
		lp: philips pergola 832 035PGY
		cd: philips mercury 434 3452

il viaggio a reims, overture
minneapolis	minneapolis	cd: minnesota orchestra centenary set
3 january	symphony	
1958		

ALBERT ROUSSEL (1869-1937)
bacchus et ariane, suite no 2
minneapolis	minneapolis	cd: minnesota orchestra centenary set
6 december	symphony	
1957		

HARALD SAEVERUD (1897-1992)
scherzo from the minneapolis symphony "gay day"
minneapolis	minneapolis	cd: minnesota orchestra centenary set
18 october	symphony	
1958		

CAMILLE SAINT-SAENS (1835-1921)
cello concerto no 1
watford	london	lp: mercury MG 50409/SR 90409
26 june	symphony	lp: mercury (france) 121 025MGL/130 025MGY
1964	starker, cello	lp: philips AL 3559/SAL 3559/A04923L/ 838 423LY
		lp: philips festivo SFM 23019/ 839 533VGY
		cd: philips mercury 432 0102

ERIK SATIE (1866-1925)
parade, ballet
watford	london	lp: mercury MG 50435/SR 90435
4-6	symphony	lp: mercury (france) 121 047MSL/131 047MSY
august		lp: philips SAL 3637/838 434LY/6747 228
1965		lp: philips sequenza 412 0281
		cd: philips mercury 434 3352
		cd: dg panorama 469 2502

ARNOLD SCHOENBERG (1874-1951)
five pieces for orchestra
watford	london	lp: mercury MG 50316/SR 90316
19-20	symphony	lp: philips AL 3539/SAL 3539/ A04909L/838 409AY
july		
1962		lp: philips festivo 839 264VGY
		cd: philips mercury 432 0062

von heute auf morgen
london	bbc symphony	unpublished radio broadcast
13 november	schmid	*recording stored in national sound archive*
1963	schachtschneider	
	olsen	

FRANZ SCHUBERT (1797-1828)
symphony no 8 "unfinished"
chicago	chicago	lp: mercury MG 50037
8-9	symphony	lp: mercury wing MGW 14018/SRW 18018
january		lp: nixa mercury MRL 2517
1954		lp: philips wing WL 1012
		lp: philips pergola 832 095PGY

overture in c in the italian style d591
amsterdam	concertgebouw	lp: philips classical favourites GBL 5581/ G03066L/G05398R
23-25	orchestra	
september		lp: epic (usa) LC 3684/BC 1078
1959		

GUNTHER SCHULLER (born 1925)
seven studies on themes of paul klee
minneapolis	minneapolis	lp: mercury MG 50282/SR 90282
16-17	symphony	lp: mercury golden imports SRI 75116
april		lp: emi mercury MMA 11151/AMS 16099
1960		lp: philips festivo 839 275DSY
		cd: philips mercury 434 3292

WILLIAM SCHUMAN (1910-1992)
new england triptych, based on hymns of william billings
washington	national	lp: london (usa) OS 26442
23-30	symphony	
april		
1975		

ROBERT SCHUMANN (1810-1856)
symphony no 4
watford	london	lp: mercury SR 90511
18-19	symphony	
july		
1963		

piano concerto
amsterdam	concertgebouw	lp: decca 411 9421
29 june-	orchestra	cd: decca 411 9422
1 july	schiff, piano	
1983		

violin concerto
watford	london	lp: mercury MG 50406/SR 90406
5 july	symphony	lp: mercury (france) 120 575MGL/130 575MGY
1964	szeryng, violin	lp: philips AL 3504/SAL 3504/ A04917L/838 417LY/6780 754
		lp: philips sequenza 6527 061
		lp: quintessence PMC 7194
		cd: philips mercury 434 3392

cello concerto
london	bbc symphony	cd: bbc legends BBCL 41332
11 november	tortelier, cello	
1962		

ROGER SESSIONS (1896-1985)
suite from the black maskers
minneapolis	minneapolis	cd: minnesota orchestra centenary set
30 december	symphony	
1955		

JEAN SIBELIUS (1865-1957)
symphony no 2

stockholm	stockholm	lp: victor VIC 1318/VICS 1318
17-18	philharmonic	lp: rca camden classics CCV 5029
october		cd: swedish society SCD 1046
1967		

luonnotar, for soprano and orchestra

wembley	london	lp: emi ASD 2486/1C063 01987
9 february	symphony	cd: emi CDM 565 1822/585 7852
1969	jones	

en saga

london	london	lp: emi ASD 2486/1C063 01987
22 august	symphony	cd: emi 585 7852
1969		*this recording replaced the originally scheduled sibelius in memoriam*

night ride and sunrise

london	london	lp: emi ASD 2486/1C063 01987
24 june	symphony	cd: emi CDM 565 1822/585 7852
1969		

the oceanides

london	london	lp: emi ASD 2486/1C063 01987
24 june	symphony	cd: emi CDM 565 1822/585 7852
1969		*recording completed on 22 august 1969*

valse triste

wembley	london	lp: mercury MG 50214/SR 90214/SR 90526
13 june	symphony	lp: mercury wing MGW 14087/SRW 18087
1960		lp: emi mercury MMA 11159/AMS 16105
		lp: philips festivo 839 819GSY
		cd: philips mercury 462 9532

BEDRICH SMETANA (1824-1884)
ma vlast

amsterdam	concertgebouw	lp: philips L09003-09004L
11-15	orchestra	lp: epic (usa) SC 6026
september		*excerpts*
1956		45: philips ABE 10032/400 030AE
		lp: philips ABL 3195/A00399L/6701 008
		lp: philips classical favourites G03135L

amsterdam	concertgebouw	lp: philips 420 6071
6-10	orchestra	cd: philips 420 6072/432 1962/442 6412
october		*excerpts*
1986		cd: philips 426 6842/438 0012/456 4322

smetana/**vltava/ma vlast**
amsterdam 21-22 february 1952	concertgebouw orchestra	lp: philips NBR 6010/N00620R/S06053R lp: epic (usa) LC 3015
wembley 9 june 1960	london symphony	lp: mercury MG 50214/SR 90214 lp: emi mercury MMA 11159/AMS 16105 lp: philips K71-B800/6747 050/6747 126 lp: metronom (germany) 140.170 cd: philips mercury 462 9532

the bartered bride, overture
minneapolis 6 april 1958	minneapolis symphony	45: emi mercury XEP 9035 lp: mercury MG 50193/MG 50323/ SR 90193/SR90323/SR 90530/OL2-107/ SR2-9007/SR2-9134/SR12-77001 lp: emi mercury MMA 11030/AMS 16047

dance of the comedians/the bartered bride
minneapolis 6 april 1958	minneapolis symphony	45: emi mercury XEP 9063/SEX 15014 lp: mercury MG 50193/MG 50327/ SR 90193/SR 90327/SR 90507/ OL2-107/SR2-9007/SR2-9130/ SR12-77001 lp: emi mercury MMA 11030/AMS 16047

polka and furiant/the bartered bride
minneapolis 6 april 1958	minneapolis symphony	45: emi mercury XEP 9035 lp: mercury MG 50193/SR 90193/OL2-107/ SR2-9007/SR12-77001 lp: emi mercury MMA 11030/AMS 16047

JOHN PHILIP SOUSA (1854-1932)
semper fidelis, march
amsterdam 25 september 1959	concergebouw orchestra	45: philips ABE 10245/SABE 2010/ SBF 182/313 122SF

WILHELM STENHAMMAR (1871-1927)
three movements from the serenade for orchestra
stockholn 4 february 1970	stockholm philharmonic	cd: bis BISCD 421-424

EDUARD STRAUSS (1835-1916)
bahn frei, polka
minneapolis   minneapolis   lp: mercury MG 50178/MG 50293/
18 december   symphony   SR 90178/SR 90293
1957
                                      lp: mercury wing MGW 14065/SRW 18065
                                      lp: emi mercury MMA 11014/AMS 16024
                                      lp: philips classical favourites GL 5816/
                                             642 232GL

doktrinen, waltz
minneapolis   minneapolis   45: emi mercury XEP 9007
18 december   symphony   lp: mercury MG 50178/MG 50289/
1957   SR 90178/SR 90289
                                      lp: mercury wing MGW 14065/SRW 18065
                                      lp: emi mercury MMA 11014/AMS 16024
                                      lp: philips classical favourites GL 5816/
                                             642 232GL
                                      cd: philips mercury 434 3382

JOHANN STRAUSS I (1804-1849)
lorelei-rheinklänge, waltz
minneapolis   minneapolis   lp: mercury MG 50178/SR 90178
18 december   symphony   lp: mercury wing MGW 14065/SRW 18065
1957   lp: emi mercury MMA 11014/AMS 16024
                                      lp: philips classical favourites GL 5816/
                                      642 232GL

JOHANN STRAUSS (1825-1899)
ägyptischer marsch
minneapolis   minneapolis   45: emi mercury XEP 9007
18 december   symphony   lp: mercury MG 50178/MG 50325/SR 90178/
1957   SR 90325
                                      lp: mercury wing MGW 14065/SRW 18065
                                      lp: emi mercury MMA 11014/AMS 16024
                                      lp: philips D88044L/6747 176
                                      lp: philips classical favourites GL 5816/642 232GL

an der schönen blauen donau, waltz
london   london   lp: decca LK 4850/PFS 4117/SPA 155/VIV 2/
6-7   philharmonic   16BB 223-232/DPA 633-634
december   lp: decca (germany) SLK 16805-P
1966   lp: london (usa) SPC 21018/STS 15545
                                      lp: pickwick IMP 2188/IMPD 203
                                      lp: castle collector CCSLP 132
                                      lp: tellydisc TELLY 13.44

johann strauss/**le beau danube, ballet arranged by desormiere**

london	london	78: hmv C 2869-2871/C 7477-7479 auto/
17 july	philharmonic	JOX 7000-7002
1936		78: electrola EH 988-990
		78: victor M 414
		lp: victor camden CAL 365
		cd: pearl GEM 0036

champagner-polka

minneapolis	minneapolis	lp: mercury MG 50131/MG 50293/
18 november	symphony	MG 50444/SR 90008/SR 90293/
1956		SR 90444
		lp: emi mercury MMA 11062/AMS 16001
		lp: philips SDAL 502/D88044L/
		K71-B 800/6736 004/6747 176
		lp: philips wing WL 1208

eljen a magyar polka

minneapolis	minneapolis	45: emi mercury XEP 9007
18 december	symphony	lp: mercury MG 50178/SR 90178
1957		lp: emi mercury MMA 11014/AMS 16024
		lp: philips D88044L/6736 004/6747 176
		lp: philips classical favourites GL 5816/
		642 232GL

frühlingsstimmen, waltz

minneapolis	minneapolis	45: emi mercury XEP 9054
18 november	symphony	lp: mercury MG 50131/MG 50289/
1956		SR 90008/SR 90289
		lp: mercury golden imports SRI 75098
		lp: emi mercury MMA 11062/AMS 16001
		lp: philips D88044L
		cd: philips mercury 434 3382
london	london	lp: decca LK 4850/PFS 4117/VIV 2
6-7	philharmonic	lp: decca (germany) SLK 16805-P
december		lp: london (usa) SPC 21018/STS 15545
1966		

johann strauss/**g'schichten aus dem wienerwald, waltz**

minneapolis	minneapolis	45: mercury EP 15023
5-7	symphony	lp: mercury MG 50019
february		lp: mercury wing MGW 14000/SRW 18000
1953		lp: emi mercury MMA 11086
		lp: philips wing WL 1000

london	london	lp: decca LK 4850/PFS 4117/SPA 205
6-7	philharmonic	VIV 2/16BB 223-232
december		lp: decca (germany) SLK 16805-P
1966		lp: london (usa) SPC 21018/STS 15545
		lp: tellydisc TELLY 13.44
		lp: trax classique TRX 108
		cd: trax classique TRXCD 108

graduation ball, ballet arranged by dorati

dallas	dallas	78: victor M 1180
february	symphony	78: hmv JOX 7006-7009
1947		lp: victor LM 1061

minneapolis	minneapolis	lp: mercury MG 50152/SR 90016
20 april	symphony	lp: mercury golden imports SRI 75014
1957		lp: mercury (france) 120 519MGL
		130 519MGY/837 894GY
		lp: emi mercury MMA 11038/AMS 16005
		lp: philips 6747 176
		lp: philips festivo 839 847GSY
		lp: philips fontana special SFL 14119/
		700 456WGY
		cd: philips mercury 434 3652
		excerpts
		lp: mercury MG 50494/SR 90494/SR2-9127

vienna	vienna	lp: decca SXL 6867
26-30	philharmonic	lp: decca (france) 7689
november		lp: london (usa) CS 7086
1976		*recording completed in june 1977*

kaiserwalzer

minneapolis	minneapolis	lp: mercury MG 50019
5-7	symphony	lp: mercury wing MGW 14000/SRW 18000
february		lp: emi mercury MMA 11086
1953		lp: philips D88044L
		lp: philips wing WL 1000

künstlerleben, waltz

minneapolis 18 november 1956	minneapolis symphony	lp: mercury MG 50131/MG 50289/ SR 90008/SR 90289 lp: mercury golden imports SRI 75098 lp: emi mercury MMA 11062/AMS 16001
london 6-7 december 1966	london philharmonic	lp: decca LK 4850/PFS 4117/VIV 2 lp: decca (germany) SLK 16805-P lp: london (usa) SPC 21018/STS 15545

künstlerleben, version for soprano and orchestra

new york september 1947	victor orchestra korjus	78: victor M 1221 78: hmv C 3898 78: hmv (switzerland) FKX 219 78: electrola EH 1361 45: victor WDM 1221 45: hmv 7EP 7039 lp: victor camden CAL 422 lp: victor (canada) CDS 1095 lp: melodiya D 034445-034446 cd: dante LYS 474-475

eine nacht in venedig, overture

minneapolis
18 december
1957
	minneapolis
	symphony
		lp: mercury MG 50178/MG 50339
		    SR 90178/SR 90339
		lp: mercury wing MGW 14065/SRW 18065
		lp: emi mercury MMA 11014/AMS 16024
		lp: philips 6747 176
		lp: philips classical favourites GL 5816/
		    642 232GL

rosen aus dem süden, waltz

minneapolis
18 november
1956
	minneapolis
	symphony
		lp: mercury MG 50131/MG 50293/
		    MG 50444/MG 50526/SR 90008/
		    SR 90293/SR 90444/SR 90526
		lp: mercury wing MGW 14087/SRW 18087
		lp: mercury golden imports SRI 75098
		lp: emi mercury MMA 11062/AMS 16001
		lp: philips SDAL 502
		lp: philips wing WL 1208
		lp: philips festivo 839 819GSY

johann strauss/**rosen aus dem süden, version for soprano and orchestra**
new york   victor   78: victor M 1221
september   orchestra   78: hmv C 3898
1947   korjus   78: hmv (switzerland) FKX 219
                                       78: electrola EH 1361
                                       45: victor WDM 1221
                                       45: hmv 7EP 7039
                                       lp: victor camden CAL 422
                                       lp: victor (canada) CDS 1095
                                       cd: dante LYS 474-475

schatzwalzer, version for soprano and orchestra
new york   victor   78: victor M 1221
september   orchestra   45: victor WDM 1221
1947   korjus   lp: victor camden CAL 422
                                       lp: victor (canada) CDS 1095
                                     lp: melodiya D 034445-034446
                                     cd: dante LYS 474-475

wein weib und gesang, waltz
minneapolis   minneapolis   lp: mercury MG 50019
5-7   symphony   lp: mercury wing MGW 14000/SRW 18000
february   lp: emi mercury MMA 11086
1953   lp: philips D88044L
                                     lp: philips wing WL 1000

london   london   lp: decca LK 4850/PFS 4117/VIV 2
6-7   philharmonic   lp: decca (germany) SLK 16805-P
december   lp: london (usa) SPC 21018/STS 15545
1966

wiener blut, waltz
minneapolis   minneapolis   lp: mercury MG 50019
5-7   symphony   lp: mercury wing MGW 14000/SRW 18000
february   lp: emi mercury MMA 11086
1953   lp: philips D88044L
                                     lp: philips wing WL 1000

wiener blut, version for soprano and orchestra
new york   victor   78: victor M 1221
september   orchestra   45: victor WDM 1221
1947   korjus   lp: victor camden CAL 411
                                     lp: victor (canada) CDS 1095
                                   lp: melodiya D 034445-034446
                                   cd: dante LYS 474-475

johann strauss/**wiener bonbons, waltz**

minneapolis	minneapolis	45: emi mercury XEP 9054
18 november	symphony	lp: mercury MG 50131/MG 50444/
1956		SR 90008/SR 90444
		lp: emi mercury MMA 11062/AMS 16001
		lp: philips SDAL 502
		lp: philips wing WL 1208

JOSEF STRAUSS (1827-1870)
aquarellen, waltz

minneapolis	minneapolis	lp: mercury MG 50178/MG 50289/SR 90178/
18 december	symphony	SR 90289
1957		lp: mercury golden imports SRI 75098
		lp: emi mercury MMA 11014/AMS 16024
		lp: philips classical favourites GL 5816/
		642 232GL
		cd: philips mercury 434 3382

dorfschwalben aus österreich, waltz

vienna	philharmonia	lp: mercury MG 50190/MG 50337/
8-9	hungarica	SR 90190/SR 90337
june		lp: mercury wing MGW 14087/SRW 18087
1958		lp: mercury (france) 120 505MGL/130 505MGY
		lp: mercury golden imports SRI 75098
		lp: emi mercury MMA 11116/AMS 16063
		lp: philips 6718 012/6736 001/K71-BC 800
		cd: philips mercury 434 3382
		cd: philips 456 4982
		mercury wing editions incorrectly described orchestra
		as minneapolis symphony

sphärenklänge, waltz

minneapolis	minneapolis	lp: mercury MG 50178/SR 90178
18 december	symphony	lp: emi mercury MMA 11014/AMS 16024
1957		lp: philips classical favourites GL 5816/
		642 232GL

RICHARD STRAUSS (1864-1949)
die ägyptische helena

detroit	detroit	lp: decca D176 D3
1-7	symphony	lp: decca (germany) 635 491GF
may	jewell chorale	lp: london (usa) OSA 13135
1979	jones	cd: decca 430 3812
	hendricks	
	finnilä	
	kastu	
	white	

richard strauss/also sprach zarathustra
detroit	detroit	lp: decca SXDL 7613
24-26	symphony	lp: decca (france) 591.350
october		lp: london (usa) LDR 71113
1982		cd: decca 410 1462/430 7082

burleske for piano and orchestra
new york	national	cd: disco archivia 1065
13 march	symphony	
1977	alpenheim, piano	

capriccio, closing scene (morgen mittag um elf)
london	royal	cd: bbc legends BBCL 41532
3 october	philharmonic	
1976	söderström	

new york	national	cd: disco archivia 1066
13 march	symphony	
1977	lear	

don juan
minneapolis	minneapolis	lp: mercury MG 50202/MG 50334/
23 december	symphony	SR 90202/SR 90334
1958		lp: mercury golden imports SRI 75015
		lp: emi mercury MMA 11125/AMS 16072
		lp: philips classical favourites GL 5831/
		SGL 5831/642 270GL/837 879GY
		lp: concert hall CM 2446/SMS 2446
		cd: philips mercury 434 3482

detroit	detroit	lp: decca SXDL 7523
30 april-	symphony	lp: london (usa) LDR 71025
7 may		cd: decca 400 0852/430 7082
1979		

don quixote
leeds	bbc symphony	unpublished radio broadcast
21 march	gendron	*recording stored in national sound aechive*
1964		

elektra, excerpt (es geht ein lärm los....orest ist tot!)
rome	rome opera	cd: ponto PD 1020
22 february	orchestra	
1965	borkh	
	eriksdotter	
	mödl	

richard strauss/**die frau ohne schatten, symphonic fantasy**

detroit	detroit	lp: decca 411 8931
14-16	symphony	cd: decca 411 8932/444 3442
november		
1983		

ein heldenleben

minneapolis	minneapolis	45: mercury EP2-501
12-14	symphony	lp: mercury MG 50012
december		lp: mercury wing MGW 14014/SRW 18014
1952		lp: nixa mercury MRL 2545
		lp: emi mercury MMA 11069
		lp: pickwick S 4041
new york	national	cd: disco archivia 1065
13 march	symphony	
1977		

macbeth

detroit	detroit	lp: decca SXDL 7613
24-26	symphony	lp: decca (france) 591.350
october		lp: london (usa) LDR 71113
1982		cd: decca 410 1462/430 7082/444 3442

der rosenkavalier, suite arranged by dorati

philadelphia	philadelphia	78: victor M 1475
july	orchestra	45: victor WDM 1475
1950		lp: victor LM 48/LM 9033
		orchestra described for this recording as robin hood dell orchestra
minneapolis	minneapolis	lp: mercury MG 50099/SR 90099
22 december	symphony	lp: mercury (france) 121 028MGL/131 028MGY
1955		lp: mercury wing MGW 14072/SRW 18072
		lp: mercury golden imports SRI 75015
		lp: nixa mercury MRL 2566
		lp: emi mercury MMA 11061/AMS 16014
		lp: philips classical favourites 837 894GY
		lp: philips festivo 839 847GSY
		lp: concert hall CM 2309/SMS 2309
		cd: philips mercury 434 3482
detroit	detroit	lp: decca 411 8931
14-16	symphony	cd: decca 411 8932/444 3442
november		
1983		

richard strauss/**dance of the seven veils/salome**
london 16-17 october 1962	royal philharmonic	lp: readers digest RDM 1027/RDS 3-15 lp: quintessence (usa) PMC 7005 cd: chesky CD 36
detroit 14-16 november 1983	detroit symphony	decca unpublished *recording probably not completed*

till eulenspiegels lustige streiche
minneapolis 22 december 1955	minneapolis symphony	45: emi mercury XEP 9033 lp: mercury MG 50099/MG 50334/SR 90334 lp: mercury wing MGW 14072/MGW 14501/ SRW 18072/SRW 18501 lp: mercury (france) 121 028MGL/131 028MGY lp: nixa mercury MRL 2566 lp: emi mercury MMA 11061/AMS 16014 lp: philips classical favourites GL 5831/ SGL 5831/642 270GL/837 879GY cd: philips mercury 434 3482 *MGW 14501/SRW 18501 has a spoken commentary dubbed over the music*
detroit 30 april- 7 may 1979	detroit symphony	lp: decca SXDL 7523 lp: london (usa) LDR 71025 cd: decca 400 0852 cd: decca belart 461 3722

tod und verklärung
minneapolis 23 december 1958	minneapolis symphony	lp: mercury MG 50202/MG 50334/ SR 90202/SR 90334 lp: emi mercury MMA 11125/AMS 16072 lp: philips classical favourites GL 5831/ SGL 5831/642 270GL/837 879GY lp: concert hall CM 2446/SMS 2446 cd: philips mercury 434 3482
detroit 30 april- 7 may 1979	detroit symphony	lp: decca SXDL 7523 lp: london (usa) LDR 71025 cd: decca 400 0852 *recording completed in may and june 1980*

4 letzte lieder
london 3 october 1976	royal philharmonic söderström	cd: bbc legends BBCL 41532

IGOR STRAVINSKY (1882-1971)

apollon musagete
detroit	detroit	lp: decca 414 4571
30 october-	symphony	cd: decca 414 4572/430 7402
1 november		
1984		

le baiser de la fée, pas de deux
comprising entrée, adagio, variation and coda
london	london	78: columbia DX 949
27 july	philharmonic	78: columbia (usa) 69840D
1939		78: columbia (canada) 15261
		78: columbia (argentina) 266.243
		78: columbia (brazil) 30.5373

le chant du rossignol
watford	london	lp: mercury MG 50387/SR 90387
22-24	symphony	lp: mercury (france) 121 030MGL/131 030MGY
june		lp: philips 838 436AY/6513 006
1964		lp: philips universo 6585 003
		cd: philips mercury 432 0122
		sacd: mercury 470 6432

four études for orchestra
watford	london	lp: mercury MG 50387/SR 90387
7 july	symphony	lp: mercury (france) 121 030MGL/131 030MGY
1964		lp: philips 838 436AY/6513 003
		cd: philips mercury 434 3312

feux d'artifice
watford	london	lp: mercury MG 50387/SR 90387
27 june	symphony	lp: mercury (france) 121 030MGL/131 030MGY
1964		lp: philips 838 436AY/6513 006
		cd: philips mercury 432 0122
		sacd: mercury 470 6432

stravinsky/**l'oiseau de feu, complete ballet**

watford	london	lp: mercury MG 50226/SR 90226
7-9	symphony	lp: mercury (france) 121 002MGL/131 002MGY
june		lp: mercury golden imports SRI 75058
1959		lp: emi mercury MMA 11089/AMS 16038
		lp: philips 6538 014
		lp: philips classical favourites GL 5827/ SGL 5827/642 238GL/837 838GY
		lp: philips fontana special 6547 003
		lp: philips fontana grandioso 894 083ZKY
		lp: contour classics 6870 574
		cd: philips mercury 432 0122
		sacd: mercury 470 6432
		excerpts
		lp: mercury SR2-9127
barking	royal	lp: enigma VAR 1022/K 53534
18-19	philharmonic	lp: asv ALH 924
july		lp: music masters (usa) 20051
1976		cd: asv CDQS 6031
		excerpts
		cd: brilliant classics 6243
		recording completed on 26 september 1976
detroit	detroit	lp: decca 410 1091
24-26	symphony	cd: decca 410 1092/421 0792/ 430 7402/448 2262
october		
1982		cd: decca belart 460 6442

l'oiseau de feu, 1919 suite

minneapolis	minneapolis	lp: mercury MG 50004/MG 50025
19-20	symphony	lp: mercury wing MGW 14010/SRW 18010
february		lp: nixa mercury MRL 2550
1952		lp: philips fontana special SFL 14026/ 700 427WGY

petrushka, 1911 version

minneapolis	minneapolis	lp: mercury MG 50058
6 april	symphony	lp: mercury wing MGW 14038/SRW 18038
1955		lp: nixa mercury MRL 2523
		lp: philips wing WL 1035
detroit	detroit	lp: decca SXDL 7521/417 2811
30 may-	symphony	lp: london (usa) LDR 71023
3 june		cd: decca 417 7582/421 0792/421 0812
1980		

stravinsky/**petrushka, 1947 version**

minneapolis	minneapolis	lp: mercury MG 50216/SR 90216
20 april	symphony	lp: mercury (france) 121 011MGL/
1959		131 011MGY
		lp: emi mercury MMA 11105/AMS 16056
		lp: philips 6567 002/6780 755
		lp: philips universo 6582 021
		cd: philips mercury 434 3312

le sacre du printemps

minneapolis	minneapolis	lp: mercury MG 50030
12-14	symphony	lp: mercury wing MGW 14027/SRW 18027
december		lp: nixa mercury MRL 2006
1953		lp: philips wing WL 1034
		lp: philips fontana special SFL 14009/
		700 422WGY

minneapolis	minneapolis	lp: mercury MG 50253/SR 90253
15 november	symphony	lp: mercury (france) 121 046MGL/131 046MGY
1959		lp: emi mercury MMA 11118/AMS 16065
		lp: philips fontana 6531 011
		lp: philips universo 6582 021
		lp: philips fontana grandioso 894 023ZKY
		cd: philips mercury 434 3312

detroit	detroit	lp: decca SXDL 7548/417 2811
11-13	symphony	lp: london (usa) LDR 71048
may		cd: decca 400 0842/417 7582/
1981		421 0792/448 2262
		cd: decca belart 460 6442

scherzo a la russe

watford	london	lp: mercury MG 50387/SR 90387
27 june	symphony	lp: mercury (france) 121 030MGL/
1964		131 030MGY
		lp: philips 838 436AY/6513 006
		cd: philips mercury 432 0122/442 5412
		sacd: mercury 470 6432

scherzo fantastique

detroit	detroit	lp: decca 414 4561
30 october-	symphony	cd: decca 414 4562
1 november		
1984		

stravinsky/**symphony no 1**
detroit detroit lp: decca 414 4561
30 october- symphony cd: decca 414 4562
1 november
1980

tango
watford london lp: mercury MG 50387/SR 90387
7 july symphony lp: mercury (france) 121 030MGL/131 030MGY
1964   lp: philips 838 436AY/6513 006
    cd: philips mercury 432 0122
    sacd: mercury 470 6432

KAROL SZYMANOWSKI (1882-1937)
symphony no 2
detroit detroit lp: decca SXDL 7524
30 may- symphony lp: london (usa) LDR 71026
3 june   cd: decca 425 6252/448 2582
1980

symphony no 3 "song of the night"
detroit detroit lp: decca SXDL 7524
30 may- symphony lp: london (usa) LDR 71026
3 june jewell chorale cd: decca 425 6252/448 2582
1980 karczykowski

PIOTR TCHAIKOVSKY (1840-1893)
symphony no 1 "winter dreams"
watford london lp: mercury OL2-115/OL 6-121/
26-27 symphony   SR2-9015/SR6-9121/SRI 3-77009
july   lp: mercury (france) 121 038MSL/131 038MSY
1965   lp: philips 6599 932/6747 195
    lp: philips (france) 800 006-800 007DTY
    lp: philips universo 6582 016
    cd: philips mercury 434 3912/475 6261

symphony no 2 "little russian"
watford london lp: mercury OL2-115/OL6-121/
29-30 symphony   SR2-9015/SR6-9121/SRI 3-77009
july   lp: philips 6599 933/6747 195
1965   lp: philips (france) 800 006-800 007DTY
    cd: philips mercury 434 3912/475 6261

symphony no 3 "polish"
watford london lp: mercury OL2-115/OL6-121/
30-31 symphony   SR2-9015/SR6-9121/SRI 3-77009
july   lp: philips 6599 934/6747 195
1965   lp: philips (france) 800 006-800 007DTY
    cd: philips mercury 434 3912/475 6261

tchaikovsky/**symphony no 4**

amsterdam 10-11 september 1956	concertgebouw orchestra	lp: philips ABL 3195/A00399L lp: philips fontana special 200 058WGL lp: epic (usa) LC 3421

wembley　　　london　　　lp: mercury MG 50279/MG 50471/SR 90279/
12 june　　　symphony　　　　SR 90471/OL6-121/SR6-9121
1960　　　　　　　　lp: mercury (france) 120 555MGL/130 555MGY
　　　　　　　　　　lp: mercury golden imports SRI 75044
　　　　　　　　　　lp: emi mercury MMA 11168/AMS 16118
　　　　　　　　　　lp: philips 838 504VY/6599 935
　　　　　　　　　　lp: philips universo 6582 022
　　　　　　　　　　lp: metronom (germany) 140.138
　　　　　　　　　　cd: philips mercury 434 3732/475 6261

washington　　national　　lp: decca SXL 6574
2-3　　　　　symphony　　lp: london (usa) CS 6793
may　　　　　　　　　　cd: decca collection classique 466 5482
1973

symphony no 5
minneapolis　　minneapolis　　lp: mercury MG 50008
27-29　　　　symphony　　　lp: mercury wing MGW 14013/SRW 18013
april　　　　　　　　　　　lp: philips wing WL 1009/BWL 004
1952　　　　　　　　　　　lp: philips fontana special 700 164WGY

watford　　　london　　　lp: mercury MG 50255/MG 50472/SR 90255/
23 june　　　symphony　　　　SR 90472/OL6-121/SR6-9121
1961　　　　　　　　lp: mercury golden imports SRI 75056
　　　　　　　　　　lp: emi mercury MMA 11175/AMS 16125
　　　　　　　　　　lp: philips 6599 936/6747 195
　　　　　　　　　　lp: philips universo 6582 013
　　　　　　　　　　cd: philips mercury 434 3052/475 6261

symphony no 6 "pathétique"
vienna　　　vienna　　　lp: philips fontana CFL 1019/698 001CL/
14-18　　　symphony　　　　697 010EL
october
1957

wembley　　　london　　　lp: mercury MG 50312/MG 50473/SR 90312/
17-18　　　symphony　　　　SR 90473/OL6-121/SR6-9121
june　　　　　　　　lp: mercury golden imports SRI 75031
1960　　　　　　　　lp: philips 6702 002/6747 195/420 0381
　　　　　　　　　　lp: philips diskothek der meister
　　　　　　　　　　　　610 904VL/838 504VY
　　　　　　　　　　lp: philips fontana grandioso 894 029ZKY
　　　　　　　　　　lp: philips universo 6582 014
　　　　　　　　　　cd: philips mercury 434 3532/475 6261

tchaikovsky/**sérénade mélancolique for violin and orchestra**
los angeles   hollywood   cd: eklipse EKR 1404
15 july   bowl symphony   cd: doremi DHR 7736-7737
1947   elman, violin

violin concerto
watford   london   lp: mercury MG 50389/SR 90389/SR 90527/
22-23   symphony   OL3-117/SR3-9017
july   szeryng,   lp: mercury (france) 120 557MGL/130 557MGY
1962   violin   lp: philips AL 3503/SAL 3503/A04924L/
                                           838 424AY/6833 120/420 0381
                                       lp: philips fontana 6598 897
                                       lp: philips universo 6582 009

london   london   lp: columbia (usa) MS 7313
16-17   symphony   lp: cbs 72768
december   zukerman,   cd: sony MBK 46268
1968   violin

rococo variations for cello and orchestra
watford   london   lp: mercury MG 50409/SR 90409
26-27   symphony   lp: mercury (france) 121 025MGL/131 025MGY
june   starker, cello   lp: philips AL 3559/SAL 3559/A04923L/
1964   838 423AY/6511 026
                                       lp: philips festivo SFM 23019/839 533VGY
                                       cd: philips mercury 432 0012

serenade for strings
vienna   philharmonia   lp: mercury MG 50200/MG 50344/
5 june   hungarica   SR 90200/SR 90344
1958   lp: emi mercury MMA 11091/AMS 16040
                                       lp: philips D88203Y/K71-BC 800
                                       lp: philips classical favourites GL 5822/642 225GL
                                       cd: philips mercury 432 7502
                                       waltz only
                                       lp: mercury MG 50395/SR 90395/SR2-9126
                                       lp: philips SDAL 503/6747 247
                                       lp: philips wing WL 1209
                                       lp: philips fontana 700 191WGY

orchestral suite no 1
watford   new   lp: mercury OL3-118/SR3-9018/SRI 3-77008
16-21   philharmonia   lp: philips SAL 3734/802 788AY/SBAL 22/
august   6703 026/6768 035/6799 002
1966   cd: philips mercury 454 2532
                                       cd: philips 456 1882

tchaikovsky/**orchestral suite no 2**
watford   new   lp: mercury OL3-118/SR3-9018/SRI 3-77008
16-21   philharmonia   lp: philips SAL 3725/802 790AY/SBAL 22/
august   6703 026/6768 035/6799 002
1966   cd: philips mercury 454 2532
                                  cd: philips 456 1882

orchestral suite no 3
watford   new   lp: mercury OL3-118/SR3-9018/SRI 3-77008/
16-21   philharmonia   SR2-9019
august   lp: philips SAL 3673/802 789AY/SBAL 22/
1966   6703 026/6768 035/6799 002
                                  cd: philips mercury 454 2532
                                  cd: philips 456 1882/464 7472

orchestral suite no 4 "mozartiana"
watford   new   lp: mercury OL3-118/SR3-9018/SRI 3-77008/
16-21   philharmonia   SR2-9019
august   lp: philips SAL 3725/802 790AY/SBAL 22/
1966   6703 026//6768 035/6799 002/6866 027
                                  cd: philips mercury 454 2532
                                  cd: philips 456 1882/464 7472

tchaikovsky/**the nutcracker, complete ballet**

minneapolis 12-14 december 1953	minneapolis symphony minneapolis university choir	lp: mercury OL2-101/OL6-114/SR6-9014 lp: nixa mercury MRL 2508-2509 lp: emi mercury MMA 11106-11107 lp: philips 6738 008 lp: philips fontana special SFL 14007-14008/ 700 420-700 421WGY *excerpts* 45: emi mercury XEP 9010 lp: mercury MG 50494/SR 90494 lp: mercury wing MGW 14011/SRW 18011 lp: mercury (france) 121 003MSL/131 003MSY lp: emi mercury MMA 11023 lp: philips wing WL 1007 lp: philips pergola 832 034PGY lp: philips universo 6582 018 lp: philips sequenza 6527 065/420 0381

watford
11-15
july
1962
	london
	symphony
	ambrosian
	singers
		lp: mercury OL2-113/SR2-9013
		lp: emi mercury MMA 11193-11194/
		    AMS 16143-16144
		lp: philips 6755 002/6780 250
		lp: philips (france) 800 002-800 003
		lp: philips classical favourites GL 5732-5733/
		    642 203GL-642 204GL
		cd: philips mercury 432 7502
		excerpts
		lp: mercury MG 50337/MG 50395/SR 90337/
		    SR 90395/SR 90528
		lp: philips K71-BC 800/6718 012/6736 004/6768 069
		lp: philips wing WL 1209
		cd: philips 422 2652/426 9752
		cd: decca belart 450 1262
		*philips classical favourites editions incorrectly described as
		the 1953 minneapolis recording*

amsterdam 30 june- 5 july 1975	concertgebouw orchestra haarlem choir	lp: philips 6747 257/6747 364 cd: philips 442 5622/464 7472 *excerpts* lp: philips 9500 697/412 9381 cd: philips 426 1772 cd: arcade (netherlands) 01.3000.32 cd: decca collection classique 468 3832

tchaikovsky/**the sleeping beauty, complete ballet**

minneapolis	minneapolis	lp: mercury OL3-103/OL6-114/SR9-9014
10-11	symphony	lp: mercury (france) 7544-7546
april		lp: nixa mercury MRL 2524-2527
1955		lp: emi mercury MMA 11113-11115
		lp: philips 6738 002
		lp: philips classical favourites GL 5706-5708/ 642 205GL-642 207GL
		lp: philips fontana special SFL 14016-14018/ 700 417-700 419WGY

excerpts
- lp: mercury MG 50118/MG 50395/MG 50493/ SR 90395/SR 90493/OLD 6
- lp: mercury wing MGW 14012/MGW 14033/ SRW 18012/SRW 18033
- lp: emi mercury MMA 11149
- lp: philips BWL 004
- lp: philips wing WL 1008/WL 1036/WL 1209
- lp: philips fontana special SFL 14010/700 423WGY
- lp: philips festivo 839 819GSY
- lp: philips pergola 832 034PGY

amsterdam	concertgebouw	lp: philips 6769 036
28 may-	orchestra	cd: philips 420 7922/446 1662
12 june		*recording completed in june 1980 and january 1981*
1979		

swan lake, complete ballet

minneapolis	minneapolis	lp: mercury MG 50068-50070/OL3-102/ OL6-114/SR6-9014
14-15	symphony	lp: nixa mercury MRL 2528-2530
december		lp: emi mercury MMA 11074-11076
1954		lp: philips 6738 004/6755 011
		lp: philips classical favourites GL 5736-5738/ 642 200-642 202GL
		lp: philips fontana special SFL 14021-14023/ 700 414-700 416WGY
		cd: philips mercury 462 9512

excerpts
- lp: mercury MG 50118/MG 50395/MG 50493/ SR 90395/SR 90493
- lp: mercury wing MGW 14025/MGW 14033/ SRW 18025/SRW 18033
- lp: emi mercury MMA 11149
- lp: philips wing WL 1017/WL 1036/WL 1209
- cd: decca collection classique 468 3832

tchaikovsky/**swan lake, ballet suite**
london   london   78: columbia DX 869-872/DX 8132-8135 auto
20 july   philharmonic   78: columbia (usa) M 349
1937   lp: columbia (usa) RL 3014
                                      recording completed on 9 august 1938

capriccio italien
minneapolis   minneapolis   lp: mercury MG 50054/SR 90054/PPS 3001
22 december   symphony   lp: mercury golden imports SRI 75001
1955   lp: mercury (denmark) 57054
                                      lp: nixa mercury MRL 2514
                                      lp: emi mercury MMA 11057/AMS 16010
                                      lp: electrola RO 60637
                                      lp: philips SDAL 503/6736 002
                                      lp: philips fontana special 700 017WGY/
                                          700 191WGY
                                      cd: philips mercury 434 3602
                                      cd: dg panorama 469 2712

detroit   detroit   lp: decca SXL 6895/417 2771
7-10   symphony   lp: decca (germany) 642 444AS
april   lp: london (usa) CS 7118
1978   lp: franklin mint FM 7011-7014
                                      cd: decca 414 4942/417 7422/443 0032/
                                          443 0042/443 0392

evgeny onegin, waltz
minneapolis   minneapolis   lp: mercury MG 50201/MG 50293/
22 december   symphony   MG 50395/SR 90201/SR 90293/
1958   SR 90395/SR2-9126
                                      lp: mercury wing MGW 14093/SRW 18093
                                      lp: emi mercury MMA 11112/AMS 16059
                                      lp: philips SDAL 503
                                      lp: philips wing WL 1209
                                      cd: philips mercury 434 3052

evgeny onegin, polonaise
minneapolis   minneapolis   lp: mercury MG 50201/MG 50293/
23 december   symphony   SR 90201/SR 90293/SR2-9126/SR2-9132
1958   lp: mercury wing MGW 14076/SRW 18076
                                      lp: emi mercury MMA 11112/AMS 16059
                                      cd: philips mercury 434 3052

fatum, symphonic poem
washington   national   lp: decca SXL 6694
5 april   symphony   lp: london (usa) CS 6891
1974   cd: decca 417 7422/443 0032/443 0392

tchaikovsky/**francesca da rimini**
minneapolis	minneapolis	lp: mercury MG 50201/MG 50345/SR 90201/
22 december	symphony	SR 90345
1958		lp: mercury wing MGW 14076/SRW 18076
		lp: emi mercury MMA 11112/AMS 16059
		cd: philips mercury 434 3732/475 6261

washington	national	lp: decca SXL 6627
10 may	symphony	lp: london (usa) CS 6841
1973		cd: decca 443 0032/443 0392

hamlet, fantasy overture
washington	national	lp: decca SXL 6627
10 may	symphony	lp: london (usa) CS 6841
1973		cd: decca 443 0032/443 0392

hamlet, overture from the incidental music
london	london	78: hmv C 3176
17 september	philharmonic	78: victor 13760
1937		78: electrola EH 1119/EB 158

marche slave
minneapolis	minneapolis	lp: mercury MG 50201/MG 50292/MG 50327/
22 december	symphony	MG 50345/SR 90201/SR 90292/SR 90327/
1958		SR 90345
		lp: mercury wing MGW 14076/SRW 18076
		lp: emi mercury MMA 11112/AMS 16059
		lp: philips K71-B 800/6736 002/6747 050
		lp: philips classical favourites GL 5837/
		SGL 5837/642 271GL/837 871GY
		lp: philips fontana special 700 191WGY
		lp: philips universo 6582 018
		cd: philips mercury 434 3052/475 6261

washington	national	lp: decca SXL 6895
7-10	symphony	lp: decca (germany) 642 444AS
april		lp: london (usa) CS 7118
1978		cd: decca 411 9542/414 4942/417 7422/
		425 0862/443 0032/443 0392

the tempest, symphonic fantasy
washington	national	lp: decca SXL 6694
5 april	symphony	lp: london (usa) CS 6891
1974		cd: decca 443 0032/443 0392

voyevoda, symphonic ballad
washington	national	lp: decca SXL 6627
10 may	symphony	lp: london (usa) CS 6841
1973		cd: decca 443 0032/443 0392

tchaikovsky/**romeo and juliet, fantasy overture**
chicago 8-9 january 1954	chicago symphony	lp: mercury MG 50037 lp: mercury wing MGW 14018/SRW 18018 lp: nixa mercury MRL 2517 lp: philips BWL 004 lp: philips wing WL 1012
watford 20 june 1959	london symphony	lp: mercury MG 50209/SR 90209 lp: emi mercury MMA 11166/AMS 16116 lp: philips SDAL 503/6585 026 lp: philips wing WL 1210 cd: philips 416 4482 cd: philips mercury 434 3532/475 6261
washington 5 april 1974	national symphony	lp: decca SXL 6694/417 2771 lp: london (usa) CS 6891 cd: decca 417 7422/443 0032/443 0392 cd: decca collection classique 466 5482

ouverture solennelle "1812"
minneapolis 4 december 1954	minneapolis symphony university of minnesota brass band	45: mercury EP 40091 45: emi mercury XEP 9092 lp: mercury MG 50054/MGD 19/GL 90 lp: mercury golden imports SRI 75142 lp: mercury (denmark) MG 57054 lp: nixa mercury MRL 2514 lp: emi mercury MMA 11057 *some issues include spoken commentary by* *deems taylor; bell effects added at a later date*

minneapolis
5 april
1958
	minneapolis
	symphony
	university of
	minnesota
	brass band
		lp: mercury SR 90054/SRD 19/GLS 90
		lp: mercury golden imports SRI 75001
		lp: mercury (france) 120 514MGL/
		   130 514MGY
		lp: emi mercury AMS 16010
		lp: electrola RO 60637
		lp: philips AL 3461/SAL 3461/A04908L/
		   838 408AY/SDAL 502/6513 007
		lp: philips fontana grandioso 894 028ZKY
		cd: philips 416 4482
		cd: philips mercury 434 3602
		cd: dg panorama 469 2712
		some issues include spoken commentary by
		deems taylor; bell effects added at a later date

detroit 7-10 april 1978	detroit symphony cathedral and liberty bells civil war cannon	lp: decca SXL 6895/417 2771 lp: decca (germany) 642 444AS lp: london (usa) CS 7118 lp: franklin mint FM 7011-7014 cd: decca 414 4942/417 7082/417 7422/ 443 0032/443 0392 *bell and cannon effects added at a later date*

JOAQUIN TURINA (1882-1949)
canto a sevilla
den haag	residentie	cd: almaviva (spain) DS 0128
31 august	orchestra	
1951	de los angeles	

GIUSEPPE VERDI (1813-1901)
la forza del destino, overture
watford	london	45: emi mercury XEP 9021
9 july	symphony	lp: mercury MG 50156/MG 50324/
1957		SR 90156/SR 90324/SR2-9134
		lp: mercury wing MGW 14053/SRW 18053
		lp: emi mercury MMA 11031/AMS 16058
		lp: philips classical favourites G06402R
		lp: philips diskothek der meister 836 602VZ
		lp: philips wing WL 1048
		lp: philips fontana special SFL 14075/700 204WGY
		lp: pickwick SPC 4043
		cd: philips mercury 434 3452

nabucco, overture
watford	london	lp: mercury MG 50156/SR 90156
9 july	symphony	lp: mercury wing MGW 14053/SRW 18053
1957		lp: emi mercury MMA 11031/AMS 16058
		lp: philips classical favourites G06402R
		lp: philips diskothek der meister 836 602VZ
		lp: philips wing WL 1048
		lp: philips fontana special SFL 14075/700 204WGY
		lp: pickwick SPC 4043
		cd: philips mercury 434 3452

rigoletto, excerpt (parmi veder)
new york	victor	78: victor M 1191/VO 13
september	orchestra	78: hmv DB 6586
1947	tagliavini	45: victor WDM 1191
		45: hmv (germany) 7RF 207
		lp: victor LM 20662
		cd: myto MCD 93382
		cd: opera CD 54508
		CD incorrectly dated 1940-1943

verdi/la traviata, act one prelude
watford   london   45: emi mercury XEP 9021
9 july   symphony   lp: mercury MG 50156/SR 90156/
1957   SR2-9130
                                     lp: mercury wing MGW 14053/SRW 18053
                                     lp: emi mercury MMA 11031/AMS 16058
                                     lp: philips classical favourites G06402R
                                     lp: philips diskothek der meister 836 602VZ
                                     lp: philips wing WL 1048
                                     lp: philips fontana special SFL 14075/700 204WGY
                                     lp: pickwick SPC 4043
                                     cd: philips mercury 434 3452

la traviata, act three prelude
watford   london   lp: mercury MG 50156/SR 90156
9 july   symphony   lp: mercury wing MGW 14053/SRW 18053
1957   lp: emi mercury MMA 11031/AMS 16058
                                     lp: philips classical favourites G06402R
                                     lp: philips diskothek der meister 836 602VZ
                                     lp: philips wing WL 1048
                                     lp: philips fontana special SFL 14075/700 204WGY
                                     lp: pickwick SPC 4043
                                     cd: philips mercury 434 3452

i vespri siciliani, overture
watford   london   lp: mercury MG 50156/MG 50361/
9 july   symphony   SR 90156/SR 90361
1957   lp: mercury wing MGW 14053/SRW 18053
                                     lp: emi mercury MMA 11031/AMS 16058
                                     lp: philips classical favourites G06402R
                                     lp: philips diskothek der meister 836 602VZ
                                     lp: philips wing WL 1048
                                     lp: philips fontana special SFL 14075/700 204WGY
                                     lp: pickwick SPC 4043
                                     cd: philips mercury 434 3452

RICHARD WAGNER (1813-1883)
a faust overture
amsterdam   concertgebouw   lp: philips 6514 219/6769 089
18 january   orchestra
1982

der fliegende holländer
london   covent garden   lp: victor LM 6156/LSC 6156/
august   orchestra   RE 25035-25037/SER 4535-4537
1961   and chorus   lp: decca 2BB 109-111
                 rysanek   cd: decca 417 3192/460 7382
                 elias   *excerpts*
                 liebl   lp: victor LM 2845/LM 9895/LSC 2845/
                 london   LSC 9895
                 tozzi   lp: decca SDD 439/414 1771
                                     lp: decca (germany) 641 975AH
                                     lp: london (usa) 1399
                                     cd: decca 452 7312

wagner/**götterdämmerung, siegfried's rhine journey**
washington	national	lp: decca SXL 6743/VIV 48
23-30	symphony	lp: london (usa) CS 6970
april		lp: rca special products RRS 11
1975		cd: decca 417 7752/444 3442

götterdämmerung, siegfried's funeral march
washington	national	lp: decca SXL 6743/VIV 48
23-30	symphony	lp: london (usa) CS 6970
april		cd: decca 417 7752/444 3442
1975		

götterdämmerung, orchestral postlude to the immolation scene
washington	national	lp: decca SXL 6743/VIV 48
23-30	symphony	lp: london (usa) CS 6970
april		cd: decca 417 7752/444 3442
1975		

lohengrin, act one prelude
wembley	london	lp: mercury MG 50287/SR 90287
4 june	symphony	lp: mercury (france) 121 005MSL/131 005MSY
1960		lp: emi mercury MMA 11176/AMS 16126
		cd: philips mercury 434 3422

lohengrin, act three prelude
watford	london	45: mercury EPS 40101
14 june	symphony	45: emi mercury XEP 9103/SEX 15042
1959		lp: mercury MG 50234/SR 90234
		lp: emi mercury MMA 11120/AMS 16067
		lp: philips fontana special SFL 14051/700 174WGY
		cd: philips mercury 434 3422

die meistersinger von nürnberg, overture
wembley	london	lp: mercury MG 50287/MG 50324/
4 june	symphony	MG 50333/SR 90287/SR 90324/
1960		SR 90333
		lp: mercury (france) 121 005MSL/131 005MSY
		lp: emi mercury MMA 11176/AMS 16126
		lp: philips classical favourites GL 5821/
		SGL 5821/642 227GL/837 827GY
		lp: philips fontana special SFL 14051/700 174WGY
		cd: philips mercury 434 3422

wagner/**parsifal, good friday music**
wembley	london	lp: mercury MG 50287/MG 50333/SR 90287/ SR 90333/SR2-9132
4 june	symphony	lp: mercury (france) 121 005MSL/131 005MSY
1960		lp: emi mercury MMA 11176/AMS 16126
		lp: philips classical favourites GL 5821/ SGL 5821/642 227GL/837 827GY
		cd: philips mercury 434 3422

das rheingold, prelude and entry of the gods into valhalla
washington	national	lp: decca SXL 6743/VIV 48
23-30	symphony	lp: london (usa) CS 6970
april		cd: decca 417 7752/444 3442
1975		

siegfried, forest murmurs
washington	national	lp: decca SXL 6743/VIV 48
23-30	symphony	lp: london (usa) CS 6970
april		cd: decca 417 7752/444 3442
1975		

tannhäuser, overture
watford	london	lp: mercury MG 50234/MG 50287/SR 90234/ SR 90287
14 june	symphony	lp: mercury (france) 121 005MSL/131 005MSY
1959		lp: emi mercury MMA 11120/MMA 11176/ AMS 16067/AMS 16126
		cd: philips mercury 434 3422

tannhäuser, venusberg music
watford	london	lp: mercury MG 50234/SR 90234
9 june	symphony	lp: mercury (france) 121 005MSL/131 005MSY
1959		lp: emi mercury MMA 11120/AMS 16067
		cd: philips mercury 434 3422

tristan und isolde, prelude and liebestod
watford	london	lp: mercury MG 50234/SR 90234
14 june	symphony	lp: emi mercury MMA 11120/AMS 16067
1959		lp: philips classical favourites GL 5821/ SGL 5821/642 227GL/837 827GY
		cd: philips mercury 434 3422
		prelude and liebestod also issued separately on mercury lps MG 50333/SR 90333 and MG 50532/SR 90532 respectively

wagner/die walküre, ride of the valkyries

washington	national	lp: decca SXL 6743/VIV 48
23-30	symphony	lp: london (usa) CS 6970
april		cd: decca 417 7752/444 3442
1975		cd: decca belart 450 0252

die walküre, wotan's farewell and magic fire music

washington	national	lp: decca SXL 6743/VIV 48
23-30	symphony	lp: london (usa) CS 6970
april		cd: decca 417 7752/444 3442
1975		

EMIL WALDTEUFEL (1837-1915)
les patineurs, waltz

vienna	philharmonia	lp: mercury MG 50190/MG 50289/
8 june	hungarica	MG 50444/SR 90190/SR 90289/
1958		SR 90444
		lp: mercury (france) 120 505MGL/130 505MGY
		lp: mercury wing MGW 14087/SRW 18087
		lp: mercury golden imports SRI 75098
		lp: emi mercury MMA 11116/AMS 16063
		lp: philips fontana 6599 900
		lp: philips wing WL 1208
		cd: philips mercury 434 3382
		mercury wing issues incorrectly describe orchestra as minneapolis symphony

CARL MARIA VON WEBER (1786-1826)
euryanthe, overture

amsterdam	concertgebouw	lp: philips 835 062AY
23-25	orchestra	lp: philips classical favourites GBL 5580/
september		G03065L/G05387R
1959		lp: philips fontana 6530 020
		lp: philips festivo 839 516VGY
		lp: philips sequenza 6527 071
		lp: epic (usa) LC 3684/BC 1078
		cd: philips 462 8682

weber/**der freischütz, overture**
amsterdam   concertgebouw   lp: philips 835 062AY/6833 154
23-25   orchestra   lp: philips classical favourites GBL 5580/
september   G03065L/G05387R
1959   lp: philips fontana 6530 020
                                      lp: philips festivo 839 516VGY
                                      lp: philips sequenza 6527 071
                                      lp: epic (usa) LC 3684/BC 1078
                                      cd: philips 462 8682

oberon, overture
minneapolis   minneapolis   cd: minnesota orchestra centenary set
30 december   symphony
1955

amsterdam   concertgebouw   lp: philips 835 062AY
23-25   orchestra   lp: philips classical favourites GBL 5580/
september   G03065L/G05387R
1959   lp: philips fontana 6530 020
                                      lp: philips festivo 839 516VGY
                                      lp: philips sequenza 6527 071
                                      lp: epic (usa) LC 3684/BC 1078
                                      cd: philips 462 8682

watford   london   lp: mercury SR 90529/SR2-9134
27 july   symphony
1962

preciosa, overture
amsterdam   concertgebouw   lp: philips 835 062AY
23-25   orchestra   lp: philips classical favourites GBL 5580/
september   G03065L/G05387R
1959   lp: epic (usa) LC 3684/BC 1078

ANTON VON WEBERN (1883-1945)
five pieces for orchestra
watford   london   lp: mercury MG 50316/SR 90316
22 july   symphony   lp: philips AL 3539/SAL 3539/
1962   A04909L/838 409AY/839 264VGY
                                      cd: philips mercury 432 0062

LEO WEINER (1885-1960)
suite on hungarian folk tunes
vienna   philharmonia   lp: philips fontana CFL 1022/698 004CL
10-11   hungarica   lp: epic (usa) LC 3513
june
1958

antal dorati
the concert register

MATINEE OP DE VRIJE ZATERDAG

AMSTERDAM CONCERTGEBOUW
(grote zaal)

ZATERDAG 9 FEBRUARI, 15.00 UUR

PHILHARMONIA HUNGARICA
DIRIGENT   **ANTAL DORATI**

JOSEPH HAYDN   SYMFONIE nr. 85 in Bes (1785/86)
1732 - 1809   „La Reine"

                         Adagio-vivace
                         Romanze : allegretto
                         Menuetto-trio
                         Finale : presto

BÉLA BARTÓK   DANSSUITE (1923)
1881 - 1945

                         Moderato-ritornel
                         Allegro molto-ritornel
                         Allegro vivace
                         Molto tranquillo-ritornel
                         Comodo
                         Finale : allegro

                         PAUZE

ANTONIN DWORSJAK   SYMFONIE nr. 6 in D, op. 60 (1880)
1841 - 1904

                         Allegro non tanto
                         Adagio
                         Scherzo
                         Finale : allegro con spirito

concert playbill by courtesy of roderick krüsemann

the kapellmeister years

1925-1927	musical assistant at the budapest opera
	preparing performances for visting conductors like franz schalk, bruno walter, erich kleiber, clemens krauss and richard strauss
1927-1929	musical assistant to fritz busch at the dresden opera
1929-1931	opera conductor at the münster opera house
	works included die toten augen (december 1929), die fledermaus (31 december 1929), friederike (1 january 1930), der fliegende holländer (27 september 1930), tiefland (19 december 1930), mignon (25 december 1930), gianni schicchi and il tabarro (18 march 1931), rigoletto (22 september 1931), carmen, fidelio, le rossignol, oedipus rex, cardillac, schwanda der dudelsackpfeifer, bluebeard's castle and l'heure espagnole
	during the münster period also guest performances in dessau *(un ballo in maschera)*, brno *(tannhäuser)* and frankfurt *(lohengrin)*
1930	conducting début with the budapest philharmonic orchestra
1932	works in berlin with a chamber orchestra preparing performances of contemporary music and with paul abraham on his operetta *ball im savoy*, conducting performances at the berlin schauspielhaus with gitta alpar in the cast
1933	performances in paris for french radio of a double bill of mozart *der schauspieldirektor* and gluck *l'ivrogne corrigé*: orchestra used later formed basis of french national radio orchestra

the ballet years

november-december 1933	first british appearances (mainly as rehearsal pianist) with the ballet russe de monte carlo (chief conductor efrem kurtz) in birmingham, bournemouth, plymouth and other centres
	works included les sylphides, le beau danube, choroeartium (brahms symphony 4), le lac des cygnes, scoula di ballo and *les présages*
1934	first american appearances (mainly as rehearsal pianist) with the ballet russe de monte carlo in new york, boston, philadelphia and pittsburgh
march 1934	ballet russe performances in monte carlo, now actually as conductor
july 1934	ballet russe performances at royal opera house covent garden and other british venues
1935	barcelona teatro del liceo (pablo casals orchestra)
july 1935	ballet russe performances in paris *l'oiseau de feu* and *les cent baisers*

the ballet years/continued

1937	beethoven concert with national symphony orchestra of washington
10 march 1937	concert with orchestra of teatro communale venice
	kodaly theatre overture/ vivaldi concerto grosso/ strauss don juan/ casella la giara/ beethoven symphony 7
16 july 1937	ballet russe at royal opera house covent garden
	the good humoured ladies/ el sombrero de 3 picos
21 july 1937	ballet russe ar royal opera house covent garden
	jeux d'enfants/ les présages/ pétrouchka
18 september 1937	ballet russe at royal opera house covent garden
	francesca da rimini/ the gods go a' begging
2 october 1937	ballet russe at royal opera house covent garden
	jeux d'enfants/ aurora's wedding/ the gods go a' begging
	numerous additional performances of these ballets given on other dates
1938	first australian tour by covent garden ballet russe opening in melbourne
	ballets included *graduation ball* and *union pacific*
may 1939	concerts with the abc symphony orchestra in sydney
20 june 1939	ballet russe at royal opera house covent garden
	the good humoured ladies/ cendrillon/ protée/ polovtsian dances
24 june 1939	ballet russe at royal opera house covent garden
	les sylphides/ l'enfant prodigue/ choreartrium
5 july 1939	ballet russe at royal opera house covent garden
	le lac des cygnes/ paganini/ le coq d'or
14 july 1939	ballet russe at royal opera house covent garden
	le lac des cygnes/ symphonie fantastique/ aurora's wedding
28 july 1939	ballet russe at royal opera house covent garden
	the good humoured ladies/ francesca da rimini/ les présages
	numerous additional performances of these ballets given on other dates
september 1939	concerts with the abc symphony orchestra in sydney
	plans to form an australian opera company were thwarted by the outbreak of second world war
17-21 november 1939	covent garden ballet russe in australia
	capriccio espagnol/ le lac des cygnes/ cendrillon/ aurora's wedding
28 february 1940	covent garden ballet russe in sydney
	graduation ball
1940	concert and ballet performances in the hollywood bowl with los angeles philharmonic orchestra
	ballet performances in new york
	ballets included la balustrade (stravinsky violin concerto)
26-27 october 1940	ballet performances in minneapolis with minneapolis symphony orchestra
	les sylphides/ le coq d'or/ graduation ball/ choroeartium/ cendrillon/ aurora's wedding
1941	concert and ballet performances with the havana symphony orchestra
1941-1945	appointment as chief conductor of american ballet theatre
8 january 1943	ballet performance with minneapolis symphony orchestra
	giselle/ three virgins and a devil/ barbe-bleue
july 1943	new york lewisohn stadium concerts
	works included first performance of copland's rodeo

the ballet years/concluded

17-19 march 1944	ballet performances with minneapolis symphony orchestra *three virgins and a devil/ dim lustre/ barbe-bleue/ casse-noisette pas de deux/ les sylphides/ gala performance/ sorochinsky fair/ billy the kid/ romeo and juliet/ sleeping beauty*
27 november 1944	ballet performance for chicago lyric opera *ballets included moonlight sonata*
15 december 1944	first orchestral concert with minneapolis symphony orchestra *beethoven leonore 3 overture/ mozart symphony 41/ ravel daphnis et chloé second suite/ strauss-dorati der rosenkavalier suite*
august 1945	concerts with havana symphony orchestra *programmes included beethoven symphony 3*

the post-war career

november-december 1945/dallas/fair park auditorium
dallas symphony	william schuman prayer in time of war/tchaikovsky romeo and juliet/brahms piano concerto 2/beethoven symphony 3 *arrau*

23 june 1946/london/royal albert hall
london symphony	bach brandenburg concerto 3/brahms violin concerto/ beethoven symphony 3 *menuhin*

30 june 1946/london/royal albert hall
london symphony	brahms haydn variations/kodaly dances of galanta/ravel la valse/tchaikovsky symphony 5

2 september 1946/salzburg/festspielhaus
mozarteum orchestra	copland quiet city/bach violin concerto 2/beethoven symphony 6 *menuhin*

5-6 september 1946/budapest
budapest philharmonic	*programmes included* bartok violin concerto 2 *menuhin*

24 september 1946/dallas/fair park auditorium
dallas symphony	ballet performance

october 1946/dallas/fair park auditorium
dallas symphony	*programmes included* kodaly peacock variations

1946 season with dallas symphony orchestra also included first american performance of bartok bluebeard's castle

15 july 1947/los angeles/hollywood bowl
hollywood bowl   bach air from suite 3/espejo airs tziganes/tchaikovsky sérénade
symphony   mélancolique/mendelssohn violin concerto
elman

8 november 1947/dallas/fair park auditorium
dallas   beethoven egmont overture/prokofiev symphony 1/berlioz
symphony   damnation de faust suite/wagner ride of the valkyries/dukas
l'apprenti sorcier/sousa semper fidelis

29 november 1947/dallas/fair park auditorium
dallas   mozart piano concerto 12/mahler symphony 3
symphony   *dorati/demond/dallas choirs*

27 december 1947/dallas/fair park auditorium
dallas   *menuhin*
symphony

1947/new york/columbia television studios
columbia   bach air from suite 3/mendelssohn violin concerto
symphony   *menuhin*

1949/oklahoma city
dallas   *programme included*
symphony   brahms symphony 2
concerts with the dallas symphony orchestra also included major choral works such as bach saint matthew passion, verdi requiem and beethoven missa solemnis

21 october 1949/minneapolis/northrop auditorium
minneapolis   mozart zauberflöte overture/strauss till eulenspiegel/
symphony   debussy la mer/beethoven symphony 7

27 october 1949/minneapolis/northrop auditorium
minneapolis   cimarosa matrimonio segreto overture/brahms haydn variations/
symphony   hindemith weber metamorphoses/tchaikovsky symphony 5

30 october 1949/minneapolis/northrop auditorium
minneapolis   weber oberon overture/villa-lobos bachianas brasileiras 2/
symphony   tchaikovsky piano concerto 1
lateiner

3 november 1949/minneapolis/northrop auditorium
minneapolis   mozart zauberflöte overture/strauss till eulenspiegel/
symphony   beethoven symphony 7
dorati also accompanied menuhin in violin solos by kreisler, paganini and wieniawski

4 november 1949/minneapolis/northrop auditorium
minneapolis symphony
bartok concerto for orchestra/beethoven violin concerto
menuhin

6 november 1949/minneapolis/northrop auditorium
minneapolis symphony
rossini cenerentola overture/falla interlude and dance from la vida breve/wagner siegfried's rhine journey/wagner forest murmurs/wagner ride of the valkyries/operatic arias by puccini, ponchielli, strauss and wagner
morris

11 november 1949/minneapolis/northrop auditorium
minneapolis symphony
tansman frescobaldi variations/sibelius violin concerto/franck symphony in d minor
druian

13 november 1949/minneapolis/northrop auditorium
minneapolis symphony
vivaldi concerto for 4 violins/mozart sinfonia concertante for wind/debussy danse sacrée et danse profane/strauss till eulenspiegel
orchestral soloists

17 november 1949/minneapolis/northrop auditorium
minneapolis symphony
mozart nozze di figaro overture/strauss till eulenspiegel/beethoven symphony 7/star-spangled banner/songs by brahms, schubert, schumann, tangström and sibelius
svanholm/oberg

18 november 1949/minneapolis/northrop auditorium
minneapolis symphony
strauss don juan/dance of the 7 veils/wagner siegfried's rhine journey and funeral march/meistersinger suite/vocal excerpts by wagner and strauss
svanholm

20 november 1949/northfield minnesota/saint olaf college
minneapolis symphony
weber oberon overture/hindemith weber metamorphoses/strauss till eulenspiegel/beethoven symphony 7/wagner ride of the valkyries

25 november 1949/minneapolis/northrop auditorium
minneapolis symphony
britten 4 sea interludes/mozart piano concerto 17/rachmaninov paganini rhapsody/mozart symphony 34
kapell

29 november 1949/minneapolis/northrop auditorium
minneapolis symphony
weber oberon overture/mozart sinfonia concertante for wind/falla interlude and dance from la vida breve/villa-lobos bachianas brasileiras 2/mussorgsky-ravel pictures from an exhibition
orchestral soloists

2 december 1949/minneapolis/northrop auditorium
minneapolis symphony
bach cantata 41/haydn symphony 96/bartok viola concerto/mussorgsky-ravel pictures from an exhibition
primrose/chorus

4 december 1949/minneapolis/northrop auditorium
minneapolis symphony
berlioz benvenuto cellini overture/strauss don juan/wieniawski violin concerto 2/ravel boléro
druian

6 december 1949/minneapolis/northrop auditorium
minneapolis symphony
weber oberon overture/falla interlude and dance from la vida breve/mozart sinfonia concertante for wind/villa-lobos bachianas brasileiras 2/haydn symphony 96/wagner ride of the valkyries
orchestral soloists

9 december 1949/minneapolis/northrop auditorium
minneapolis symphony
gluck iphigenie in aulis overture/tchaikovsky romeo and juliet/barber violin concerto/brahms symphony 3
posselt

11 december 1949/saint peter minnesota
minneapolis symphony
mozart zauberflöte overture/falla interlude and dance from la vida breve/tchaikovsky romeo and juliet/gluck iphigenie in aulis overture/schubert symphony 9

16 december 1949/minneapolis/northrop auditorium
minneapolis symphony
vivaldi sinfonia in g/schubert symphony 9/stravinsky le sacre du printemps

22 december 1949/minneapolis/northrop auditorium
minneapolis symphony
handel messiah
glaz/bollinger/sullivan/pease/minneapolis university choir

30 december 1949/minneapolis/northrop auditorium
minneapolis symphony
prokofiev symphony 1/ravel rapsodie espagnole/messiaen l'ascension/tchaikovsky violin concerto
stern

17 january 1950/saint paul minnesota/auditorium theatre
minneapolis symphony
weber oberon overture/falla interlude and dance from la vida breve/smetana moldau/wagner siegfried's rhine journey/brahms symphony 3

20 january 1950/minneapolis/northrop auditorium
minneapolis symphony
wagner tristan und isolde, scenes
traubel/melchior

26 january 1950/minneapolis/northrop auditorium
minneapolis symphony
brahms symphony 3/falla interlude and dance from la vida breve/smetana moldau/j.strauss fledermaus overture/star-spangled banner/piano solos by chopin
serkin

27 january 1950/minneapolis/northrop auditorium
minneapolis symphony
mozart maurerische trauermusik/brahms piano concerto 2/beethoven symphony 6
serkin

28 january 1950/milwaukee wisconsin/city auditorium
minneapolis symphony
berlioz benvenuto cellini overture/debussy prélude a l'apres-midi/hindemith weber metamorphoses/strauss dance of the 7 veils/tchaikovsky symphony 5

29 january 1950/chicago/civic opera house
minneapolis symphony
mozart zauberflöte overture/debussy prélude a l'apres-midi/tchaikovsky violin concerto/bartok concerto for orchestra
stern

1 february 1950/fort wayne indiana/quimby auditorium
minneapolis symphony
berlioz benvenuto cellini overture/hindemith weber metamorphoses/mozart zauberflöte overture/wagner ride of the valkyries/strauss dance of the 7 veils/schubert symphony 9

2 february 1950/toledo ohio/peristyle museum
minneapolis symphony

4 february 1950/buffalo new york/klinehans music hall
minneapolis symphony

7 february 1950/saint paul minnesota/city auditorium
minneapolis symphony
nicolai merry wives of windsor overture/wagner forest murmurs/j.strauss schatzwalzer/britten young persons guide

10 february 1950/minneapolis/northrop auditorium
minneapolis symphony
berlioz benvenuto cellini overture/debussy prélude a l'apres-midi/poulenc sinfonietta/strauss don quixote
orchestral soloists

11 february 1950/minneapolis/northrop auditorium
minneapolis symphony
cimarosa matrimonio segreto overture/handel concerto grosso op 6 no 7/bartok concerto for orchestra
radio concert

17 february 1950/minneapolis/ northrop auditorium
minneapolis symphony purcell trumpet voluntary/mahler symphony 3
johnson/ saint john's boys choir/ cecilian singers

19 february 1950/minneapolis/northrop auditorium
minneapolis symphony *gershwin programme*
porgy and bess suite/rhapsody in blue/piano concerto/an american in paris
levant

24 february 1950/minneapolis/northrop auditorium
minneapolis symphony wagner tannhäuser overture/william schuman symphony 3/ beethoven piano concerto 5
michelangeli

26 february 1950/minneapolis/northrop auditorium
minneapolis symphony mozart eine kleine nachtmusik/boccherini cello concerto/ choral works
hubert/ saint olaf choir

2-3 march 1950/minneapolis/northrop auditorium
minneapolis symphony mozart ave verum corpus/verdi requiem mass
yeend/ heidt/ carelli/ scott/ minneapolis university choir

6 march 1950/des moines indiana
minneapolis symphony

7-8 march 1950/ames iowa/iowa state university
minneapolis symphony

10 march 1950/madison wisconsin/university of wisconsin
minneapolis symphony cimarosa matrimonio segreto overture/falla interlude and dance from la vida breve/hindemith weber metamorphoses

12 march 1950/la crosse wisconsin/vocational high school
minneapolis symphony weber oberon overture/strauss dance of the 7 veils/wagner tannhäuser overture/schubert symphony 9

15 march 1950/minneapolis/northrop auditorium
minneapolis symphony nicolai merry wives overture/smetana moldau/britten young person's guide/tchaikovsky symphony 6

16 march 1950/minneapolis/northrop auditorium
minneapolis symphony nicolai merry wives overture/wagner forest murmurs/ britten young person's guide/j.strauss schatzwalzer/star-spangled banner

17 march 1950/minneapolis/northrop auditorium
minneapolis symphony
mozart nozze di figaro overture/mozart symphony 31/bach cantata 53/mahler kindertotenlieder/scriabin poeme de l'extase
anderson

19 march 1950/minneapolis/northrop auditorium
minneapolis symphony
bach passacaglia and fugue bwv 582/beethoven symphony 7/vocal works by liszt and schubert/spirituals
anderson/rupp

24 march 1950/minneapolis/northrop auditorium
minneapolis symphony
persichetti dance overture/vaughan williams tallis fantasia/kodaly hary janos suite/brahms symphony 1

25 march 1950/moorhead minnesota/armory hall
minneapolis symphony

26 march 1950/grand forks north dakota/central high school
minneapolis symphony

27 march 1950/minot north dakota/teachers college
minneapolis symphony

28 march 1950/moose jaw saskatchewan
minneapolis symphony
berlioz benvenuto cellini overture/debussy prélude a l'apres-midi/falla interlude and dance from la vida breve/gershwin porgy and bess suite/j.strauss schatzwalzer/franck symphony in d minor

29 march 1950/calgary/palace theatre
minneapolis symphony

30 march 1950/edmonton
minneapolis symphony

31 march 1950/saskatoon/saskatoon arena
minneapolis symphony
programme as for 28 march

1 april 1950/regina/regina arena
minneapolis symphony
weber oberon overture/schubert rosamunde entr'acte 3/smetana moldau/tchaikovsky romeo and juliet/j.strauss schatzwalzer/beethoven symphony 7

3-4 april 1950/winnipeg/auditorium
minneapolis symphony

7 april 1950/minneapolis/northrop auditorium
minneapolis symphony
rimsky-korsakov russian easter overture/rachmaninov piano concerto 2/debussy le martyre de saint sébastien/strauss tod und verklärung
trepel

9 april 1950/minneapolis/northrop auditorium
minneapolis symphony
wagner ride of the valkyries/liszt piano concerto 2/brahms symphony 1
lindsay

12 april 1950/mankato minnesota/teachers college
minneapolis symphony

14 april 1950/minneapolis/northrop auditorium
minneapolis symphony
bach toccata adagio and fugue bwv 564/bartok divertimento/wagner tristan prelude and liebestod/beethoven symphony 5

16 april 1950/minneapolis/northrop auditorium
minneapolis symphony
offenbach belle hélène suite/mozart symphony 31/glazunov violin concerto/tchaikovsky 1812 overture

24 may 1950/berlin/titania palast
rias-orchester
beethoven symphony 4/beethoven piano concerto 4/bartok concerto for orchestra
gieseking

20 october 1950/minneapolis/northrop auditorium
minneapolis symphony
beethoven leonore 3 overture/falla sombrero de 3 picos/ravel daphnis et chloé second suite/brahms symphony 2

22 october 1950/minneaplois/northrop auditorium
minneapolis symphony
weber euryanthe overture/saint-saens piano concerto 2/mussorgsky-ravel pictures from an exhibition/star-spangled banner
graham

27 october 1950/minneapolis/northrop auditorium
minneapolis symphony
corelli concerto grosso op 6 no 1/prokofiev scythian suite/sibelius symphony 2

2 november 1950/minneapolis/northrop auditorium
minneapolis symphony — beethoven leonore 3 overture/corelli concerto grosso op 6 no 1/ravel daphnis et chloé second suite/sibelius symphony 2

4 november 1950/minneapolis/northrop auditorium
minneapolis symphony — grétry céphale et procris/honegger pacific 231/bloch schelomo/beethoven symphony 4
piatigorsky

5 november 1950/saint peter minnesota
minneapolis symphony — weber euryanthe overture/grétry céphale et procris/ravel daphnis et chloé second suite/brahms symphony 2

9 november 1950/saint paul minnesota/civic auditorium
minneapolis symphony — beethoven leonore 3 overture/honegger pacific 231/ravel daphnis et chloé second suite/piano solos by chopin, liszt and mozart
arrau

10 november 1950/minneapolis/northrop auditorium
minneapolis symphony — earl introduction and allegro/brahms piano concerto 1/strauss also sprach zarathustra
arrau

12 november 1950/minneapolis/northrop auditorium
minneapolis symphony — purcell trumpet voluntary/offenbach belle hélene suite/britten young person's guide/ravel piano concerto in g
j.casadesus

16 november 1950/minneapolis/northrop auditorium
minneapolis symphony — beethoven prometheus overture/respighi pini di roma/star-spangled banner/vocal works by bizet, brahms and tchaikovsky
thebom/oberg

17 november 1950/minneapolis/northrop auditorium
minneapolis symphony — beethoven prometheus overture/mozart symphony 36/mahler lieder eines fahrenden gesellen/schoenberg lied der waldtaube/respighi pini di roma
thebom

19 november 1950/northfield minnesota/saint olaf college
minneapolis symphony

24 november 1950/minneapolis/northrop auditorium
minneapolis symphony — menotti amelia al ballo overture/prokofiev violin concerto 2/berlioz symphonie fantastique
druian

30 november 1950/minneapolis/northrop auditorium
minneapolis symphony
wagner meistersinger overture/mozart symphony 36/menotti amelia al ballo overture/j.strauss rosen aus dem süden/ mussorgsky-ravel pictures from an exhibition

1 december 1950/minneapolis/northrop auditorium
minneapolis symphony
bach orchestral suite 4/beethoven piano concerto 3/ hindemith sinfonia serena
hess

3 december 1950/minneapolis/northrop auditorium
minneapolis symphony
smetana bartered bride overture/falla el amor brujo/ tchaikovsky symphony 5
johnson

5 december 1950/saint paul minnesota/civic auditorium
minneapolis symphony
rossini signor bruschino overture/grétry céphale et procris/ falla pantomime and dance from el amor brujo/offenbach belle hélene suite/beethoven symphony 4

8 december 1950/minneapolis/northrop auditorium
minneapolis symphony
rossini signor bruschino overture/haydn symphony 31/kodaly peacock variations/tchaikovsky violin concerto
spivakovsky

15 december 1950/minneapolis/northrop auditorium
minneapolis symphony
mendelssohn hebrides overture/brahms double concerto/ strauss-dorati rosenkavalier suite
druian/munroe

22 december 1950/minneapolis/northrop auditorium
minneapolis symphony
rimsky-korsakov introduction and wedding march from le coq d'or/rachmaninov piano concerto 1/schubert symphony 5/ j.strauss annen polka/j.strauss wine women and song/j.strauss spitzentuch der königin
janis

12 january 1951/minneapolis/northrop auditorium
minneapolis symphony
berlioz carnaval romain overture/brahms violin concerto/bartok concerto for orchestra
heifetz

16 january 1951/saint paul minnesota/civic auditorium
minneapolis symphony
smetana bartered bride overture/mozart german dances k605/wagner meistersinger overture/j.strauss spitzentuch der königin/j.strauss annen polka/brahms symphony 4

19 january 1951/minneapolis/northrop auditorium
minneapolis symphony
hander water music suite/veretti sinfonia sacra/brahms symphony 4
apollo club chorus

21 january 1951/winona minnesota/winona high school
minneapolis symphony
wagner meistersinger overture/falla 3 dances from el sombrero de 3 picos/ravel daphnis et chloé second suite/tchaikovsky symphony 5

23 january 1951/minneapolis/northrop auditorium
minneapolis symphony
purcell trumpet voluntary/debussy prélude a l'apres-midi/tchaikovsky symphony 6/vocal works by brahms, donizetti and massenet
anderson

25 january 1951/minneapolis/northrop auditorium
minneapolis symphony
purcell trumpet voluntary/debussy ibéria/milhaud scaramouche for 2 pianos and orchestra/strauss rosenkavalier suite
nemenoff/luboshetz

26 january 1951/minneapolis/northrop auditorium
minneapolis symphony
rameau dardanus suite/martinu concerto for 2 pianos/mozart concerto for 2 pianos/debussy images
nemenoff/luboshetz

27 january 1951/milwaukee wisconsin/city auditorium
minneapolis symphony
beethoven leonore 3 overture/franck symphony in d minor/falla ritual fire dance/mozart nozze di figaro overture/respighi pini di roma

29 january 1951/detroit michigan/masonic temple
minneapolis symphony
beethoven leonore 3 overture/grétry céphale et procris/mozart nozze di figaro overture/prokofiev violin concerto 2/tchaikovsky symphony 5
druian

30 january 1951/toledo ohio/peristyle museum
minneapolis
symphony

1 february 1951/jackson michigan/jackson high school
minneapolis mendelssohn hebrides overture/j.strauss annen polka/j.strauss
symphony rosen aus dem süden/mussorgsky-ravel pictures from an
    exhibition/sibelius symphony 2

2 february 1951/east lansing michigan/michigan stadium
minneapolis
symphony

5 february 1951/syracuse new york/central high school
minneapolis
symphony

6 february 1951/ithaca new york/cornell university
minneapolis beethoven leonore 3 overture/brahms symphony 4/grétry céphale
symphony et procris/falla el sombrero de 3 picos/ravel daphnis et chloé
    second suite/j.strauss spitzentuch der königin

7 february 1951/hamilton ontario/palace theatre
minneapolis
symphony

8 february 1951/saginaw michigan/saginaw auditorium
minneapolis wagner meistersinger overture/tchaikovsky symphony 5/
symphony falla ritual fire dance/el sombrero de 3 picos/ravel daphnis
    et chloé second suite/j.strauss rosen aus dem süden

9 february 1951/bay city michigan/central high school
minneapolis
symphony

10 february 1951/midland michigan/midland high school
minneapolis
symphony

13 february 1951/freeport illinios/the consistory
minneapolis
symphony

14 february 1951/beverly hills illinios/fenger high school
minneapolis
symphony

15 february 1951/appleton wisconsin/appleton high school
minneapolis
symphony

17 february 1951/ishpeming michigam/ishpeming high school
minneapolis
symphony

18 february 1951/wausau wisconsin/city hall auditorium
minneapolis
symphony

23 february 1951/minneapolis/northrop auditorium
minneapolis   bach magnificat/bach wir glauben all an einen gott/
symphony   beethoven symphony 9
paige/alberts/johnson/lloyd/harrell/minnesota university choir

25 february 1951/minneapolis/northrop auditorium
minneapolis   haydn symphony 85/sibelius violin concerto/
symphony   kodaly hary janos suite
telmanyi

27 february 1951/saint paul minnesota/civic auditorium
minneapolis   mozart nozze di figaro overture/tchaikovsky violin concerto/
symphony   kodaly hary janos suite/strauss-dorati rosenkavalier suite
druain

3 march 1951/minneapolis/northrop auditorium
minneapolis   chasins period suite/dvorak violin concerto/mendelssohn
symphony   symphony 3
milstein

5 march 1951/winnipeg/winnipeg auditorium
minneapolis
symphony

6 march 1951/grand forks north dakota/central high school
minneapolis
symphony

7 march 1951/minot north dakota/teachers college
minneapolis
symphony

8 march 1951/moorhead minnesota/armory auditorium
minneapolis
symphony

13 march 1951/minneapolis/northrop auditorium
minneapolis   mendelssohn hebrides overture/falla el sombrero de 3 picos/
symphony   grétry céphale et procris/schubert symphony 5/rimsky-korsakov
introduction and wedding march from le coq d'or

15 march 1951/minneapolis/northrop auditorium
minneapolis   weber euryanthe overture/haydn symphony 85/tchaikovsky
symphony   violin concerto/stravinsky petrushka
druain

16 march 1951/minneapolis/northrop auditorium
minneapolis   mozart idomeneo overture/haydn symphony 85/falla noches en
symphony   los jardines de espana/rachmaninov paganini rhapsody/
stravinsky petrushka
rubinstein

18 march 1951/minneapolis/northrop auditorium
minneapolis   wagner tannhäuser overture and venusberg music/
symphony   tchaikovsky piano concerto 1/beethoven symphony 5
rubinstein

23 march 1951/minneapolis/northrop auditorium
minneapolis   bartok music for strings percussion and celesta/bruch violin
symphony   concerto 1/schumann symphony 2
morini

30 march 1951/minneapolis/northrop auditorium
minneapolis   brahms academic festival overture/piston symphony 4/hail
symphony   minnesota/beethoven symphony 3

31 march 1951/la crosse wisconsin/vocational high school
minneapolis   wagner meistersinger overture/tchaikovsky violin concerto/
symphony   j.strauss annen polka/brahms symphony 4/smetana bartered
bride overture
druain

1 april 1951/madison wisconsin/university of wisconsin
minneapolis
symphony

2 april 1951/urbana illinios/university of illinois
minneapolis
symphony

3 april 1951/saint louis missouri/kiel opera house
minneapolis
symphony

4-5 april 1951/columbia missouri/university of missouri
minneapolis
symphony

6 april 1951/burlington iowa/memorial auditorium
minneapolis
symphony

8 april 1951/ames iowa/iowa state university
minneapolis
symphony

9 april 1951/waverly iowa/wartburg college
minneapolis
symphony

10-11 april 1951/iowa city
minneapolis
symphony

12 april 1951/cedar rapids iowa/veterans music hall
minneapolis
symphony

14 april 1951/minneapolis/northrop auditorium
minneapolis   smetana bartered bride overture/debussy prélude a l'apres-midi/
symphony   britten young person's guide/wagner meistersinger overture

28 august 1951/scheveningen/kurzaal
residentie   schubert symphony 8/tchaikovsky violin concerto/orthel
orchestra   symphony 2/ravel la valse
                   stern

31 august 1951/scheveningen/kurzaal
residentie   mozart nozze di figaro overture/mozart serenata notturna/
orchestra   mahler symphony 1/vocal works by mozart and turina
                   de los angeles

18 october 1951/minneapolis/northrop auditorium
minneapolis   weber euryanthe overture/mendelssohn violin concerto/
symphony   dukas apprenti sorcier/strauss don juan/j.strauss rosen aus
                   dem süden
                   druian

2 november 1951/minneapolis/northrop auditorium
minneapolis   beethoven egmont overture/casella paganiniana/ravel la valse/
symphony   brahms symphony 1

4 november 1951/minneapolis/northrop auditorium
minneapolis   berlioz carnaval romain overture/mendelssohn violin concerto/
symphony   beethoven symphony 5
                   druian

9 november 1951/minneapolis/northrop auditorium
minneapolis   handel concerto grosso op 6 no 8/martin concerto for 7 winds/
symphony   mozart symphony 40/strauss till eulenspiegel

11 november 1951/minneapolis/northrop auditorium
minneapolis   rossini gazza ladra overture/schubert symphony 8/tchaikovsky
symphony   piano concerto 1
                   bolet

13 november 1951/minneapolis/northrop auditorium
minneapolis   handel concerto grosso op 6 no 8/casella paganiniana/strauss
symphony   till eulenspiegel/schubert symphony 8/wagner meistersinger
                   overture

15 november 1951/minneapolis/northrop auditorium
minneapolis   beethoven egmont overture/casella paganiniana/schubert
symphony   symphony 8/ravel daphnis et chloé second suite/piano solos
                   by debussy and liszt
                   kapell

16 november 1951/minneapolis/northrop auditorium
minneapolis symphony
haydn symphony 48/debussy jeux/prokofiev piano concerto 3/stravinsky firebird suite
kapell

18 november 1951/northfield minnesota/saint olaf college
minneapolis symphony
berlioz carnaval romain overture/strauss don juan/ravel la valse/brahms symphony 1

23 november 1951/minneapolis/northrop auditorium
minneapolis symphony
lalande sinfonies pour les soupers du roi/bach violin concerto 2/mozart violin concerto 7/borodin symphony 2
menuhin

25 november 1951/minneapolis/northrop auditorium
minneapolis symphony
haydn die schöpfung

28 november 1951/minneapolis/northrop auditorium
minneapolis symphony

29 november 1951/international falls minnesota
minneapolis symphony

2 december 1951/la crosse wisconsin/vocational high school
minneapolis symphony

6 december 1951/minneapolis/northrop auditorium
minneapolis symphony

7 december 1951/minneapolis/northrop auditorium
minneapolis symphony
strauss salome
dow/johnson/fredericks/rothmüller
concert performance of the opera

9 december 1951/minneapolis/northrop auditorium
minneapolis symphony dukas apprenti sorcier/gershwin piano concerto/ravel daphnis et chloé second suite/strauss don juan
johannesen

12 december 1951/elmhurst illinois/york community hall
minneapolis symphony

13 december 1951/saint paul minnesota/civic auditorium
minneapolis symphony

14 december 1951/minneapolis/northrop auditorium
minneapolis symphony cherubini ali baba overture/hindemith violin concerto/frid paradou/beethoven symphony 2
druian

17 december 1951/minneapolis/northrop auditorium
minneapolis symphony handel messiah
bollinger/alberts/poleri/pease/minneapolis high school choir

28 december 1951/minneapolis/northrop auditorium
minneapolis symphony dvorak slavonic rhapsody 3/martinu piano concerto/tchaikovsky symphony 4
firkusny

4 january 1952/minneapolis/northrop auditorium
minneapolis symphony berlioz carnaval romain overture/debussy 3 nocturnes/ravel alborada del gracioso/ravel pavane pour une infante défunte/berlioz harold en italie
persinger/cecilian singers

17 january 1952/saint paul minnesota/civic auditorium
minneapolis symphony debussy fetes/ravel alborada del gracioso/stravinsky firebird suite/piano solos by chopin and weber
serkin

18 january 1952/minneapolis/northrop auditorium
minneapolis symphony creston choric dance 2/beethoven piano concerto 5/prokofiev symphony 5
serkin

25 january 1952/minneapolis/northrop auditorium
minneapolis symphony *wagner programme*
entry of the gods/rhine journey and funeral march/tristan prelude and liebestod/isolde's narration and curse/tristan act 3 prelude/brünnhilde's immolation
flagstad

26 january 1952/milwaukee wisconsin/city auditorium
minneapolis symphony

28 january 1952/minneapolis/northrop auditorium
minneapolis symphony beethoven egmont overture/mozart symphony 40/rachmaninov piano concerto 2/stravinsky firebird suite
janis

29 january 1952/minneapolis/northrop auditorium
minneapolis symphony

30 january 1952/battle creek michigan/kellog auditorium
minneapolis symphony

5 february 1952/minneapolis/northrop auditorium
minneapolis symphony weber euryanthe overture/handel concerto grosso op 6 no 8/prokofiev peter and the wolf/beethoven symphony 2

7 february 1952/minneapolis/northrop auditorium
minneapolis symphony berlioz carnaval romain/wagner entry of the gods/violin solos by dinicu, gluck, kreisler and saint-saens
stern

8 february 1952/minneapolis/northrop auditorium
minneapolis symphony beethoven namensfeier overture/beethoven violin concerto/piston symphony 4/albeniz ibéria
stern

13-17 february 1952/amsterdam/concertgebouw
concertgebouw   beethoven prometheus overture/schubert symphony 9/
orchestra   mussorgsky-ravel pictures from an exhibition

20-21 february 1952/amsterdam/concertgebouw
concertgebouw   vivaldi concerto op 3 no 11/beethoven symphony 4/liszt piano
orchestra   concerto 1/kodaly hary janos suite
de groot

23 february 1952/den haag/gebouw voor kunsten en wetenschappen
concertrgebouw   beethoven prometheus overture/beethoven symphony 4/
orchestra   mendelssohn violin concerto/mussorgsky-ravel pictures
from an exhibition
martzy

24 february 1952/amsterdam/concertgebouw
concertgebouw   beethoven prometheus overture/schubert symphony 9/
orchestra   mussorgsky-ravel pictures from an exhibition

29 february 1952/minneapolis/northrop auditorium
minneapolis   rossini italiana in algeri overture/brahms piano concerto 2/
symphony   dvorak symphony 8
curzon

6-7 march 1952/minneapolis/northrop auditorium
minneapolis   beethoven missa solemnia
symphony   *moudry/faull/carelli/ligeti/minnesota university choir*

9 march 1952/bismarck north dakota/war memorial auditorium
minneapolis
symphony

10 march 1952/regina sakatchewan/exhibition auditorium
minneapolis
aymphony

11 march 1952/lethbridge alberta/civic auditorium
minneapolis
symphony

12 march 1952/calgary alberta/stampede auditorium
minneapolis
symphony

14 march 1952/edmonton alberta
minneapolis
symphony

15 march 1952/saskatoon alberta/university auditorium
minneapolis
symphony

17-18 march 1952/winnipeg ontario
minneapolis
symphony

19 march 1952
minneapolis
symphony

20 march 1952/moorhead minnesota/armory auditorium
minneapolis
symphony

23 march 1952/minneapolis/northrop auditorium
minneapolis
symphony

27 march 1952/minneapolis/northrop auditorium
minneapolis   mozart symphony 35/respighi gli uccelli/borodin polovtsian
symphony   dances/works for viola and piano by bach and borodin
primrose/knardahl

28 march 1952/minneapolis/northrop auditorium
minneapolis   purcell suite for strings/walton viola concerto/schubert
symphony   symphony 9
primrose

30 march 1952/rochester minnesota/mayo civic auditorium
minneapolis   berlioz carnaval romain overture/copland hoedown/dukas
symphony   apprenti sorcier/mendelssohn violin concerto/
tchaikovsky symphony 4
druian

1 april 1952/saint paul minnesota/civic auditorium
minneapolis symphony mendelssohn hebrides overture/prokofiev peter and the wolf/rimsky-korsakov scheherazade

3 april 1952/minneapolis/northrop auditorium
minneapolis symphony strauss till eulenspiegel/stravinsky firebird suite/mussorgsky-ravel pictures from an exhibition/tchaikovsky symphony 4

4 april 1952/minneapolis/northrop auditorium
minneapolis symphony shulman laurentian overture/respighi gli uccelli/mussorgsky-ravel pictures from an exhibition/mendelssohn symphony 4

6 april 1952/minneapolis/northrop auditorium
minneapolis symphony dukas apprenti sorcier/purcell trumpet voluntary/rimsky-korsakov scheherazade/songs and arias by dvorak, hageman, handel, schubert and wagner
melton

11 april 1952/minneapolis/northrop auditorium
minneapolis symphony mozart symphony 35/beethoven symphony 8/tchaikovsky symphony 5

13 april 1952/minneapolis/northrop auditorium
minneapolis symphony *tchaikovsky programme*
oprochnik overture/piano concerto 1/symphony 4
levant

14 april 1952/minneapolis/northrop auditorium
minneapolis symphony berlioz carnaval romain overture/debussy nuages et fetes/schubert rosamunde 3 entr'actes/strauss till eulenspiegel/tchaikovsky symphony 5

15 april 1952/sioux falls south dakota/coliseum
minneapolis symphony

16 april 1952/cedar rapids iowa/veterans auditorium
minneapolis symphony

18 april 1952/galesburg illinois/knox college
minneapolis
symphony

20 april 1952/ames iowa/iowa state university
minneapolis
symphony

21 april 1952/columbia missouri/university of columbia
minneapolis
symphony

22-23 april 1952/iowa city/university of iowa
minneapolis
symphony

19 june 1952/scheveningen/kurzaal
residentie orchestra   bach brandenburg concerto 4/schoenberg verklärte nacht/ bartok bluebeard's castle
lipton/kraus/retel

25 june 1952/haarlem/concertgebouw
residentie
orchestra

3 september 1952/scheveningen/kurzaal
residentie orchestra   mozart zauberflöte overture/mozart piano concerto 20/ bruckner symphony 3
askenase

5 september 1952/scheveningen/kurzaal
residentie orchestra   *beethoven programme*
symphony 8/symphony 9
spoorenberg/hermes/scheffer/ravelli/toonkunst koor

4 and 9-11 october 1952/amsterdam/concertgebouw
concertgebouw orchestra   smetana moldau/bartok piano concerto 2/beethoven symphony 3
loriod

1 november 1952/minneapolis/northrop auditorium
minneapolis symphony — wagner meistersinger overture/debussy la mer/beethoven symphony 3

7 november 1952/minneapolis/northrop auditorium
minneapolis orchestra — mozart symphony 37/weber konzertstück/strauss ein heldenleben
arrau

9 november 1952/minneapolis/northrop auditorium
minneapolis orchestra — rossini william tell overture/lalo symphonie espagnole/respighi pini di roma
druian

11 november 1952/minneapolis/northrop auditorium
minneapolis symphony

12 november 1952/minneapolis/northrop auditorium
minneapolis symphony

13 november 1952/minneapolis/northrop auditorium
minneapolis symphony — mozart symphony 37/dukas apprenti sorcier/gershwin american in paris/lalo symphonie espagnole
druian

16 november 1952/minneapolis/northrop auditorium
minneapolis symphony — beethoven coriolan overture/respighi pini di roma/beethoven symphony 3

20 november 1952/minneapolis/northrop auditorium
minneapolis symphony — brahms haydn variations/mendelssohn violin concerto/creston symphony 3/falla sombrero de 3 picos
milstein

21 november 1952/excelsior minnesota/minnetonka high school
minneapolis symphony — wagner meistersinger overture/schubert symphony 8/dukas apprenti sorcier/gershwin american in paris/respighi pini di roma

23 november 1952/minneapolis/northrop auditorium
minneapolis symphony schubert rosamunde overture/schubert symphony 8/j.strauss kaiserwalzer/wiener blut/wine women and song

25 november 1952/saint paul minnesota/saint paul auditorium
minneapolis symphony *programme as for 23 november*

28 november 1952/minneapolis/northrop auditorium
minneapolis symphony beethoven coriolan overture/beethoven symphony 5/ bartok bluebeard's castle
dow/london/matthews

30 november 1952/minneapolis/northrop auditorium
minneapolis symphony mozart eine kleine nachtmusik/mozart violin concerto 3/ dukas apprenti sorcier/ravel tzigane/respighi fontane di roma
grumiaux

1 december 1952/austin minnesota/austin central hall
minneapolis symphony

2 december 1952/la crosse wisconsin/vocational high school
minneapolis symphony

3 december 1952/milwaukee wisconsin/city auditorium
minneapolis symphony

4 december 1952/green bay wisconsin/west high school
minneapolis symphony

5 december 1952/oshkosh wisconsin/south park auditorium
minneapolis symphony

7 december 1952/minneapolis/northrop auditorium
minneapolis symphony
wagner lohengrin prelude/liszt piano concerto 1/strauss ein heldenleben
sandor

9 december 1952/minneapolis/northrop auditorium
minneapolis symphony

11 december 1952/minneapolis/northrop auditorium
mineapolis symphony
bach concerto bwv 1061/lopatnikov concerto for 2 pianos/ mahler symphony 1
vronsky and babin

19 december 1952/minneapolis/northrop auditorium
minneapolis symphony
schumann konzertstück for 4 horns/brahms violin concerto/ honegger symphony 5/ravel daphnis et chloé second suite
druian

9 january 1953/minneapolis/northrop auditorium
minneapolis symphony
kodaly psalmus hungaricus/strauss tod und verklärung/ walton belshazzar's feast
carelli/smith/minneapolis university choir

13 january 1953/saint paul minnesota/civic auditorium
minneapolis symphony

15 january 1953/minneapolis/northrop auditorium
minneapolis symphony
beethoven leonore 3 overture/hindemith cello concerto/ dvorak symphony 9
jamieson

20 january 1953/minneapolis/northrop auditorium
minneapolis symphony
strauss till eulenspiegel/j.strauss tales from the vienna woods/ tchaikovsky casse-noisette suite

23 january 1953/minneapolis/northrop auditorium
minneapolis symphony
geminiani introduction and allegro/sibelius violin concerto/ berlioz symphonie fantastique
heifetz

27 january 1953/saint paul minnesota/civic auditorium
minneapolis symphony

29 january 1953/minneapolis/northrop auditorium
minneapolis symphony — geminiani introduction and allegro/j.strauss wiener blut/schubert symphony 9

30 january 1953/minneapolis/northrop auditorium
minneapolis symphony — prokofiev march and scherzo from love of 3 oranges/copland symphony 3/brahms piano concerto 2
rubinstein

3 february 1953/minneapolis/northrop auditorium
minneapolis symphony — mendelssohn elijah
moudry/carr/fredericks/sudler/minneapolis high school choir

9 february 1953/toledo ohio/peristyle museum
minneapolis symphony

10 february 1953/findlay ohio/senior high school
minneapolis symphony

11 february 1953/columbus ohio/veterans memorial
minneapolis symphony

12 february 1953/ann arbor michigan/university of michigan
minneapolis symphony — beethoven egmont overture/mozart eine kleine nachtmusik/debussy la mer/brahms symphony 1

14 february 1953/chicago/orchestra hall
minneapolis symphony — beethoven egmont overture/strauss till eulenspiegel/ravel daphnis et chloé second suite/beethoven symphony 3

15 february 1953/madison wisconsin/university of wisconsin
minneapolis symphony

16 february 1953/fond du lac wisconsin/roosevelt auditorium
minneapolis symphony — beethoven egmont overture/schubert symphony 8/brahms haydn variations/dukas apprenti sorcier/gershwin porgy and bess suite

17 february 1953/appleton wisconsin/appleton high school
minneapolis symphony

19 february 1953/minneapolis/northrop auditorium
minneapolis *programme included*
symphony milhaud percussion concerto/dvorak symphony 9

20 february 1953/minneapolis/northrop auditorium
minneapolis *johann strauss programme*
symphony overtures, polkas, waltzes and arias
petina

24 february 1953/minneapolis/northrop auditorium
minneapolis rossini william tell overture/prokofiev peter and the wolf/
symphony dukas apprenti sorcier/wagner ride of the valkyries

27 february 1953/minneapolis/northrop auditorium
minneapolis bach toccata adagio and fugue bwv 564/milhaud suite provencale/
symphony mozart eine kleine nachtmusik/pizzetti symphony in a minor

1 march 1953/minneapolis/northrop auditorium
minneapolis beethoven leonore 3 overture/schumann piano concerto/
symphony gershwin porgy and bess suite
laszlo

6 march 1953/minneapolis/northrop auditorium
minneapolis wagner parsifal, scenes
symphony *harshaw/svanholm/ligeti/rothmüller/cecilian singers*

15 march 1953/minneapolis/northrop auditorium
minneapolis purcell trumpet voluntary/beethoven symphony 5/choral works
symphony *saint olaf choir*

17 march 1953/saint paul minnesota/civic auditorium
minneapolis *programme included*
symphony milhaud percussion concerto

19 march 1953/minneapolis/northrop auditorium
minneapolis vivaldi concerto for 2 trumpets/ives the fourth of july/falla
symphony el sombrero de 3 picos/wagner meistersinger overture
orchestral soloists

20 march 1953/minneapolis/northrop auditorium
minneapolis prokofiev symphony 1/mozart andante k285e/vivaldi concerto
symphony for 2 trumpets/bruckner symphony 9
orchestral soloists

23 march 1953/albert lea minnesota
minneapolis geminiani introduction and allegro/ravel daphnis et chloé second
symphony suite/strauss till eulenspiegel/beethoven symphony 3

27 march 1953/minneapolis/northrop auditorium
minneapolis	berlioz damnation de faust suite/franck variations symphoniques/
symphony	rivier piano concerto 1/bizet symphony in c
	de la bruchollerie

3 april 1953/minneapolis/northrop auditorium
minneapolis	rossini semiramide overture/respighi fontane di roma/petrassi
symphony	concerto for orchestra/beethoven violin concerto
	francescatti

10 april 1953/minneapolis/northrop auditorium
minneapolis	mozart symphony 41/beethoven symphony 9
symphony	*scheunemann/bomar/lloyd/schon/macalester college choir*
	concert marking the orchestra's fiftieth jubilee

12 april 1953/ames iowa/iowa state university
minneapolis	mozart eine kleine nachtmusik/j.strauss annen polka/
symphony	debussy la mer/brahms symphony 1

13 april 1953/des moines iowa/krnt radio auditorium
minneapolis
symphony

14 april 1953/galesburg/knox college
minneapolis	geminiani introduction and allegro/berlioz damnation de
symphony	faust suite/ravel daphnis et chloé second suite/strauss till
	eulenspiegel/beethoven symphony 3

15 april 1953/iowa city/university of iowa
minneapolis
symphony

16 april 1953/vermillion south dakota/university of south dakota
minneapolis
symphony

17 april 1953/sioux falls south dakota/coliseum
minneapolis
symphony

18 april 1953/mitchell south dakota/corn palace
minneapolis
symphony

20 april 1953/winnipeg ontario/winnipeg auditorium
minneapolis
symphony

21 april 1953/grand forks north dakota/central high school
minneapolis
symphony

22 april 1953/minot north dakota/teachers college
minneapolis
symphony

23 april 1953/moorhead minnesota/concordia college
minneapolis
symphony

24 april 1953/rochester minnesota/mayo civic auditorium
minneapolis   prokofiev symphony 1/prokofiev march and scherzo from
symphony   love of 3 oranges/berlioz damnation de faust suite/
                beethoven symphony 3

25 june 1953/scheveningen/kurzaal
residentie   kodaly psalmus hungaricus/bartok bluebeard's castle
orchestra   *lipton/ svanholm/ scott/ toonkunstkoor/ matrosenkoor*

26 august 1953/scheveningen/kurzaal
residentie   mendelssohn symphony 4/mahler das lied von der erde
orchestra   *nikolaidi/ fehenberger*

7 november 1953/minneapolis/northrop auditorium
minneapolis   wagner meistersinger overture/schubert symphony 8/prokofiev
symphony   symphony 7/liszt les préludes

8 november 1953/minneapolis/northrop auditorium
minneapolis   grieg holberg suite/grieg piano concerto/gershwin rhapsody in
symphony   blue/gershwin american in paris
                lowenthal/ knardahl

10 november 1953/saint paul minnesota/civic auditorium
minneapolis   grieg holberg suite/prokofiev symphony 7/j.strauss blue danube/
symphony   tchaikovsky casse noisette suite

13 november 1953/minneapolis/northrop auditorium
minneapolis   fetler gothic variations/strauss don quixote/beethoven
symphony   symphony 6
                jamieson

15 november 1953/minneapolis/northrop auditorium
minneapolis symphony	schubert symphony 5/overtures, waltzes and polkas by johann strauss

19 november 1953/minneapolis/northrop auditorium
minneapolis symphony	j.strauss waldmeister overture/schubert symphony 5/ tchaikovsky casse noisette excerpts/bartok concerto for orchestra

20 november 1953/minneapolis/northrop auditorium
minneapolis symphony	bach brandenburg concerto 6/brahms violin concerto/ bartok concerto for orchestra *menuhin*

22 november 1953/northfield minnesota/saint olaf college
minneapolis
symphony

24 november 1953/saint paul minnesota/civic auditorium
minneapolis symphony	j.strauss künstlerleben/tchaikovsky casse noisette excerpts/ wagner meistersinger overture/bartok concerto for orchestra

27 november 1953/minneapolis/northrop auditorium
minneapolis symphony	telemann suite for oboe and strings/hindemith harmonie der welt/sibelius symphony 1

29 november 1953/minneapolis/northrop auditorium
minneapolis symphony	tchaikovsky casse noisette *complete concert performance*

2 december 1953/saint paul minnesota/civic auditorium
minneapolis symphony	schubert symphony 8/mendelssohn violin concerto/mozart adagio k261/wieniawski polonaise brillante/respighi pini di roma *spivakovsky*

3 december 1953/saint paul minnesota/civic auditorium
minneapolis symphony	mozart nozze di figaro overture/gershwin rhapsody in blue/ bartok concerto for orchestra/beethoven symphony 6

4 december 1953/minneapolis/northrop auditorium
minneapolis honegger jeanne d'arc au bucher
symphony *zorina/hobson/jordan/renan/lishner/saint marks cathedral and minneapolis university choirs*

8 december 1953/minneapolis/northrop auditorium
minneapolis mozart symphony 33/gershwin american in paris/j.strauss
symphony thunder and lightning/j.strauss tritsch-tratsch polka/tchaikovsky waltz from casse noisette

10 december 1953/minneapolis/northrop auditorium
minneapolis gershwin rhapsody in blue/strauss don quixote
symphony *knardahl/jamieson*

11 december 1953/minneapolis/northrop auditorium
minneapolis mozart symphony 33/mozart piano concerto 24/stravinsky
symphony le sacre du printemps
  casadesus

18 december 1953/minneapolis/northrop auditorium
minneapolis haydn symphony 98/debussy prélude a l'apres-midi/thomson
symphony 3 pieces/thomson louisiana story/ravel la valse

21 december 1953/minneapolis/university of minneapolis
minneapolis rossini italiana in algeri overture/mozart notturno for 4
symphony orchestras/ginastera variaciones concertantes/debussy danse sacrée et danse profane/schubert symphony 5
  mainzer

27 december 1953/minneapolis/northrop auditorium
minneapolis *beethoven programme*
symphony leonore 3 overture/violin concerto/symphony 5
  druian

2 january 1954/minneapolis/northrop auditorium
minneapolis verdi luisa miller overture/ginastera variaciones concertantes/
symphony respighi ancient airs and dances suite 2/tchaikovsky violin concerto
  druian

12 january 1954/saint paul minnesita/civic auditorium
minneapolis beethoven egmont overture/mozart symphony 33/ravel
symphony introduction and allegro for harp/wagner siegfried's rhine journey
  mainzer

13 january 1954/faribault minnesota/faribault high school
minneapolis
symphony

15 january 1954/minneapolis/northrop auditorium
minneapolis symphony
berg lulu suite/brahms piano concerto 1/mozart haffner serenade
serkin

28 january 1954/minneapolis/northrop auditorium
minneapolis symphony
berlioz carnaval romain overture/wagner ride of the valkyries/beethoven symphony 7

29 january 1954/minneapolis/northrop auditorium
minneapolis symphony
weber euryanthe overture/mozart symphony 40/bartok miraculous mandarin suite/mussorgsky-ravel pictures from an exhibition

30 january 1954/la crosse wisconsin/vocational high school
minneapolis symphony

31 january 1954/wausau wisconsin/central high school
minneapolis symphony

1 february 1954/winona minnesota/winona high school
minneapolis symphony

2 february 1954/terre haute indianapolis/students union
minneapolis symphony

3 february 1954/louisville kentucky/memorial auditorium
minneapolis symphony

4 february 1954/bloomington indianapolis/indiana uiversity
minneapolis symphony

5 february 1954/fort wayne indianapolis/quimby auditorium
minneapolis symphony

6 february 1954/saginaw minnesota/saginaw auditorium
minneapolis
symphony

8 february 1954/midland minnesota/midland high school
minneapolis
symphony

9 february 1954/detroit michigan/masonic temple
minneapolis
symphony

10 february 1954/toledo ohio/peristyle museum
minneapolis
symphony

12 february 1954/hanover new hampshire/dartmouth college
minneapolis
symphony

14 february 1954/boston massachusetts/symphony hall
minneapolis   beethoven leonore 3 overture/mozart symphony 40/
symphony   bartok miraculous mandarin suite/mussorgsky-ravel
pictures from an exhibition

15 february 1954/amherst massachusetts/university of massachusetts
minneapolis
symphony

16 february 1954/providence rhode island/veterans memorial auditorium
minneapolis
symphony

18 february 1954/norwalk connecticut/norwalk high school
minneapolis
symphony

19 february 1954/stamford connecticut/stamford high school
minneapolis
symphony

22 february 1954/white plains new york/white plains auditorium
minneapolis
symphony

23 february 1954/new york/carnegie hall
minneapolis   rossini italiana in algeri overture/mozart symphony 40/
symphony   berg lulu suite/bartok concerto for orchestra

24 february 1954/scranton pennsylvania/masonic temple
minneapolis
symphony

25 february 1954/hazleton pennsylvania/hazleton high school
minneapolis
symphony

26 february 1954/york pennsylvania/william penn high school
minneapolis
symphony

27 february 1954/warren ohio/harding auditorium
minneapolis
symphony

1 march 1954/park forest illinios/rich township auditorium
minneapolis
symphony

4-5 march 1954/minneapolis/northrop auditorium
minneapolis   mendelssohn midsummer night's dream overture/beethoven
symphony   piano concerto 4/haydn piano sonata 7/brahms symphony 2
                hess

7 march 1954/minneapolis/northrop auditorium
minneapolis   brahms ein deutsches requiem
symphony   *gustafson/daniels/university choir*

8 march 1954/excelsior minnesota/minnetonka high school
minneapolis
symphony

12 march 1954/minneapolis/northrop auditorium
minneapolis   brahms haydn variations/bartok violin rhapsody 1/mendelssohn
symphony   violin concerto/veress sinfonia minneapolitana
                stern

14 march 1954/minneapolis/northrop auditorium
minneapolis   *gershwin programme*
symphony   cuban overture/piano concerto/porgy and bess suite
                weiser

21 march 1954/minneapolis/northrop auditorium
minneapolis   weber oberon overture/ravel la valse/mozart symphony 40/
symphony   choral works
                saint olaf choir

23 march 1954/minneapolis/northrop auditorium
minneapolis symphony — beethoven egmont overture/britten young persons's guide/ j.strauss blue danube/tchaikovsky casse noisette suite

26 march 1954/minneapolis/northrop auditorium
minneapolis symphony — bloch concerto grosso 2/tchaikovsky piano concerto 1/ schumann symphony 3
de la bruchollerie

28 march 1954/minneapolis/northrop auditorium
minneapolis symphony — *programme of scandinavian music*
riefling

30 march 1954/davenport iowa/orpheum theatre
minneapolis symphony

31 march 1954/iowa city/university of iowa
minneapolis symphony

1 april 1954/burlington iowa/memorial auditorium
minneapolis symphony

3 april 1954/beloit wisconsin/memorial high school
minneapolis symphony

4 april 1954/madison wisconsin/university of wisconsin
minneapolis symphony

7 april 1954/edina minnesota/morningside auditorium
minneapolis symphony

9 april 1954/minneapolis/northrop auditorium
minneapolis symphony — ravel introduction and allegro for harp/ives new england holiday/schubert symphony 9
mainzer

11 april 1954/minneapolis/northrop auditorium
minneapolis   puccini crisantemi/puccini suor angelica
symphony   *hurley/norton/johnson/hennig/west/cecilian singers*

16 april 1954/minneapolis/northrop auditorium
minneapolis   beethoven egmont overture/mahler symphony 2
symphony   *hurley/west/university choir*

17 april 1954/new london connecticut/connecticut college
minneapolis
symphony

18 april 1954/bismarck north dakota/war memorial auditorium
minneapolis
symphony

19 april 1954/minot north dakota/teachers college
minneapolis
symphony

20 april 1954/regina saskatchewan/exhibition auditorium
minneapolis   berlioz marche hongroise/debussy prélude a l'apres-midi/
symphony   mussorgsky-ravel pictures from an exhibition/brahms
                           symphony 2

21 april 1954/lethbridge alberta/civic auditorium
minneapolis
symphony

23 april 1954/edmonton alberta
minneapolis
symphony

26 april 1954/saskatoon saskatchewan/university auditorium
minneapolis
symphony

27 april 1954/winnipeg ontario/winnipeg auditorium
minneapolis   weber euryanthe overture/ravel la valse/mussorgsky-ravel
symphony   pictures from an exhibition/brahms symphony 2

28 april 1954/winnipeg ontario/winnipeg auditorium
minneapolis
symphony

29 april 1954/moorhead minnesota/concordia college
minneapolis symphony
mozart symphony 40/ravel la valse/mendelssohn symphony 4/ bartok concerto for orchestra

30 april 1954/minneapolis/northrop auditorium
minneapolis symphony

28 october 1954/minneapolis/northrop auditorium
minneapolis symphony

30 october 1954/minneapolis/northrop auditorium
minneapolis symphony
mozart march k249/brahms symphony 3/beethoven symphony 3

31 october 1954/minneapolis/northrop auditorium
minneapolis symphony
tchaikovsky programme
romeo and juliet/violin concerto/rococo variations/1812 overture
druian/jamieson

2 november 1954/rochester minnesota/mayo civic auditorium
minneapolis symphony
brahms academic festival overture/ginastera variaciones concertantes/ravel daphnis et chloé second suite/beethoven symphony 7

5 november 1954/minneapolis/northrop auditorium
minneapolis symphony
strauss elektra
diw/yeend/lipton/curtis/winters
concert performance of the opera

9 november 1954/minneapolis/northrop auditorium
minneapolis symphony
dukas la péri fanfare/ginastera variaciones concertantes/ gould inventions for 4 pianos
first piano quartet

12 november 1954/minneapolis/northrop auditorium
minneapolis symphony
prokofiev love of 3 oranges suite/toch symphony 2/ tchaikovsky symphony 6

14 november 1954/minneapolis/northrop auditorium
minneapolis symphony
programme of waltzes by délibes, dohnanyi, lanner, lehar, ravel, johann strauss, richard strauss and tchaikovsky

18 november 1954/minneapolis/northrop auditorium
minneapolis symphony
britten young person's guide/prokofiev love of 3 oranges suite/respighi feste romane

19 november 1954/minneapolis/northrop auditorium

minneapolis symphony
brahms academic festival overture/brahms violin concerto/respighi vetrate di chiesa/respighi feste romane
francescatti

21 november 1954/northfield minnesota/saint olaf college

minneapolis symphony

23 november 1954/saint paul minnesota/civic auditorium

minneapolis symphony

26 november 1954/minneapolis/northrop auditorium

minneapolis symphony
programme of american music
william schuman american festival overture/copland rodeo excerpts/cowell hymn and fuguing tune 3/george violin concerto/creston symphony 2
druian

28 november 1954/minneapolis/northrop auditorium

minneapolis symphony
grieg programme
peer gynt suite 1/piano concerto/4 lyric pieces/sigurd jorsalfar
knardahl

30 november and 2 december 1954/saint paul minnesota/civic auditorium

minneapolis symphony
mozart march k249/ravel daphnis et chloé/tchaikovsky 1812 overture
macalester college choir

3 december 1954/minneapolis/northrop auditorium

minneapolis symphony
bach concerto for 2 violins bwv 1043/ravel daphnis et chloé
druian/akos/macalester choir

7 december 1954/minneapolis/northrop auditorium

minneapolis symphony

10 december 1954/minneapolis/northrop auditorium

minneapolis symphony
smetana moldau/dvorak cello concerto/vaughan williams sinfonia antartica
rose/richter/cecilian singers

12 december 1954/minneapolis/northrop audiorium
minneapolis   tchaikovsky casse noisette
symphony   *cecilian singers/complete concert performance*

14 december 1954/minneapolis/northrop auditorium
minneapolis
symphony

17 december 1954/minneapolis/northrop auditorium
minneapolis   mozart cosi fan tutte overture/mozart violin concerto 5/mozart
symphony   symphony 38/strauss frau ohne schatten fantasy/strauss till
     eulenspiegel
     carol

21-22 december 1954/minneapolis/northrop auditorium
minneapolis   debussy l'enfant prodigue/menotti amahl and the night visitors
symphony   *smith/crain/felsted/andrews/woodworth*

30 december 1954/minneapolis/northrop auditorium
minneapolis   wagner tannhäuser overture/bach-dorati suite from cantatas/
symphony   hindemith mathis der maler/beethoven symphony 8

6 january 1955/saint paul minnesota/civic auditorium
minneapolis   mozart cosi fan tutte overture/mendelssohn symphony 4/
symphony   mussorgsky-ravel pictures from an exhibition

28 january 1955/minneapolis/northrop auditorium
minneapolis   orrego-salas festive overture/brahms piano concerto 1/
symphony   beethoven symphony 5
     rubinstein

30 january 1955/minneapolis/northrop auditorium
minneapolis   orrego-salas festive overture/caturla 3 cuban dances/
symphony   ginastera estancia ballet suite/chavez sinfonia india/guarnieri
     3 dances for orchestra

1 february 1955/richfield minnesota/richfield high school
minneapolis
symphony

4 february 1955/minneapolis/northrop auditorium
minneapolis   prokofiev unidentified work/rachmaninov piano concerto 3/
symphony   tchaikovsky symphony 4
     janis

5 february 1955/rochester minnesota/mayo civic auditorium
minneapolis
symphony

6 february 1955/lawrence kansas/university of kansas
minneapolis
symphony

7 february 1955/wichita kansas/wichita high school
minneapolis
symphony

8 february 1955/tulsa oklahoma/municipal theatre
minneapolis   brahms academic festival overture/ravel daphnis et chloé second
symphony   suite/strauss till eulenspiegel

9 february 1955/abilene texas/radford student auditorium
minneapolis
symphony

10 february 1955/midland texas/midland high school
minneapolis
symphony

12 february 1955/dallas texas/mcfarlin memorial
minneapolis
symphony

13 february 1955/fort worth texas/will rogers auditorium
minneapolis
symphony

14 february 1955/houston texas/music hall
minneapolis
symphony

15 february 1955/beaumont texas/city auditorium
minneapolis
symphony

16 february 1955/galveston texas/municipal auditorium
minneapolis
symphony

17 february 1955/corpus christi texas/del mar auditorium
minneapolis
symphony

18 february 1955/laredo texas/martin frank high school
minneapolis
symphony

19 february 1955/harlingen texas/municipal auditorium
minneapolis
symphony

21 february 1955/venue not certain
minneapolis
symphony

22 february 1955/shreveport louisiana/municipal auditorium
minneapolis
symphony

23 february 1955/monroe louisiana/neville high school
minneapolis
symphony

24 february 1955/vicksburg missouri/municipal auditorium
minneapolis
symphony

25 february 1955/lafayette louisiana/campus auditorium
minneapolis
symphony

27 february 1955/new orleans louisiana/municipal auditorium
minneapolis
symphony

28 february 1955/hattiesburg mississippi
minneapolis
symphony

1 march 1955/memphis tennessee
minneapolis
symphony

2 march 1955/evansville indiana/coliseum
minneapolis
symphony

3 march 1955/springfield illinios/orpheum theatre
minneapolis
symphony

4 march 1955/decatur illinios/masonic temple
minneapolis
symphony

6 march 1955/madison wisconsin/university of wisconsin
minneapolis
symphony

8 march 1955/faribault minnesota/faribault high school
minneapolis
symphony

11 march 1955/minneapolis/northrop auditorium
minneapolis   pergolesi concertino in g/mozart symphony 35/mahler
symphony   das lied von der erde
                  nikolaidi/svanholm

12 march 1955/edina minnesota/morningside auditorium
minneapolis
symphony

15 march 1955/minneapolis/northrop auditorium
minneapolis   mozart cosi fan tutte overture/j.strauss kaiserwalzer/
symphony   brahms symphony 3

16 march 1955/saint paul minnesota/civic auditorium
minneapolis
symphony

18 march 1955/minneapolis/northrop auditorium
minneapolis   brahms tragic overture/beethoven piano concerto 5/
symphony   mendelssohn symphony 3
                  gieseking

20 march 1955/minneapolis/northrop auditorium
minneapolis   beethoven leonore 3 overture/bach-dorati suite from cantatas/
symphony   brahms haydn variations/choral works
                  saint olaf choir

22 march 1955/minneapolis/northrop auditorium
minneapolis   bach concerto for 2 violins bwv 1043/purcell trumpet
symphony   voluntary/sanjuan iniciacion from liturgia negra/
                  tchaikovsky nutcracker suite
                  orchestral soloists

171

25 march 1955/minneapolis/northrop auditorium
minneapolis	purcell trumpet voluntary/haydn sinfonia concertante/blacher
symphony	paganini variations/beethoven symphony 7
	orchestra soloists

27 march 1955/minneapolis/northrop auditorium
minneapolis	copland rodeo suite/falla el sombrero de 3 picos/ravel daphnis
symphony	et chloé second suite/stravinsky petrushka

28 march 1955/fergus falls minnesota/roosevelt auditorium
minneapolis
symphony

29 march 1955/winnipeg ontario/winnipeg auditorium
minneapolis	copland hoedown/britten young person's guide/berlioz
symphony	damnation de faust suite/brahms symphony 3

31 march 1955/minot north dakota/teachers college
minneapolis
symphony

1 april 1955/moorhead minnesota/concordia college
minneapolis
symphony

4 april 1955/minneapolis/northrop auditorium
minneapolis
symphony

8 april 1955/minneapolis/northrop auditorium
minneapolis	bach matthäus-passion
symphony	*bible/moll/lloyd/smith/schuessler/gramm/roosevelt, saint marks and
	university choirs*

11 april 1955/excelsior minnesota/minnetonka high school
minneapolis
symphony

12 april 1955/rochester minnesota/mayo civic auditorium
minneapolis
symphony

13 april 1955/la crosse wisconsin/vocational high school
minneapolis
symphony

14 april 1955/glen ellyn illinois/glenbard high school
minneapolis
symphony

15 april 1955/appleton wisconsin/appleton high school
minneapolis
symphony

17 april 1955/galesburg illinios/knox college
minneapolis
symphony

18 april 1955/ottumwa iowa/ottumwa high school
minneapolis
symphony

19 april 1955/iowa city/university of iowa
minneapolis
symphony

20 april 1955/waterloo iowa/paramount theatre
minneapolis
symphony

21 april 1955/dubuque iowa/dubuque senior school
minneapolis
symphony

22 april 1955/cedar rapids iowa/veterans auditorium
minneapolis
symphony

1955/scheveningen/kurzaal
residentie   bruckner symphony 8
orchestra

3 november 1955/minneapolis/northrop auditorium
minneapolis
symphony

4 november 1955/minneapolis/northrop auditorium
minneapolis   beethoven fidelio overture/beethoven symphony 4/bach air
symphony   from third suite/elgar enigma variations/ravel rapsodie
                     espagnol

6 november 1955/northfield minnesota/saint olaf college
minneapolis
symphony

8 november 1955/rochester minnesota/mayo civic auditorium
minneapolis
symphony

11 november 1955
minneapolis symphony — rossini scala di seta overture/schubert symphony 2/strauss don quixote

13 november 1955/saint louis park minnesota/saint louis park theatre
minneapolis symphony

15 november 1955/minneapolis/northrop auditorium
minneapolis symphony — rossini scala di seta overture/bartok hungarian sketches/berlioz damnation de faust suite/beethoven symphony 4/j.strauss tales from the vienna woods

18 november 1955/minneapolis/northrop auditorium
minneapolis symphony — bartok suite 2/bartok hungarian sketches/bartok rumanian folk dances/brahms piano concerto 2
anda

21 november 1955/saint paul minnesota/civic auditorium
minneapolis symphony

22 november 1955/richfield minnesota/richfield high school
minneapolis symphony

25 november 1955/minneapolis/northrop auditorium
minneapolis symphony — bach-weiner toccata adagio and fugue bwv 564/fetler symphony 3/mennin folk overture/dvorak symphony 9

2 december 1955/minneapolis/northrop auditorium
minneapolis symphony — berlioz carnaval romain overture/tchaikovsky violin concerto/copland appalachian spring/strauss-dorati rosenkavalier suite
oistrakh

4 december 1955/minneapolis/northrop auditorium
minneapolis symphony — schubert rosamunde overture/strauss-dorati rosenkavalier suite/j.strauss fledermaus overture/pizzicato polka/tales from the vienna woods/voices of spring

5 december 1955/saint paul minnesota/civic auditorium
minneapolis symphony

9 december 1955/minneapolis/northrop auditorium
minneapolis symphony — *sibelius nintieth birthday programme* swan of tuonela/violin concerto/symphony 2
heifetz

11 december 1955/minneapolis/northrop auditorium
minneapolis symphony
tchaikovsky casse noisette
cecilian singers/ complete concert performance

13 december 1955/minneapolis/northrop auditorium
minneapolis symphony
mendelssohn hebrides overture/prokofiev symphony 1/ sibelius swan of tuonela/stravinsky firebird suite

16 december 1955/minneapolis/northrop auditorium
minneapolis symphony
handel concerto grosso op 6 no 9/haydn symphony 102/ prokofiev symphony 5

19 december 1955/minneapolis/university of minneapolis
minneapolis symphony
britten young person's guide/strauss-dorati rosenkavalier suite/ strauss till eulenspiegel/tchaikovsky capriccio italien

30 december 1955/minneapolis/northrop auditorium
minneapolis symphony
weber oberon overture/debussy prélude a l'apres-midi/sessions black maskers suite/chopin piano concerto no 1/falla sombrero de 3 picos
uninsky

6 january 1956/minneapolis/northrop auditorium
minneapolis symphony
mozart symphony 25/beethoven piano concerto 4/brahms piano concerto 1
arrau

8 january 1956/minneapolis/northrop auditorium
minneapolis symphony
sullivan the mikado
palmer/ bellino/ johnson/ culhane/ walker/ bruce/ maxeiner/ chorus concert performance

15 january 1956/minneapolis/northrop auditorium
minneapolis symphony
wolf-ferrari segreto di susanna overture/rachmaninov piano concerto 2/dvorak 3 slavonic dances/ravel boléro
kunin

20 january 1956/minneapolis/northrop auditotium
minneapolis symphony
mozart bi-centenary programme
cosi fan tutte
curtin/ hobson/ george/ lloyd/ morgan/ smith/ chorus concert performance of the opera

22 january 1956/minneapolis/northrop auditorium
minneapolis symphony
weber oberon overture/liszt hungarian fantasia for piano and orchestra/victor herbert cello concerto and other works
engdahl/ blitz

26 january 1956/minneapolis/northrop auditorium
minneapolis symphony
mozart zauberflöte overture/mozart serenata notturna/
gershwin american in paris/ravel rapsodie espagnole

27 january 1956/minneapolis/northrop auditorium
minneapolis symphony
mozart bi-centenary programme
zauberflöte overture/symphony 1/piano concerto 21/serenata notturna/symphony 41
casadesus

3 february 1956/minneapolis/northrop auditorium
minneapolis symphony
brahms haydn variations/brahms 4 ernste gesänge/villa-lobos bachianas brasilieras 5/brahms alto rhapsody/debussy la mer
thebom/ macalester choir

5 february 1956/minneapolis/northrop auditorium
minneapolis symphony
tchaikovsky programme
capriccio italien/piano concerto 1/violin concerto
knardahl/ druian

7 february 1956/minneapolis/northrop auditorium
minneapolis symphony
rossini scala di seta overture/bach brandenburg concerto 2/
mozart sinfonia concertante for wind/j.strauss voices of spring
orchestral soloists

10 february 1956/minneapolis/northrop auditorium
minneapolis symphony
cimarosa giannina e bernadone overture/casella la giara/
mendelssohn violin concerto/berlioz symphonie fantastique
druian

11 february 1956/white bear lake minnesota
minneapolis symphony

17 february 1956/minneapolis/northrop auditorium
minneapolis symphony
beethoven leonore 3 overture/beethoven violin concerto/
orrego-salas symphony 2/stravinsky firebird suite
menuhin

19 february 1956/madison wisconsin/university of wisconsin
minneapolis symphony

20 february 1956/janesville wisconsin/janesville junior school
minneapolis symphony
beethoven leonore 3 overture/debussy la mer/tchaikovsky symphony 5

22 february 1956/louisville kentucky/memorial auditorium
minneapolis symphony berlioz carnaval romain overture/mendelssohn violin concerto/mozart symphony 40/ravel daphnis et chloé second suite
druian

23 february 1956/nashville tennessee/war memorial auditorium
minneapolis symphony beethoven egmont overture.bartok concerto for orchestra/mozart symphony 40/ravel daphnis et chloé second suite

24 february 1956/auburn alabama/auburn university
minneapolis symphony rossini italiana in algeri overture/brahms symphony 1/elgar enigma variations/ravel dephnis et chloé second suite

25 february 1956/montgomery alabama
minneapolis symphony mozart zauberflöte overture/sibelius symphony 2/falla sombrero de 3 picos/tchaikovsky romeo and juliet

27 february 1956/mobile alabama/saenger theatre
minneapolis symphony beethoven leonore 3 overture/debussy la mer/brahms symphony 1

28 february 1956
minneapolis symphony beethoven egmont overture/beethoven symphony 4/ravel rapsodie espagnole/strauss-dorati rosenkavalier suite

29 february 1956/tallahassee florida/westcott auditorium
minneapolis symphony

1 march 1956/gainsville florida/university of florida
minneapolis symphony beethoven egmont overture/bartok concerto for orchestra/mozart symphony 40/ravel daphnis et chloé second suite

2 march 1956
minneapolis symphony beethoven egmont overture/beethoven symphony 4/ravel rapsodie espagnole/strauss-dorati rosenkavalier suite

3 march 1956/miami florida/dade county auditorium
minneapolis symphony — brahms tragic overture/dvorak symphony 9/falla sombrero de 3 picos/tchaikovsky romeo and juliet

5 march 1956/sarasota florida/municipal auditorium
minneapolis symphony — mozart zauberflöte overture/sibelius symphony 2/falla sombrero de 3 picos/tchaikovsky romeo and juliet

6 march 1956/daytona beach florida/peabody auditorium
minneapolis symphony — beethoven egmont overture/bartok concerto for orchestra/mozart symphony 40/ravel daphnis et chloé second suite

7 march 1956/macon georgia/wesleyan college
minneapolis symphony — brahms academic festival overture/strauss till eulenspiegel/berlioz symphonie fantastique

8 march 1956/columbus georgia/jordan high school
minneapolis symphony — beethoven egmont overture/brahms symphony 1/ravel rapsodie espagnole/strauss-dorati rosenkavalier suite

10 march 1956/charleston south carolina
minneapolis symphony — beethoven leonore 3 overture/brahms symphony 1/ravel daphnis et chloé second suite/strauss till eulenspiegel

12 march 1956/savannah georgia/municipal auditorium
minneapolis symphony — brahms academic festival overture/beethoven symphony 4/stravinsky firebird suite/tchaikovsky romeo and juliet

13 march 1956/clemson south carolina/clemson agricultural auditorium
minneapolis symphony — berlioz carnaval romain overture/mendelssohn violin concerto/mozart symphony 40/stravinsky firebird suite
druian

14 march 1956/lynchburg vitginia
minneapolis symphony — mozart zauberflöte overture/handel concerto grosso op 6 no 9/haydn symphony 102/ravel daphnis et chloé second suite/strauss till eulenspiegel

15 march 1956/zanesville ohio/municipal auditorium
minneapolis symphony — rossini italiana in algeri overture/brahms symphony 1/elgar enigma variations/ravel daphnis et chloé second suite

16 march 1956/marietta ohio/college field auditorium
minneapolis symphony — brahms academic festival overture/strauss till eulenspiegel/berlioz symphonie fantastique

17 march 1956/sharon philadelphia/sharon senior high school
minneapolis symphony — beethoven leonore 3 overture/debussy la mer/brahms symphony 1

19 march 1956/delaware ohio/ohio wesleyan auditorium
minneapolis symphony — rossini scala di seta overture/bartok concerto for orchestra/beethoven symphony 8/strauss till eulenspiegel

20 march 1956/toledo ohio/peristyle museum
minneapolis symphony

21 march 1956/detroit michigan/masonic temple
minneapolis symphony — rossini scala di seta overture/brahms symphony 3/ravel daphnis et chloé second suite/strauss-dorati rosenkavalier suite

23 march 1956/minneapolis/northrop auditorium
minneapolis symphony — franklin suite for strings/brahms violin concerto/tchaikovsky symphony 5
stern

25 march 1956/minneapolis/northrop auditorium
minneapolis symphony — mozart zauberflöte overture/haydn cello concerto 2/ravel daphnis et chloé second suite/choral works
jamieson/saint olaf choir

30 march 1956/minneapolis/northrop auditorium
minneapolis symphony — barber medea's dance of vengeance/wagner good friday music/respighi fontane di roma/schubert symphony 9

6 april 1956/minneapolis/northrop auditorium
minneapolis symphony — *beethoven programme*
symphony 1/symphony 9
marshall/sachs/mccollum/harrell/university choir

8 april 1956/minneapolis/northrop auditorium
minneapolis symphony — *evening of musical comedy and operetta*
works by coward, friml, kern, loewe, porter, rodgers, millöcker and j.strauss
rice/paige/nielsen/university glee club

10 april 1956/rochester minnesota/mayo civic auditorium
minneapolis   mozart symphony 1/mozart violin concerto 4/mozart
symphony   symphony 41/tchaikovsky symphony 5
               druian

11 april 1956/iowa city/university of iowa
minneapolis
symphony

12 april 1956/bloomington illinois/scottish rite auditorium
minneapolis   brahms academic festival overture/strauss till eulenspiegel/
symphony   berlioz symphonie fantastique

13 april 1956/lafayette indiana/purdue university
minneapolis
symphony

14 april 1956/wheaton illinois/wheaton college
minneapolis   beethoven egmont overture/bartok concerto for orchestra/
symphony   mozart symphony 40/ravel daphnis et chloé second suite

15 april 1956/chicago illinois/orchestra hall
minneapolis   barber medea's dance of vengeance/mozart symphony 40/
symphony   bartok violin concerto 2/casella la giara
               spivakovsky

16 april 1956/south bend indiana/john adam auditorium
minneapolis   mozart cosi fan tutte overture/ravel rapsodie espagnole/
symphony   brahms symphony 3/stravinsky firebird suite

17 april 1956/milwaukee wisconsin/city auditorium
minneapolis   rossini italiana in algeri overture/brahms symphony 1/elgar
symphony   enigma variations/ravel daphnis et chloé second suite

18 april 1956/la crosse wisconsin/vocational high school
minneapolis   rossini scala di seta overture/bartok concerto for orchestra/
symphony   tchaikovsky symphony 5

19 april 1956/austin minnesota/central high school
minneapolis   rossini scala di seta overture/brahms haydn variations/
symphony   falla sombrero de 3 picos/prokofiev symphony 5

20 april 1956/charles city iowa/city auditorium
minneapolis   mozart zauberflöte overture/falla sombrero de 3 picos/tchaikovsky
symphony   romeo and juliet/sibelius symphony 2

21 april 1956/new ulm minnesota
minneapolis   mozart zauberflöte overture/beethoven symphony 4/ravel
symphony   rapsodie espagnole/strauss-dorati rosenkavalier suite

25 april 1956/moorhead minnesota/concordia college
minneapolis
symphony

26 and 29 april 1956/minneapolis/northrop auditorium
minneapolis   beethoven egmont overture/beethoven symphony 4/ravel
symphony   rapsodie espagnole/strauss-dorati rosenkavalier suite

27 june 1956/scheveningen/kurzaal
concertgebouw   smetana vysherad/kodaly peacock variations/bartok bluebeard's
orchestra   castle
                  palankay/szekely/retel

28 june 1956/amsterdam/concertgebouw
concertrgebouw   *programme as for 27 june*
orchestra

29 june 1956/enschede/de twentse schouwburg
concertgebouw   beethoven egmont overture/smetana vysherad/kodaly peacock
orchestra   variations/brahms symphony 1

1 july 1956/amsterdam/concertgebouw
concertgebouw   *programme as for 27 june*
orchestra

5 september 1956/scheveningen/kurzaal
concertgebouw   clarke trumpet voluntary/van lier de dijk/mozart violin
orchestra   concerto 3/tchaikovsky symphony 4
                  stern/lutz

7 september 1956/scheveningen/kurzaal
concertgebouw   beethoven leonore 3 overture/brahms violin concerto/bartok
orchestra   miraculous mandarin suite/strauss till eulenspiegel
                  stern

8 september 1956/amsterdam/concertgebouw
concertgebouw   beethoven leonore 3 overture/van lier de dijk/tchaikovsky
orchestra   symphony 4
                  lutz

12 september 1956/scheveningen/kurzaal
concertgebouw   beethoven leonore 3 overture/brahms violin concerto/
orchestra   bartok miraculous mandarin suite/strauss till eulenspiegel
                  krebbers

13 september 1956/nijmegen/de vereniging
concertgebouw *programme as for 12 september*
orchestra

15 september 1956/amsterdam/concertgebouw
concertgebouw smetana from bohemia's woods and fields/brahms violin
orchestra concerto/bartok miraculous mandarin suite/strauss till eulenspiegel
krebbers

24 october 1956/minneapolis/northrop auditorium
minneapolis mozart nozze di figaro overture/haydn symphony 99/debussy
symphony clarinet rhapsody 1/gershwin american in paris/beethoven
symphony 3
williams

25 october 1956/anoka minnesota/anoka senior high school
minneapolis
symphony

26 october 1956/minneapolis/northrop auditorium
minneapolis strauss don juan/bartok concerto for orchestra/
symphony beethoven symphony 3

28 october 1956/northfield minnesota/saint olaf college
minneapolis
symphony

30 october 1956/rochester minnesota/mayo civic auditorium
minneapolis rossini gazza ladra overture/casella la giara/strauss don juan/
symphony schubert symphony 9

1 november 1956/saint paul minnesota
minneapolis
symphony

3 november 1956/minneapolis/northrop auditorium
minneapolis creston dance overture/debussy clarinet rhapsody 1/prokofiev
symphony violin concerto 1/brahms symphony 2
senofsky/williams

7 november 1956/minneapolis/northrop auditorium
minneapolis creston dance overture/beethoven 12 contredances/kodaly
symphony hary janos suite

9 november 1956/minneapolis/northrop auditorium
minneapolis mendelssohn midsummer night's dream overture/dallapiccola
symphony partita/schumann symphony 1/tchaikovsky romeo and juliet

11 november 1956/minneapolis/northrop auditotium
minneapolis beethoven 12 contredances/mozart minuet k320a/schubert
symphony rosamunde excerpts/j.strauss artists life/voices of spring/roses
  from the south/leichtes blut/champagne polka/wiener bonbons/
  fledermaus overture/music of the spheres

15 november 1956/saint paul minnesota
minneapolis
symphony

16 november 1956/minneapolis/northrop auditorium
minneapolis haydn symphony 99/beethoven piano concerto 4/riegger dance
symphony rhythms/kodaly hary janos suite
  curzon

23 november 1956/minneapolis/northrop auditorium
minneapolis george thanksgiving overture/hindemith hérodiade/schoenberg
symphony moderner psalm/stravinsky perséphone
  lee/zorina/paige/macelester choir

26 november 1956/minneapolis/northrop auditorium
minneapolis rossini william tell overture/haydn symphony 99/grieg peer gynt
symphony suite 2

28 november 1956/excelsior minnesota/minnetonka high school
minneapolis
symphony

30 november 1956/minneapolis/northrop auditorium
minneapolis torelli sinfonia con 2 trombe/barber medea's dance of vengeance/
symphony brahms piano concerto 1/dvorak symphony 8
  firkusny

1 december 1956/saint louis park minnesota/saint louis auditorium
minneapolis
symphony

7 december 1956/minneapolis/northrop auditorium
minneapolis mozart symphony 35/mendelssohn violin concerto/bartok
symphony miraculous mandarin suite
  milstein

14 december 1956/minneapolis/northrop auditorium
minneapolis schubert rosamunde overture/j.strauss blue danube/artists life/
symphony kaiserwalzer/mahler symphony 4
  rice

16 december 1956/minneapolis/northrop auditorium
minneapolis   tchaikovsky casse noisette
symphony   *complete concert performance*

17 december 1956/minneapolis/northrop auditorium
minneapolis   rossini signor bruschino overture/bach orchesttral suite 2/telemann
symphony   concerto for 2 horns/mozart sinfonia concertante for violin and
              viola/ravel rapsodie espagnole/dvorak 2 slavonic dances
              orchestral soloists

19 december 1956/minneapolis/northrop auditorium
minneapolis   beethoven egmont overture/bartok hungarian sketches/kodaly
symphony   hary janos suite/liszt les préludes/berlioz marche hongroise

30 december 1956/minneapolis/northrop auditorium
minneapolis   weber freischütz overture/ponchielli dance of the hours/fauré
symphony   pavane/bizer l'arlésienne suite 2/offenbach gaité parisienne/
              kreisler works for violin and orchestra
              druian

14 january 1957/saint paul minnesota/civic auditorium
minneapolis
symphony

19 january 1957/rochester minnesota/mayo civic auditorium
minneapolis   creston dance overture/debussy ibéria/bartok miraculous
symphony   mandarin suite/tchaikovsky symphony 4

20 january 1957/park forest illinois/rich township high school
minneapolis
symphony

21 january 1957/wauwatosa wisconsin/east high school
minneapolis
symphony

22 january 1957/iowa city/university of iowa
minneapolis
symphony

23 january 1957/decorah iowa/luther college
minneapolis
symphony

24 january 1957/fairmont minnesota
minneapolis
symphony

25 january 1957/mankato minnesota/mankato high school
minneapolis
symphony

26 january 1957/winona minnesota/winona high school
minneapolis
symphony

29 january 1957/minneapolis/northrop auditorium
minneapolis   smetana bartered bride overture/tchaikovsky symphony 4
symphony

1 february 1957/minneapolis/northrop auditorium
minneapolis   gould spirituals/beethoven piano concerto 2/rachmaninov
symphony   paganini rhapsody/tchaikovsky symphony 4
     rubinstein

3 february 1957/elmhurst illinois/york community auditorium
minneapolis   creston dance overture/mozart symphony 35/ravel rapsodie
symphony   espagmole/brahms symphony 1

4 february 1957/freeport illinois/the consistory
minneapolis   rossini cenerentola overture/riegger dance rhythms/strauss don
symphony   juan/ravel daphnis et chloé second suite/brahms symphony 2

5 february 1957/canton illinois/canton high school
minneapolis   mozart nozze di figaro overture/debussy ibéria/tchaikovsky
symphony   romeo and juliet/beethoven symphony 3

6 february 1957/carbondale illinois/southern illinois university
minneapolis
symphony

7 february 1957/evansville indiana/coliseum
minneapolis   *programme as for 5 february*
symphony

8 february 1957/muncie indiana/ball state university
minneapolis   *programme as for 4 february*
symphony

10 february 1957/findlay ohio/findlay senior school
minneapolis   *programme as for 5 february*
symphony

12 february 1957/lima ohio/lima high school
minneapolis   *programme as for 4 february*
symphony

13 february 1957/west chester philadelphia/philips memorial auditorium
minneapolis   *programme as for 3 february*
symphony

14 february 1957/white plains new york/white plains auditorium
minneapolis   brahms academic festival overture/beethoven symphony 6/bartok
symphony   hungarian sketches/riegger dance rhythms/stravinsky firebird
                suite

15 february 1957/bethlehem philadelphia/moravian college
minneapolis   beethoven egmont overture/brahms symphony 1/barber medea
symphony   ballet suite/debussy la mer

16 february 1957/brooklyn new york/brooklyn college
mineapolis   rossini scala di seta overture/casella la giara/barber medea ballet
symphony   suite/strauss till eulenspiegel/schubert symphony 9

17 february 1957/new york/carnegie hall
minneapolis   *bartok programme*
symphony   miraculous mandarin suite/violin concerto 2/concerto for
                orchestra
                menuhin

18 february 1957/southampton new york
minneapolis   *programme as for 5 february*
symphony

20 february 1957/hartford connecticut/bushnell memorial auditorium
minneapolis   rossini scala di seta overture/mozart violin concerto 4/riegger
symphony   dance rhythms/bartok miraculous mandarin suite/beethoven
                symphony 8
                druian

21 february 1957/schenectady new york/plaza theatre
minneapolis   *programme as for 3 february*
symphony

22 february 1957/lewisburg philadelphia/brucknell university
minneapolis   *programme as for 4 february*
symphony

23 february 1957/olean new york/olean high school
minneapolis symphony — *programme as for 5 february*

24 february 1957/jamestown new york/jamestown high school
minneapolis symphony — rossini cenerentola overture/mozart symphony 25/mendelssohn violin concerto/bartok concerto for orchestra
druian

25 february 1957/lockport new york/lockport high school
minneapolis symphony — *programme as for 4 february*

26 february 1957/mount clemens michigan/mount clemens auditorium
minneapolis symphony — *programme as for 5 february*

27 february 1957/muskegon michigan/central campus auditorium
minneapolis symphony — *programme as for 4 february*

28 february 1957/peoria illinois/shrine mosque
minneapolis symphony — casella la giara/debussy ibéria/mozart symphony 35/mendelssohn violin concerto/strauss till eulenspiegel
druian

1 march 1957/wilmette illinois/junior high school
minneapolis symphony — *programme as for 4 february*

3 march 1957/madison wisconsin/university of wisconsin
minneapolis symphony

4 march 1957/dubuque iowa/dubuque senior school
minneapolis symphony — *programme as for 4 february*

187

5 march 1957/la crosse wisconsin/vocational high school
minneapolis symphony — rossini scala di seta overture/beethoven symphony 4/kodaly hary janos suite/ravel daphnis et chloé second suite

9 march 1957/edina minnesota/morningside auditorium
minneapolis symphony — *programme as for 16 february*

12 march 1957/minneapolis/northrop auditorium
minneapolis symphony — rossini barbiere di siviglia overture/mozart flute concerto 2/ prokofiev peter and the wolf/strauss till eulenspiegel
swanson

15 march 1957/minneapolis/northrop auditorium
minneapolis symphony — rossini signor bruschino overture/beethoven violin concerto/ dohnanyi symphony 2
francescatti

16 march 1957/bemidji minnesota/bemidji high school
minneapolis symphony — *programme as for 5 february*

17 march 1957/international falls minnesota
minneapolis symphony — *programme as for 5 february*

18 march 1957/winnipeg ontario/winnipeg auditorium
minneapolis symphony

19 march 1957/brandon ontario
minneapolis symphony — berlioz carnaval romain overture/copland appalachian spring/ ravel daphnis et chloé second suite/beethoven symphony 6

20 march 1957/regina alberta
minneapolis symphony — schubert rosamunde overture/bartok concerto for orchestra/ tchaikovsky symphony 4

21 march 1957/lethbridge alberta/civic auditorium
minneapolis symphony — rossini gazza ladra overture/gould spirituals/debussy la mer/ brahms symphony 2

22 march 1957/calgary/stampede auditorium
minneapolis symphony — mozart symphony 35/albeniz iberia/kodaly hary janos suite/strauss don juan

23 march 1957/edmonton alberta/jubilee auditorium
minneapolis symphony *programme as for 19 march*

25 march 1957/saskatoon saskatchewan/university auditorium
minneapolis symphony *programme as for 21 march*

26 march 1957/devil's lake north dakota/central high school
minneapolis symphony beethoven leonore 3 overture/bartok concerto for orchestra/tchaikovsky symphony 4

27 march 1957/grand forks north dakota/central high school
minneapolis symphony *programme as for 4 february*

28 march 1957/moorhead minnesota/concordia college
minneapolis symphony *programme as for 16 february*

29 march 1957/wadena minnesota/memorial auditorium
minneapolis symphony *programme as for 5 february*

2 april 1957/minneapolis/northrop auditorium
minneapolis symphony mozart nozze di figaro overture/beethoven violin concerto/prokofiev peter and the wolf/tchaikovsky swan lake suite
druian

11 april 1957/rochester minnesota/mayo civic auditorium
minneapolis symphony *beethoven programme*
leonore 3 overture/violin concerto/symphony 3
druian

12 april 1957/minneapolis/northrop auditorium
minneapolis symphony vivaldi sinfonia in g/bach brandenburg concerto 2/mozart violin concerto 4/william schuman new england triptych
orchestral soloists

14 april 1957/minneapolis/northrop auditorium
minneapolis rossini gazza ladra overture/albeniz iberia/copland appalachian
symphony spring/choral works
saint olaf choir

15 april 1957/white bear lake minnesota/white bear auditorium
minneapolis
symphony

19 april 1957/minneapolis/northrop auditorium
minneapolis dorati the way of the cross cantata
symphony *smith/macneil/langstaff/university choir*

3 july 1957/london/royal festival hall
london mozart symphony 33/mozart piano concerto 23/bartok
symphony concerto for orchestra
matthews

30 july 1957/london/royal albert hall
london brahms haydn variations/kodaly dances of galanta/ravel
symphony la valse/tchaikovsky symphony 5

7 september-7 october first overseas tour by minneapolis symphony orchestra
7 september 1957/athens/herodes atticus theatre
minneapolis mozart nozze di figaro overture/barber medea's dance of
symphony vengeance/ravel daphnis et chloé second suite/beethoven
 symphony 3

8 september 1957/athens/herodes atticus theatre
minneapolis rossini gazza ladra overture/cowell music for orchestra/
symphony debussy la mer/bartok concerto for orchestra

10 september 1957/salonnika/royal theatre
minneapolis *programme as for 7 september*
symphony

14 september 1957/baghdad
minneapolis mozart symphony 35/cowell music for orchestra/bartok
symphony miraculous mandarin suite/beethoven symphony 5

16 september 1957/teheran/golestan palace
minneapolis rossini gazza ladra overture/mozart symphony 35/cowell
symphony persian set/beethoven symphony 5

17 september 1957/lahore
minneapolis beethoven leonore 3 overture/strauss till eulenspiegel/
symphony dvorak symphony 9

20 september 1957/karachi
minneapolis symphony   *programme as for 7 september*

25 september 1957/bombay/eros theatre
minneapolis symphony   rossini gazza ladra overture/william schuman new england triptych/debussy la mer/beethoven symphony 7

26 september 1957/bombay/eros theatre
minneapolis symphony   creston dance overture/bartok concerto for orchestra/dvorak symphony 9

28 september 1957/beirut/unesco hall
minneapolis symphony   weber oberon overture/copland appalachian spring/bartok miraculous mandarin suite/beethoven symphony 5

29 september 1957/beirut/unesco hall
minneapolis symphony   rossini gazza ladra overture/mozart symphony 40/cowell music for orchestra/fuleihan invocation/debussy la mer

1 october 1957/ankara/devlet open air theatre
minneapolis symphony   *programme as for 7 september*

2 october 1957/ankara/devlet open air theatre
minneapolis symphony   cowell music for orchestra/bartok concerto for orchestra/dvorak symphony 9

3 october 1957/istanbul/atlas theatre
minneapolis symphony   beethoven leonore 3 overture/cowell music for orchestra/strauss till eulenspiegel/brahms symphony 2

4 october 1957/istanbul/atlas theatre
minneapolis symphony

6 october 1957/zagreb
minneapolis symphony   mozart symphony 35/gould spirituals/bartok miraculous mandarin suite/beethoven symphony 5

7 october 1957/belgrade
minneapolis symphony   mozart nozze di figaro overture/cowell music for orchestra/bartok concerto for orchestra/brahms symphony 2

15 october 1957/vienna/musikvereinssaal
philharmonia gluck orfeo ed euridice overture/haydn symphony 99/bartok
hungarica divertimento/weiner suite/berlioz marche hongroise/kodaly
  intermezzo from hary janos

20 october 1957/amsterdam/concertgebouw
concertgebouw weber oberon overture/mozart violin concerto 5/kodaly
orchestra peacock variations/berlioz damnation de faust suite
  milstein

23-25 october 1957/amsterdam/concertgebouw
concertgebouw handel concerto grosso op 6 no 10/mozart piano concerto 24/
orchestra poot symphony 3/ravel daphnis et chloé second suite
  hess

30 october 1957/minneapolis/northrop auditorium
minneapolis beethoven leonore 3 overture/william new england triptych/
symphony beethoven symphony 5

1 and 5 november 1957/minneapolis/northrop auditorium
minneapolis beethoven weihe des hauses overture/beethoven symphony 5/
symphony cowell music for orchestra/mussorgsky-ravel pictures from
  an exhibition

8 november 1957/minneapolis/northrop auditorium
minneapolis mozart march k320a/bach double violin concerto/bartok
symphony violin concerto 2/brahms symphony 2
  menuhin/druian

10 november 1957/minneapolis/northrop auditorium
minneapolis works by the strauss family
symphony

15 november 1957/minneapolis/northrop auditorium
minneapolis mozart piano concerto 25/dohnanyi symphony 2
symphony *dohnanyi*

17 november 1957/minneapolis/northtrop auditorium
minneapolis *sibelius programme*
symphony finlandia/violin concerto/symphony 2
  druian

19 november 1957/saint paul minnesota/civic auditorium
minneapolis
symphony

22 november 1957/minneapolis/northrop auditorium
minneapolis weber preciosa overture/tchaikovsky violin concerto/ravel
symphony ma mere l'oye/toch symphony 4
  stern

29 november 1957/mineapolis/northrop auditorium
minneapolis berlioz grande messe des morts
symphony *lloyd/ university concert band and choir*

1 december 1957/saint louis park minnesota/saint louis park auditorium
minneapolis berlioz carnaval romain overture/gould spirituals/ravel ma mere
symphony l'oye/beethoven symphony 5

3 december 1957/minneapolis/northrop auditorium
minneapolis beethoven egmont overture/copland rodeo/grieg peer gynt
symphony suite 1/sibelius symphony 1

6 december 1957/minneapolis/northrop auditorium
minneapolis roussel bacchus et ariane suite 2/saint-saens piano concerto 4/
symphony haydn symphony 86/stravinsky firebird suite
  casadesus

8 december 1957/minneapolis/northrop auditorium
minneapolis sibelius finlandia/tchaikovsky casse noisette ballet
symphony

12 december 1957/saint paul/saint paul auditorium
minneapolis
symphony

13 december 1957/minneapolis/northrop auditorium
minneapolis bach sinfonia from weihnachtsoratorium/tachmaninov piano
symphony concerto 2/william schuman credendum/beethoven suymphony 6
  entremont

16 december 1957/minneapolis/northrop auditorium
minneapolis copland el salon mexico/gershwin american in paris/dorati
symphony cello concerto/copland danzon cubano/creston dance overture
  jamieson

27 december 1957/minneapolis/northrop auditorium
minneapolis schubert symphony 8/mendelssohn piano concerto 1/ravel piano
symphony concerto for left hand/debussy la mer
  barber-samuelis

3 january 1958/minneapolis/northrop auditorium
minneapolis   rossini viaggio a reims overture/beethoven violin concerto/
symphony   prokofiev symphony 3
                   druian

7 january 1958/rochester minnesota/mayo civic auditorium
minneapolis   smetana bartered bride overture/falla sombrero de 3 picos/
symphony   ravel ma mere l'oye/prokofiev symphony 3

8 january 1958/saint paul minnesota/saint paul auditorium
minneapolis
symphony

10 january 1958/minneapolis/northrop auditorium
minneapolis   cherubini ali baba overture/gabrieli sonata pian e forte/
symphony   castelnuovo-tedesco guitar concerto/helm divertimento/
                   brahms symphony 4
                   segovia

14 january 1958/minneapolis/northrop auditorium
minneapolis   rossini viaggio a reims overture/haydn symphony 86/mendelssohn
symphony   piano concerto 1/falla sombrero de 3 picos
                   margolis

17 january 1958/minneapolis/northrop auditorium
minneapolis   mozart symphony 29/dvorak 4 slavonic dances/orbon 3 versiones
symphony   sinfonicas/strauss tod und verklärung

26 january 1958/amsterdam/concertgebouw
concerrtgebouw   beethoven symphony 3/bartok miraculous mandarin suite/
orchestra   kodaly dances of marossek

29-30 january 1958/amsterdam/concertgebouw
concertgebouw   mozart symphony 35/mendelssohn violin concerto/veress threnos
orchestra   in memoriam bela bartok/bartok miraculous mandarin suite
                   spivakovsky

1-2 february 1958/amsterdam/concertgebouw
concertgebouw   frid cäcilia overture/schumann piano concerto/dvorak
orchestra   symphony 8
                   haas

4 february 1958/rotterdam/schouwburg
concertgebouw   mozart symphony 35/bartok miraculous mandarin suite/dvorak
orchestra   symphony 8

5-6 february 1958/amsterdam/concertgebouw
concertgebouw   beethoven symphony 1/strauss tod und verklärung/ravel ma mere
orchestra   l'oye/roussel bacchus et ariane second suite

8 february 1958/den haag/gebouw voor kunsten en wetenschappen
concertgebouw   *programme as for 5-6 february*
orchestra

10 february 1958/lawrence kansas/university of kansas
minneapolis   rossini gazza ladra overture/hovhaness prelude and fugue/ravel
symphony   daphnis et chloé second suite/strauss till eulenspiegel/beethoven
                 symphony 7

11 february 1958/topeka kansas/municipal auditorium
minneapolis   *programme as for 10 february*
symphony

12 february 1958/garden city kansas/clifford hope auditorium
minneapolis
symphony

13 february 1958/great bend kansas/city auditorium
minneapolis   rossini scala di seta overture/copland rodeo/ravel daphnis et
symphony   chloé second suite/beethoven symphony 6

14 february 1958/hutchinson kansas/richardson auditorium
minneapolis   weber oberon overture/strauss tod und verklärung/stravinsky
symphony   firebird suite/dvorak symphony 8

15 february 1958/dallas texas/mcfarlin auditorium
minneapolis   creston dance overture/prokofiev symphony 3/brahms
symphony   symphony 2

17 february 1958/fort worth texas/will rogers auditorium
minneapolis   hovhaness prelude and fugue/beethoven symphony 6/
symphony   mussorgsky-ravel pictures from an exhibition

18 february 1958/houston texas/music hall
minneapolis   *programme as for 14 february*
symphony

19 february 1958/corpus christi texas/del mar auditorium
minneapolis symphony berlioz carnaval romain overture/beethoven symphony 5/ copland rodeo/ravel ma mere l'oye

20 february 1958/harlingen texas/municipal auditorium
minneapolis symphony *programme as for 10 february*

21 february 1958/brownsville texas/fort brown auditorium
minneapolis symphony mozart symphony 35/beethoven symphony 5/brahms symphony 1

22 february 1958/galveston texas/municipal auditorium
minneapolis symphony *programme as for 14 february*

24 february 1958/temple texas/lamar junior high school
minneapolis symphony *programme as for 10 february*

25 february 1958/lake charles louisiana/mcneese auditorium
minneapolis symphony mozart nozze di figaro overture/mendelssohn violin concerto/ ravel ma mere l'oye/brahms symphony 2
druian

26 february 1958/port arthur texas/woodrow auditorium
minneapolis symphony *programme and soloist as for 25 february*

27 february 1958/new orleans louisiana/municipal auditorium
minneapolis symphony creston dance overture/mozart symphony 35/tchaikovsky violin concerto/debussy la mer
stern

1 march 1958/baton rouge louisiana
minneapolis symphony creston dance overture/debussy la mer/falla sombrero de 3 picos/ brahms symphony 2

2 march 1958/shreveport louisiana/municipal auditorium
minneapolis symphony berlioz carnaval romain overture/copland rodeo/ravel ma mere l'oye/ brahms symphony 4

3 march 1958/little rock arkansas/robinson suditorium
minneapolis symphony *programme as for 10 february*

4 march 1958/oxford mississipi/fulton chapel
minneapolis
symphony

5 march 1958/cape girardeau missouri
minneapolis   *programme as for 14 february*
symphony

6 march 1958/paducah kentucky/tilghman high school
minneapolis   *programme as for 2 march*
symphony

7 march 1958/louisville kentucky/memorial auditorium
minneapolis   *programme as for 14 february*
symphony

9 march 1958/athens ohio/memorial auditorium
minneapolis   *programme as for 14 february*
symphony

10 march 1958/delaware ohio/ohio wesleyan auditorium
minneapolis
symphony

11 march 1958/port huron michigan/desmond theatre
minneapolis   *programme as for 2 march*
symphony

12 march 1958/saginaw michigan/saginaw auditorium
minneapolis   *programme as for 10 february*
symphony

13 march 1958/milwaukee wisconsin/oriental theatre
minneapolis   *programme as for 2 march*
symphony

15 march 1958/janesville wisconsin/janesville high school
minneapolis   *programme as for 10 february*
symphony

16 march 1958/madison wisconsin/university of wisconsin
minneapolis
symphony

17 march 1958/la crosse wisconsin/vocational high school
minneapolis   *programme as for 14 february*
symphony

18 march 1958/mason city iowa/mason city high school
minneapolis   berlioz carnaval romain overture/copland rodeo/debussy
symphony   fetes/brahms symphony 4

19 march 1958/albert lea minnesota
minneapolis   creston dance overture/bizet carmen suite/beethoven fidelio
symphony   overture/brahms symphony 2

21 march 1958/minneapolis/northrop auditorium
minneapolis   hovhaness prelude and fugue/brahms piano concerto 1/
symphony   dvorak symphony 8
   fleisher

28 march 1958/minneapolis/northrop auditorium
minneapolis   weber oberon overture/falla sombrero de 3 picos/mozart
symphony   violin concerto 5/mennin symphony 5
   goldberg

30 march 1958/minneapolis/northrop auditorium
minneapolis   smetana bartered bride overture/rachmaninov paganini
symphony   rhapsody/dvorak 4 slavonic dances
   janis

4 april 1958/minneapolis/northrop auditorium
minneapolis   berlioz carnaval romain overture/schumann cello concerto/
symphony   labroca 8 madrigals/mendelssohn symphony 4
   jamieson/ langstaff

8 april 1958/minneapolis/museum
members of   dorati 2 enchantments of lo-tay-pe
minneapolis   *langstaff*
symphony

11 april 1958/minneapolis/northrop auditorium
minneapolis   *beethoven programme*
symphony   symphony 8/symphony 9
   stader/ hobson/ lloyd/ treigle/ malacester choir

12 april 1958/minneapolis/northrop auditorium
minneapolis   mozart symphony 29/beethoven symphony 9
symphony   *stader/ hobson/ lloyd/ treigle/ malacester choir*

13 april 1958/ames iowa/iowa state university
minneapolis   creston dance overture/falla sombrero de 3 picos/debussy
symphony   la mer/brahms symphony 2

14 april 1958/des moines iowa
minneapolis
symphony

15 april 1958/iowa city/university of iowa
minneapolis
symphony

16 april 1958/rockford illinios/coronado theatre
minneapolis   creston dance overture/chopin piano concerto 1/brahms
symphony   symphony 2
                  brailowsky

18 april 1958/urbana illinois/university of illinois
minneapolis   creston dance overture/mozart symphony 29/dvorak
symphony   4 slavonic dances/prokofiev symphony 3

19 april 1958/detroit michigan/masonic temple
minneapolis   rossini scala di seta overture/copland rodeo/ravel daphnis
symphony   et chloé second suite/beethoven symphony 6

20 april 1958/chicago/orchestra hall
minneapolis   berlioz carnaval romain overture/william schuman new england
symphony   triptych/chopin piano concerto 1/dvorak symphony 8
                  brailowsky

21 april 1958/racine wisconsin/memorial hall
minneapolis   *programme as for 19 april*
symphony

22 april 1958/austin minnesota/austin central high school
minneapolis   berlioz carnaval romain overture/copland rodeo/ravel ma mere
symphony   l'oye/brahms symphony 4

23 april 1958/mankato minnesota/mankato high school
minneapolis
symphony

24 april 1958/moorhead minnesota/concordia college
minneapolis   *programme as for 13 april*
symphony

27 april 1958/saint cloud minnesota/technical high school
minneapolis
symphony

13 may 1958/brescia/teatro grande
philharmonia respighi gli uccelli/mendelssohn symphony 4/bartok divetimento/
hungarica kodaly dances of galanta/berlioz marche hongroise

14 may 1958/verona/teatro nova
philharmonia rossini scala di seta overture/bartok divertimento/kodaly dances
hungarica of galanta/kodaly intermezzo from hary janos

15 may 1958/aquila/teatro communale
philharmonia beethoven symphony 2/mendelssohn symphony 4/kodaly dances
hungarica of galanta/kodaly intermezzo from hary janos

16 may 1958/napoli/teatro san carlo
philharmonia *programme as for 15 may*
hungarica

17 may 1958/palermo/teatro biondo
philharmonia *programme as for 14 may*
hungarica

20 may 1958/amsterdam/concertgebouw
philharmonia bartok divertimento/liszt hungarian fantasia for piano and
hungarica orchestra/kodaly dances of galanta/berlioz marche hongroise
de groot

21 may 1958/hilversum
philharmonia mozart symphony 39/bartok divertimento/kodaly dances of
hungarica galanta
radio concert with audience

22 may 1958/den haag/gebouw voor kunsten en wetenschappen
philharmonia beethoven egmont overture/bartok violin concerto 2/
hungarica mendelssohn symphony 4/kodaly dances of galanta
menuhin

27 may 1958/paris/salle pleyel
philharmonia beethoven egmont overture/bartok violin concerto 2/
hungarica bartok divertimento
menuhin

28 may 1958/bad godesberg/stadthalle
philharmonia beethoven egmont overture/brahms violin concerto/kodaly
hungarica dances of galanta/berlioz marche hongroise
szigeti

30 may 1958/vienna/musikvereinssaal
philharmonia　*programme and soloist as for 28 may*
hungarica　*concert televised by orf-fernsehen*

15 june 1958/vienna/konzerthaus
philharmonia　*beethoven programme*
hungarica　egmont overture/violin concerto/symphony 4
　　　　　schneiderhan

13 august 1958/passau/domhof
philharmonia　bartok divertimento/bartok 2 portraits/weiner suite/kodaly
hungarica　dances of galanta/berlioz marche hongroise

15 august 1958/brussels/théatre américan
philharmonia　beethoven egmont overture/mendelssohn symphony 4/
hungarica　bartok divertimento/kodaly dances of galanta/kodaly
　　　　　intermezzo from hary janos

16 october 1958/excelsior minnesota/minnetonka high school
minneapolis　william schuman american festival overture/strauss don juan/
symphony　beethoven symphony 3

18 october 1958/minneapolis/northrop auditorium
minneapolis　william schuman american festival overture/saeverud minnesota
symphony　symphony/beethoven symphony 3

19 october 1958/northfield minnesota/saint olaf college
minneapolis　*programme as for 18 october*
symphony

20 october 1958/minneapolis/northrop auditorium
minneapolis　*programme as for 18 october*
symphony

25 october 1958/minneapolis/northrop auditorium
minneapolis　handel concerto grosso op 6 no 4/mozart symphony 34/peterson
symphony　free variations/strauss don juan./ravel daphnis et chloé
　　　　　second suite

29 october 1958/edina minnesota/morningside auditorium
minneapolis
symphony

31 october 1958/minneapolis/northrop auditorium
minneapolis symphony
tchaikovsky romeo and juliet/prokofiev piano concerto 2/brahms symphony 1
ashkenazy

2 november 1958/minneapolis/northrop auditorium
minneapolis symphony
schubert rosamunde excerpts/lanner schönbrunner waltzes/kreisler works for violin and orchestra/works by j.strauss
druian

4 november 1958/saint paul minnesota/saint paul auditorium
minneapolis symphony

5 november 1958/saint paul minnesota/womens institute
minneapolis symphony

7 november 1958/minneapolis/northrop auditorium
minneapolis symphony
rossini turco in italia overture/lalo symphonie espagnole/fetler contrasts/haydn symphony 95
stern

11 november 1958/rochester minnesota/mayo civic auditorium
minneapolis symphony
rossini turco in italia overture/haydn symphony 95/fetler contrasts/brahms symphony 1

14 november 1958/minneapolis/northrop auditorium
minneapolis symphony
berlioz benvenuto cellini overture/debussy ibéria/kodaly dances of galanta/rachmaninov piano concerto 2
janis

19 november 1958/minneapolis/northrop auditorium
minneapolis symphony
berlioz l'enfance du christ
allen/mccollum/sze/macalester choir

21 november 1958/minneapolis/northrop auditorium
minneapolis symphony
mozart symphony 39/strauss 4 letzte lieder/beethoven symphony 2/arias by mozart and puccini
della casa

24 november 1958/minneapolis/northrop auditorium
minneapolis symphony
beethoven egmont overture/mozart symphony 39/mendelssohn violin concerto/beethoven symphony 2/tchaikovsky romeo and juliet
druian

28 november 1958/minneapolis/northrop auditorium

minneapolis symphony	mendelssohn midsummer night's dream music/mendelssohn violin concerto/copland symphony 3 *druian*

2 december 1958/minneapolis/northrop auditorium

minneapolis symphony	weber euryanthe overture/mozart sinfonia concertante for wind/ britten young person's guide/j.strauss voices of spring *orchestral soloists*

5 december 1958/minneapolis/northrop auditorium

minneapolis symphony	beethoven prometheus overture/bach orchestral suite 2/ bruckner symphony 8

11 december 1958/saint paul minnesota/civic auditorium

minneapolis symphony

12 december 1958/minneapolis/northrop auditorium

minneapolis symphony	puccini crisantemi/lamontaine piano concerto/schubert symphony 9 *bolet*

15 december 1958/minneapolis/university of minnesota

minneapolis symphony	tchaikovsky francesca da rimini/strauss tod und verklärung/ rimsky-korsakov scheherazade

28 december 1958/minneapolis/northrop auditorium

minneapolis symphony	tchaikovsky casse noisette *complete concert performance*

2 january 1959/minneapolis/northrop auditorium
minneapolis stevens symphonic dances/beethoven piano concerto 4/brahms
symphony   symphony 2
            gould

18 january 1959/minneapolis/northrop auditorium
minneapolis song of norway
symphony   *rice/jonson/fullmer/abelson/university glee club*
            concert version of the musical

22 january 1959/faribault minnesota/faribault high school
minneapolis mozart symphony 38/strauss-dorati rosenkavalier suite/brahms
symphony   symphony 2

1 february 1959/saint louis patk minnesota/saint louis park auditorium
minneapolis beethoven egmont overture/strauss don juan/tchaikovsky
symphony   romeo and juliet/brahms symphony 2

2 february 1959/saint paul minnesota/macalester college
minneapolis
symphony

3 february 1959/rochester minnesota/mayo civic auditorium
minneapolis weber euryanthe overture/beethoven symphony 2/wagner tristan
symphony   prelude and liebestod/strauss don juan

6 february 1959/minneapolis/northrop auditorium
minneapolis dorati way of the cross cantata
symphony   *forrester/treigle/langstaff/university choir*

8 february 1959/minneapolis/northrop auditorium
minneapolis *tchaikovsky programme*
symphony   romeo and juliet/ftancesca da rimini/piano concerto 1
            cliburn

9 february 1959/minneapolis/northrop auditorium
minneapolis gershwin american in paris
symphony   *programme also included anna russell's version of wagner's ring cycle and*
            other items involving anna russell

10 february 1959/minneapolis/northrop auditorium
minneapolis mozart nozze di figaro overture/tchaikovsky evgeny onegin
symphony   excerpts/beethoven symphony 5

13 february 1959/minneapolis/northrop auditorium
minneapolis nabokov sinfonia biblica/brahms violin concerto/beethoven
symphony   symphony 5
            francescatti

16 february 1959/orlando florida/municipal auditorium
minneapolis symphony
rossini turco in italia overture/haydn symphony 95/strauss don juan/
tchaikovsky romeo and juliet/wagner tristan prelude and liebestod

17 february 1959/tampa florida/city auditorium
minneapolis symphony *programme as for 16 february*

18 february 1959/saint petersburg florida/senior high school
minneapolis symphony *programme as for 16 february*

19 february 1959/west palm beach florida/palm beach auditorium
minneapolis symphony *programme as for 16 february*

20 february 1959/miami florida/dade county auditorium
minneapolis symphony *programme as for 16 february*

21 february 1959/miami beach florida/theatre forum
minneapolis symphony
mozart symphony 34/strauss don juan/ravel daphnis et chloé
second suite/beethoven piano concerto 5
kentner

23 february 1959/minneapolis/northrop auditorium
minneapolis symphony
beethoven leonore 3 overture/beethoven piano concerto 5/
tchaikovsky symphony 5
kentner

24 february 1959/daytona beach florida/peabody auditorium
minneapolis symphony *programme as for 16 february*

25 february 1959/jacksonville florida/civic auditorium
minneapolis symphony *programme as for 3 february*

26 february 1959/charleston south carolina/meminger beach auditorium
minneapolis symphony *programme as for 16 february*

27 february 1959/savannah georgia/municipal auditorium
minneapolis symphony   strauss don juan/debussy la mer/brahms symphony 1

28 february 1959/brunswick georgia/memorial high school
minneapolis symphony   *programme as for 16 february*

2 march 1959/albany georgia
minneapolis symphony   berlioz benvenuto cellini overture/debussy la mer/brahms symphony 1

3 march 1959/auburn alabama/auburn university
minneapolis symphony   *programme as for 16 february*

4 march 1959/montgomery alabama
minneapolis symphony   *programme as for 3 february*

5 march 1959/florence alabama/coffee auditorium
minneapolis symphony   *programme as for 16 february*

6 march 1959/birmingham alabama/municipal auditorium
minneapolis symphony   berlioz benvenuto cellini overture/fetler contrasts/tchaikovsky romeo and juliet/brahms symphony 2

7 march 1959/spartanburg south connecticut/converse auditorium
minneapolis symphony   weber euryanthe overture/fetler contrasts/debussy la mer/brahms symphony 1

9 march 1959/clemson south connecticut/agricultural auditorium
minneapolis symphony   strauss don juan/debussy la mer/beethoven symphony 5

11 march 1959/knoxville tennessee/university auditorium
minneapolis symphony   *programme as for 2 march*

15 march 1959/madison wisconsin/university of wisconsin
minneapolis symphony

17 march 1959/la crosse wisconsin/vocational high school
minneapolis symphony   *programme as for 16 february*

19 march 1959/mankato minnesota/mankato high school
minneapolis symphony   *programme as for 16 february*

20 march 1959/minneapolis/northrop auditorium
minneapolis symphony   bach brandenburg concerto 3/foss piano concerto 2/brahms double concerto
foss/druian/jamieson

22 march 1959/minneapolis/northrop auditorium
minneapolis symphony   wagner meistersinger overture/khachaturian piano concerto/choral works
johnson/saint olaf choir

27 march 1959/minneapolis/northrop auditorium
minneapolis symphony   *wagner programme*
tristan prelude and liebestod/parsifal karfreitagszauber/die walküre act 1
raitt/kaart/abelson

30 march 1959/windom minnesota/windom high school
minneapolis symphony   *programme as for 16 february*

31 march 1959/rochester minnesota/mayo civic auditorium
minneapolis symphony   mozart symphony 34/dorati cello concerto/stravinsly petrouchka
jamieson

1 april 1959/iowa city/university of iowa
minneapolis symphony

2 april 1959/macomb illinios/western hall
minneapolis symphony   *programme as for 2 march*

3 april 1959/kewanee illinois
minneapolis symphony   *programme as for 2 march*

4 april 1959/wilmette illinois/junior high school
minneapolis symphony   mozart symphony 34/beethoven symphony 5/brahms symphony 2

5 april 1959/glen ellyn illinois/glenbard high school
minneapolis symphony   *programme as for 16 february*

6 april 1959/elkhart indiana/elkhart high school
minneapolis symphony   *programme as for 16 february*

7 april 1959/valparaiso indiana
minneapolis symphony   weber euryanthe overture/strauss tod und verklärung/ravel daphnis et chloé second suite/beethoven symphony 2

8 april 1959/freeport illinois/the consistory
minneapolis symphony   *programme as for 16 february*

9 april 1959/fond du lac wisconsin/fond du lac auditorium
minneapolis symphony   *programme as for 16 february*

10 april 1959/wauwatosa wisconsin/east high school
minneapolis syumphony   *programme as for 16 february*

12 april 1959/sheboygan wisconsin/urban junior school
minneapolis symphony   *programme as for 7 april*

13 april 1959/ripon wisconsin/ripon college
minneapolis symphony   strauss don juan/stravinsky petrouchka/dvorak symphony 9

14 april 1959/green bay wisconsin/west high school
minneapolis symphony   weber euryanthe overture/beethoven violin concerto/tchaikovsky symphony 5
druian

15 april 1959/wausau wisconsin/central high school
minneapolis symphony   *programme as for 16 february*

16 april 1959/moorhead minnesota/concordia college
minneapolis symphony   beethoven symphony 2/dorati cello concerto/stravinsky petrouchka
jamieson

28-29 may 1959/munich/herkulessaal
bavarian radio orchestra   haydn symphony 95/bartok dance suite/tchaikovsky symphony 5

5 june 1959/london/royal festival hall
london symphony   purcell suite/brahms violin concerto/schubert symphony 9
szeryng

12 june 1959/london/royal festival hall
london symphony	mozart 2 marches/mozart symphony 34/mahler symphony 4 *brockless*

24 june 1959/london/royal festival hall
london symphony	pergolesi concertino 2/stravinsky concerto for strings/mahler das lied von der erde *heynis/dickie*

29 june 1959/hilversum
residentie orchestra

30 june 1959/utrecht/tivoli
residentie orchestra	bartok dance suite/bartok violin concerto 2/brahms symphony 4 *menuhin*

1 july 1959/scheveningen/kurzaal
residentie orchestra	*programme and soloist as for 30 june*

2 july 1959/scheveningen/kurzaal
residentie orchestra	bartok dance suite/bartok violin concerto/berlioz symphonie fantastique *menuhin*

3 july 1959/hilversum
residentie orchestra

17, 24 and 28 august 1959/salzburg/festspielhaus
vienna philharmonic	erbse julietta *streich/knoll/wagner/höngen/stolze/majkut/berry/pernerstorfer/jerger/ vienna opera chorus*

8 september 1959/montreux
concertgebouw orchestra	mozart zauberflöte overture/pijper 6 adagios/schumann piano concerto/dvorak symphony 9 *kempff*

14 september 1959/venice/teatro la fenice
philharmonia hungarica	*programme included* jolivet sinfonia

19 september 1959/amsterdam/concertgebouw
concertgebouw orchestra	mozart zauberflöte overture/pijper 6 adagios/prokofiev violin concerto 2/dvorak symphony 9 *krachmalik*

29 september 1959/montreal/forum hall
philharmonia   beethoven egmont overture/bartok dance suite/kodaly dances
hungarica   of galanta/kodaly intermezzo from hary janos/berlioz marche
                 hongroise

30 september 1959/ottowa/ottowa theatre
philharmonia   *programme as for 29 september*
hungarica

1 october 1959/toronto/massey hall
philharmonia   *programme as for 29 september*
hungarica

4 october 1959/new york/carnegie hall
philharmonia   mendelssohn symphony 4/bartok divertimento/kodaly peacock
hungarica   variations/berlioz marche hongroise

5 october 1959/new brunswick new jersey/rutgers auditorium
philharmonia   *programme as for 29 september*
hungarica

6 october 1959/milwaukee wisconsin/garfield theatre
philharmonia   beethoven symphony 2/kodaly peacock variations/berlioz
hungarica   marche hongroise

7 october 1959/chicago/orchestra hall
philharmonia   *programme as for 4 october*
hungarica

8 october 1959/minneapolis/northrop auditorium
philharmonia   *programm as for 4 october*
hungarica

15 october 1959/anoka minnesota/anoka senior school
minneapolis   beethoven leonore 3 overture/debussy la mer/brahms
symphony   symphony 1

18 october 1959/northfield minnesota/saint olaf college
minneapolis   verdi forza del destino overture/bartok concerto for orchestra/
symphony   brahms symphony 1

20 october 1959/saint paul minnesota/saint paul auditorium
minneapolis
symphony

23 october 1959/minneapolis/northrop auditorium
minneapolis   beethoven leonore 3 overture/bartok concerto for orchestra/
symphony   brahms symphony 1

31 october 1959/minneapolis/northrop auditorium
minneapolis symphony
bach orchestral suite 3/mozart piano concerto 27/prokofiev symphony 5
haebler

1 november 1959/minneapolis/northrop auditorium
minneapolis symphony
schubert rosamunde overture/schubert symphony 8/works by j.strauss

5 november 1959/minneapolis/northrop auditorium
minneapolis symphony
verdi forza del destino overture/prokofiev peter and the wolf/strauss till eulenspiegel

10 november 1959/rochester minnesota/mayo civic auditorium
minneapolis symphony
berlioz carnaval romain overture/prokofiev symphony 5/stravinsky le sacre du printemps

13 november 1959/minneapolis/northrop auditorium
minneapolis symphony
berlioz carnaval romain overture/beethoven violin concerto/stravinsky le sacre du printemps
menuhin

20 november 1959/minneapolis/northrop auditorium
minneapolis symphony
mozart symphony 25/mozart concerto for 2 pianos/ravel concerto for the left hand/casadesus orchestral suite 2
duo casadesus

22 november 1959/minneapolis/northrop auditorium
minneapolis symphony
britten young person's guide/copland rodeo/saint-saens introduction and rondo capriccioso/prokofiev peter and the wolf/strauss till eulenspiegel
druian

27 november 1959/minneapolis/northrop auditorium
minneapolis symphiony
programme of american music
gutche holofernes overture/schuller paul klee studies/creston janus/william schuman violin concerto
druian

28 november 1959/edina minnesota/morningside auditorium
minneapolis symphony
berlioz carnaval romain overture/beethoven symphony 6/mussorgsky-ravel pictures from an exhibition

4 december 1959/minneapolis/northrop auditorium
minneapolis symphony
serebrier elegy/rachmaninov piano concerto 3/mahler symphony 4
s.fleming/pennario

14 december 1959/minneapolis/northrop auditorium
minneapolis symphony
wagner lohengrin act 3 prelude/brahms double concerto/
debussy clarinet rhapsody/liebermann festival concerto/
seiber notturno/berlioz marche hongroise
orchestral soloists

18 december 1959/minneapolis/northrop auditorium
minneapolis symphony
corelli christmas concerto/brahms haydn variations/beethoven symphony 9
curtin/hobson/lloyd/treigle/university chorus

20 december 1959/minneapolis/northrop auditorium
minneapolis symphony
tchaikovsky casse noisette
complete concert performance

2 january 1960/minneapolis/northrop auditorium
minneapolis symphony
barbirolli elizabethan suite/brahms piano concerto 2/falla sombrero de 3 picos/sessions symphony 4
arrau

3 january 1960/saint louis patk minnesota/saint louis park high school
minneapolis symphony
beethoven leonore 3 overture/brahms symphony 1/mussorgsky-ravel pictures from an exhibition

7 january 1960/minneapolis/northrop auditorium
minneapolis symphony
mozart nozze di figaro overture/mozart flute concerto 1/
schuller paul klee studies/tchaikovsky symphony 5
anderson

8 january 1960/minneapolis/northrop auditorium
minneapolis symphony
beethoven prometheus overture/haydn symphony 101/ravel daphnis et chloé second suite/shifrin 3 pieces/strauss don juan

10 january 1960/minneapolis/northrop auditorium
minneapolis symphony
pergolesi la serva padrona/menotti old maid and the thief
jenkins/jonson/gustafson/woodworth/verdak/abelson
fully-staged performances with designs by the conductor's daughter

2 february 1960/rochester minnesota/mayo civic auditorium
minneapolis symphony
weber euryanthe overture/sessions symphony 4/schuller paul klee studies/brahms symphony 2

5 february 1960/minneapolis/northrop auditorium
minneapolis symphony
mozart symphony 35/schumann piano concerto/debussy 3 nocturnes/borodin polovtsian dances
istomin/central lutheran choir

8 february 1960/ann arbor michigan/university of michigan
minneapolis
symphony

9 february 1960/toledo ohio/peristyle musrum
minneapolis
symphony

10 february 1960/dayton ohio
minneapolis
symphony

13 february 1960/brooklyn new york/brooklyn college
minneapolis
symphony

14 february 1960/new york/carnegie hall
minneapolis   berlioz carnaval romain overture/schuller paul klee studies/
symphony   sessions symphony 4/brahms symphony 2

15 february 1960/white plains new york/white plains auditorium
minneapolis   weber euryanthe overture/debussy la mer/strauss don juan/
symphony   brahms symphony 1

16 february 1960/pittsfield massachusetts/pittsfield high school
minneapolis   beethoven leonore 3 overture/debussy nuages et fetes/haydn
symphony   symphony 101/falla sombrero de 3 picos/strauss till eulenspiegel

17 february 1960/portland maine/city hall auditorium
minneapolis   berlioz carnaval romain overture/prokofiev symphony 5/
symphony   beethoven symphony 5

18 february 1960/providence rhode island/veterans memorial auditorium
minneapolis   purcell trumpet voluntary/mozart symphony 35/brahms haydn
symphony   variations/prokofiev symphony 5

19 february 1960/plainfield new jersey/plainfield high school
minneapolis   weber euryanthe overture/strauss don juan/debussy la mer/
symphony   beethoven symphony 6

20 february 1960/milford connecticut/millford high school
minneapolis
symphony

22 february 1960/stamford connecticut/stamford high school
minneapolis symphony *programme as for 17 february*

23 february 1960/rome new york/capitol theatre
minneapolis symphony weber oberon overture/debussy la mer/tchaikovsky symphony 4

24 february 1960/scranton philadelphia/masonic temple
minneapolis symphony bach brandenburg concerto 3/bartok concerto for orchestra/beethoven symphony 7

25 february 1960/williamsport philadelphia/roosevelt junior school
minneapolis symphony weber euryanthe overture/debussy la mer/strauss don juan/beethoven symphony 6

26 february 1960/binghampton new york/capitol theatre
minneapolis symphony *programme as for 23 february*

29 february 1960/jamestown new york/jamestown high school
minneapolis symphony verdi forza del destino overture/brahms symphony 1/mussorgsky-ravel pictures from an exhibition

1 march 1960/lorain ohio/palace theatre
minneapolis symphony *programme as for 23 february*

3 march 1960/holland michigan/holland civic centre
minneapolis symphony *programme as for 19 february*

4 march 1960/south bend indiana/saint mary's college
minneapolis symphony purcell trumpet voluntary/mozart symphony 35/brahms haydn variations/prokofiev symphony 5

5 march 1960/waukegan illinois/west campus auditorium
minneapolis symphony *programme as for 16 february*

7 march 1960/janesville wisconsin/janesville junior school
minneapolis symphony *programme as for 25 february*

8 march 1960/la crosse wisconsin/vocational high school
minneapolis symphony *programme as for 24 february*

11 march 1960/minneapolis/northrop auditorium
minneapolis symphony purcell trumpet voluntary/beethoven symphony 6/overtures by rossini and verdi/operatic arias by bellini, rossini, donizetti and verdi
simionato

18 march 1960/minneapolis/northrop auditorium
minneapolis symphony dvorak carnival overture/brahms violin concerto/dorati symphony 1
goldberg

21 march 1960/regina saskatchewan/regina arena
minneapolis symphony *programme as for 16 february*

22 march 1960/calgary alberta/jubilee auditorium
minneapolis symphony *programme as for 29 february*

23 march 1960/edmonton alberta
minneapolis symphony *programme as for 25 february*

24 march 1960/saskatoon sakatchewan/sakatoon arena
minneapolis symphony *programme as for 17 february*

25 march 1960/winnipeg manitoba/winnipeg auditorium
minneapolis symphony *programme as for 25 february*

26 march 1960/moorhead minnesota/concordia college
minneapolis symphony bach brandenburg concerto 3/brahms double concerto/bartok concerto for orchestra
druian/jamieson

28 march 1960/fairmont minnesota/fairmont senior school
minneapolis symphony *programme as for 25 february*

29 march 1960/rochester minnesota/mayo civic auditorium
minneapolis symphony
beethoven leonore 3 overture/brahms double concerto/debussy nuages et fetes/strauss till eulenspiegel
druian/jamieson

30 march 1960/minneapolis/northrop auditorium
minneapolis symphony
fetler contrasts/brahms double concerto/beethoven symphony 7
druian/jamieson

31 march 1960/dubuque iowa/loras college
minneapolis symphony
beethoven leonore 3 overture/haydn symphony 101/falla sombrero de 3 picos/debussy nuages et fetes/strauss till eulenspiegel

3 april 1960/hinsdale illinois/junior high school
minneapolis symphony
programme as for 25 february

4 april 1960/goshen indiana/goshen college
minneapolis symphony

5 april 1960/wilmette illinois/junior high school
minneapolis symphony
programme as for 29 february

6 april 1960/skokie illinois/niles high school
minneapolis symphony
programme as for 31 march

7 april 1960/austin minnesota/austin central high school
minneapolis symphony
programme as for 25 february

8 april 1960/winona minnesota/winona high school
minneapolis symphony
programme as for 23 february

10 april 1960/minneapolis/northrop auditorium
minneapolis symphony
verdi forza del destino overture/prokofiev piano concerto 3/ norton partita/choral works
simpson/saint olaf choir

15 april 1960/minneapolis/northrop auditorium
minneapolis symphony
verdi messa da requiem
yeend/madeira/carelli/tozzi/university choir

11 june 1960/london/kenwood concert bowl
london symphony
smetana bartered bride overture/borodin polovtsian dances/beethoven symphony 6
open-air concert which also included bliss suite from things to come conducted by the composer

24 june 1960/london/royal festival hall
london symphony
pergolesi concertino in g/stravinsky concerto in d/mahler das lied von der erde
heynis/petrak

11 october 1960/swansea/brangwyn hall
london symphony
strauss don juan/sibelius violin concerto/berlioz symphonie fantastique
staryk

12 october 1960/swansea/brangwyn hall
london symphony
pergolesi concertino in g/mozart sinfonia concertante for violin and viola/schubert symphony 9
maguire/streatfield

6 november 1960/hamburg/staatstheater
philharmonisches staatsorchester
strauss der rosenkavalier

12 november 1960/london/royal festival hall
london symphony
dvorak carnival overture/dukas l'apprenti sorcier/britten pas de deux from prince of the pagodas/tchaikovsky symphony 4

14 november 1960/london/royal festival hall
london symphony
bartok music for strings percussion and celesta/falla 7 popular spanish songs/stravinsky le sacre du printemps
berganza

25-27 november 1960/madrid
madrid philharmonic beethoven leonore 3 overture/brahms symphony 2/bartok miraculous mandarin suite/ravel daphnis et chloé second suite

30 november 1960/hamburg/staatstheater
philharmonisches staatsorchester mozart die zauberflöte

6 december 1960/hamburg/musikhalle
philharmonisches staatsorchester webern passacaglia/stravinsky monumentum pro gesualdo/bartok concerto for orchestra/brahms symphony 2

8-10 december 1960/tel aviv/mann auditorium
london symphony dvorak carnival overture/britten pas de deux from prince of the pagodas/mozart symphony 34/shostakovich symphony 5

11 december 1960/jerusalem/bim om auditorium
london symphony *programme as for 8-10 december*

12-13 december 1960/tel aviv/mann auditorium
london symphony *programme as for 8-10 december*

14-15 december 1960/haifa/armon theatre
london symphony *programme as for 8-10 december*

17 december 1960/tel aviv/mann auditorium
london symphony boyce symphony 5/britten young persons's guide/beethoven symphony 3

18-19 december 1960/tel aviv/mann auditorium
london symphony walton portsmouth point overture/beethoven symphony 8/bartok concerto for orchestra

20 december 1960/haifa/armon theatre
london symphony *programme as for 18-19 december*

21 december 1960/tel aviv/mann auditorium
london symphony dvorak symphony 8/mahler symphony 4
davrath

22 december 1960/tel aviv/mann auditorium
london beethoven leonore 3 overture/mozart sinfonia concertante
symphony for wind/tchaikovsky symphony 4
orchestral soloists

december 1960/athens
london britten young person's guide/beethoven symphony 8/
symphony shostakovich symphony 5

8 january 1961/paris/salle pleyel
conservatoire *works by dvorak, brahms and beethoven*
orchestra

3, 5, 13 and 16 february 1961/amsterdam/stadschouwburg
residentie verdi simon boccanegra
orchestra *tiemessen/d.bartoli/oppicelli/trama/gorin/netherlands opera chorus*

22-23 february 1961/utrecht/tivoli
utrecht mozart schauspieldirektor overture/mozart symphony 41/
symphony mahler symphony 1

27 february 1961/amsterdam/stadschouwburg
residentie verdi simon boccanegra
orchestra *tiemessen/d.bartoli/oppicelli/trama/gorin/netherlands opera chorus*

12 march 1961/amsterdam/stadschouwburg
residentie verdi simon boccanegra
orchestra *tiemessen/d.bartoli/oppicelli/trama/gorin/netherlands opera chorus*

7 april 1961/london/royal festival hall
london berlioz grande messe des morts
symphony *mcalpine/ lso chorus*

11 april 1961/london/royal festival hall
london seiber besardo suite/berg wozzeck fragments/stravinsky
symphony the firebird
pilarczyk

15 april 1961/tokyo
tokyo *beethoven programme*
philharmonic leonore 3 overture/symphony 8/symphony 3

april 1961/tokyo
tokyo berlioz benvenuto cellini overture/bartok concerto for orchestra/
philharmonic brahms symphony 1

april 1961/tokyo
tokyo dvorak carnival overture/mozart symphony 40/strauss till
philharmonic eulenspiegel/barber medea's dance of vengeance/ravel daphnis
et chloé second suite

6 may 1961/vienna/staatsoper
vienna beethoven fidelio
philharmonic *goltz/ güden/ beirer/ dickie/ böhme/ schöffler/ wiener/ vienna opera chorus*

7 may 1961/vienna/staatsoper
vienna verdi otello
philharmonic *jurinac/ a.ludwig/ mccracken/ dermota/ protti/ welter/ vienna opera chorus*

10 may 1961/vienna/staatsoper
vienna wagner der fliegende holländer
philharmonic *goltz/ höngen/ uhl/ dermota/ fliether/ kreppel/ vienna opera chorus*

16 may 1961/vienna/staatsoper
vienna strauss der rosenkavalier
philharmonic *della casa/ dvorakova/ lipp/ dickie/ böhme/ poell/ vienna opera chorus*

20 may 1961/vienna/staatsoper
vienna wagner der fliegende holländer
philharmonic *zadek/ höngen/ windgassen/ terkal/ hotter/ böhme/ vienna opera chorus*

29 may 1961/vienna/konzerthaus
vienna schoenberg gurrelieder
symphony *wiener singakademie/ wiener singverein/ wiener kammerchor*

4 june 1961/lisbon
lisbon　　　　　　　*beethoven programme*
philharmonic

june 1961/lisbon
lisbon　　　　　　　verdi messa da requiem
philharmonic　　　*philharmonic choir*

18 june 1961/london/crystal palace concert bowl
london　　　　　　beethoven symphony 3/tchaikovsky romeo and juliet/
symphony　　　　 tchaikovsky 1812 overture
　　　　　　　　　open-air concert

21 june 1961/london/royal festival hall
london　　　　　　prokofiev symphony 1/rachmaninov piano concerto 2/
symphony　　　　 tchaikovsky symphony 5
　　　　　　　　　janis

28 june 1961/london/royal festival hall
london　　　　　　britten young person's guide/rachmaninov paganini rhapsody/
symphony　　　　 dvorak symphony 9
　　　　　　　　　ogdon

1 july 1961/amsterdam/stadsschouwburg
residentie　　　　 verdi simon boccanegra
orchestra　　　　　*tiemessen/d.bartoli/oppicelli/trama/walters/netherlands opera chorus*

3 july 1961/den haag/koninklijke schouwburg
residentie　　　　 *programme as for 1 july*
orchestra

7 july 1961/cheltenham/town hall
london　　　　　　boyce symphony 5/beethoven symphony 8/shostakovich
symphony　　　　 symphony 5/newton work for wind and lower strings

10 july 1961/hilversum

11 july 1961/scheveningen/kurzaal
concertgebouw　　haydn symphony 101/bartok bluebeard's castle
orchestra　　　　　*pilarczyk/szekely/fiolet*

12 july 1961/amsterdam/stadschouwburg
residentie　　　　 *programme as for 1 july*
orchestra

13 july 1961/amsterdam/concertgebouw
concertgebouw   *programme and soloists as for 11 july*
orchestra

14 july 1961/hilversum

2 august 1961/venice/teatro la fenice
la fenice
orchestra

24 september 1961/montreux
orchestre   barber adagio for strings/bach violin concerto in a/bruch
national   violin concerto no 1/beethoven symphony 6
                milstein

22 october 1961/paris/théatre des champs-élysées
orchestre   beethoven egmont overture/beethoven violin concerto/
national   dvorak symphony 9
                milstein

26 october 1961/luxembourg
orchestre   mozart symphony 34/bartok suite 2/beethoven symphony 2
national

5 november 1961/tel aviv/mann auditorium
israel   pergolesi concertino in g/haydn symphony 96/bartok
philharmonic   bluebeard's castle
                wien/ernster

november 1961/tel aviv/mann auditorium
israel   partos images/mozart a piano concerto/tchaikovsky symphony 4
philharmonic   *barenboim*

17 november 1961/tel aviv/mann auditorium
israel   *programme and soloists as for 5 november*
philharmonic

20 november 1961/tel aviv/mann auditorium
israel   bach brandenburg concerto 1/schoenberg piano concerto/
philharmonic   tchaikovsky symphony 5
                pelleg

20-23 january 1962/concerts in switzerland
london
symphony

24 january 1962/basel
london   elgar enigma variations/weber clarinet concerto/tchaikovsky
symphony   symphony 4
                de peyer

25 january 1962/strasbourg
london symphony berlioz benvenuto cellini overture/bartok concerto for orchestra
concert also included bliss colour symphony conducted by the composer

29 january 1962/bonn
london symphony dvorak carnival overture/kodaly peacock variations/schubert symphony 9

4 february 1962/paris/salle pleyel
orchestre national

5 february 1962/london/royal festival hall
philharmonia bartok dance suite/rachmaninov piano concerto 2/falla nights in the gardens of spain/tchaikovsky romeo and juliet
rubinstein

9 february 1962/paris/théatre des champs-élysées
orchestre national kodaly peacock variations/casella la giara/smetana moldau/ravel alborada del gracioso/ravel daphnis et chloé second suite

13 february 1962/paris/théatre des champs-élysées
orchestre national messiaen chronochomie/ravel piano concerto in g/brahms symphony 1
henriot-schweitzer

19-22 february 1962/brussels/palais des beaux-arts
orchestre national de belgique clementi symphony in b flat/bach piano concerto/franck variations symphoniques/strauss also sprach zarathustra

3 march 1962/berlin/hochschule für musik
rias-orchester liszt christus
lear/cervena/caposy/fischer-dieskau/saint hedwig's choir

11 march 1962/paris/théatre des champs-élysées
conservatoire orchestra mozart overture/chopin piano concerto 1/bartok concerto for orchestra

19 march 1962/copenhagen/odd fellow palaet
royal danish orchestra mozart symphony 34/stravinsky le sacre du printemps/beethoven symphony 7

23 march 1962/copenhagen/odd fellow palaet
royal danish orchestra tchaikovsky romeo and juliet/stravinsky firebird suite/beethoven symphony 5

3 april 1962/palermo/teatro massimo
teatro massimo orchestra kodaly dances of galanta/beethoven symphony 6

15 april 1962/london/royal festival hall
london symphony berlioz benvenuto cellini overture/bartok concerto for orchestra/beethoven symphony 5

19 april 1962/london/royal festival hall
london symphony *stravinsky programme*
symphony in c/violin concerto/petrouchka
gitlis

26 april 1962/huddersfield/town hall
london symphony *programme as for 15 april*

27 april 1962/newcastle-upon-tyne/city hall
london symphony *programme as for 15 april*

28 april 1962/leeds/town hall
london symphony *programme and soloist as for 19 april*

3 may 1962/london/royal festival hall
london symphony boyce symphony 5/boccherini guitar concerto/guitar solos/brahms symphony 2
segovia

8 may 1962/london/royal festival hall
london symphony *bartok programme*
music for strings percussion and celesta/bluebeard's castle
szönyi/szekely

10 may 1962/oxford/sheldonian theatre
london symphony boyce symphony 5/stravinsky petrouchka/brahms symphony 2

21 may 1962/prague/rudolfinum
czech philharmonic mozart zauberflöte overture/bartok music for strings percussion and celesta/debussy 3 nocturnes/roussel bacchus et ariane suite 2

29 may 1962/marl/stadttheater
philharmonia hungarica beethoven leonore 3 overture/bartok violin concerto 2/kodaly dances of galanta
menuhin
televised concert to mark five years of zdf television

16 june 1962/amsterdam/stadschouwburg
utrecht dallapiccola il prigioniero/monteverdi il ritorno d'ulisse
symphony *delorie/bossy/sante/colombo/corradi/ghitti/koopman/netherlands opera chorus*

18 june 1962/den haag/gebouw voor kunsten en wetenschappen
utrecht *programme as for 16 june*
symphony

20 june 1962/utrecht/tivoli
utrecht *programme as for 16 june*
symphony

22-23 june 1962/strasbourg
london bartok/beethoven/bliss/boyce/debussy
symphony

25-26 june 1962/paris/salle pleyel
london *programmes included*
symphony brahms symphony 2

27 june 1962/scheveningen/kurzaal
residentie debussy ibéria/bartok-kodaly 5 songs/stravinsky the firebird
orchestra *pilarczyk*

29 june 1962/rotterdam/rotterdamse schouwburg
utrecht *programme as for 16 june*
symphony

30 june 1962/haarlem/concertgebouw
residentie *programme and soloist as for 27 june*
orchestra

2 july 1962/cheltenham/town hall
london berlioz benvenuto cellini overture/goehr violin concerto/
symphony stravinsky symphony in c
  parikian

8 july 1962/amsterdam/stadschouwburg
utrecht *programme as for 16 june*
symphony

12 july 1962/den haag/gebouw voor kunsten en wetenschappen
utrecht *programme as for 16 june*
symphony

1 september 1962/montreux
orchestre de la   *programme included*
suisse romande   bartok concerto for orchestra

6 september 1962/besancon
orchestre   *programme included*
national   dorati symphony 1/kodaly dances of galanta

3 october 1962/london/royal festival hall
bbc symphony   bach cantata 50/bach double violin concerto/beethoven symphony 9
maguire/nelson/spoorenberg/veasey/young/bell/bbc chorus

8-10 october 1962/swansea/brangwyn hall
london   *programmes included*
symphony   brahms symphony 2/stravinsky petrouchka

14 october 1962/london/royal festival hall
bbc symphony   tippett praeludium/bartok cantata profana/schoenberg dance of the golden calf/stravinsky le sacre du printemps
handt/hemsley/bbc chorus

22 and 24 november 1962/london/royal opera house
covent garden   rimsky-korsakov le coq d'or
orchestra   *grist/vaughan/sinclair/macdonald/lanigan/savoie/robinson/kelly/covent garden chorus*
the opera was sung in english translation

26 november 1962/london/royal festival hall
philharmonia   stravinsly firebird suite/prokofiev piano concerto 2/walton belshazzar's feast
cherkassky/glossop/philharmonia chorus

27 and 29 november 1962/london/royal opera house
covent garden   *programme and cast as for 22 and 24 november*
orchestra

december 1962/concerts in israel
israel   *programmes included works by*
philharmonic   dorati/frid/partos/serly/veress

january 1963/concerts in paris
orchestre   *programmes included*
national   dorati the way of the cross

19 january 1963/london/maida vale studios
bbc symphony   hindemith concert music/brandenburg concerto 6/bartok concerto for orchestra

23 january 1963/london/royal festival hall
bbc symphony berlioz benvenuto cellini
*carlyle/pashley/veasey/lewis/mitchinson/kentish/cameron/noble/ward/
garrard/bbc chorus
concert performance of the opera*

26 january 1963/london/maida vale studios
bbc symphony tippett praeludium/bartok cantata profana/schubert symphony 9
mitchinson/hemsley/bbc chorus

27 january 1963/oxford/new theatre
bbc symphony bach brandenburg concerto 6/beethoven piano concerto 5/
bartok concerto for orchestra
wayenberg

30 january 1963/bristol/colston hall
bbc symphony beethoven weihe des hauses overture/brahms piano concerto 2/
stravinsky le sacre du printemps
wayenberg

6 february 1963/london/royal festival hall
bbc symphony mozart clemenza di tito overture/schubert symphony 9/
britten spring symphony
vyvyan/proctor/young/bbc and emanuel choirs

february 1963/concerts in paris
orchestre *programmes included*
national and works by liszt and franck
conservatoire *cziffra*
orchestra

2 april 1963/london/royal festival hall
london berlioz carnaval romain overture/schumann piano concerto/
symphony beethoven symphony 3
cherkassky

8 april 1963/copenhagen/odd fellow palaet
royal danish brahms symphony 2/haydn symphony 98/bartok miraculous
orchestra mandarin suite

14 april 1963/osaka/festival hall
london
symphony

16 april 1963/hiroshima/public hall
london
symphony

17 april 1963/yawaka/public hall
london
symphony

22 april 1963/nagoya
london
symphony

23 april 1963/tokyo/kaikan hall
london
symphony

28 april 1963/tokyo/kaikan hall
london
symphony

30 april 1963/tokyo/kaikan hall
london
symphony

1 june 1963/london/maida vale studios
bbc symphony   *bartok programme*
               divertimento/village scenes/miraculous mandarin suite
               bbc chorus

2 june 1963/london/maida vale studios
bbc symphony   beethoven symphony 2/bartok miraculous mandarin suite/
               elgar enigma variations

9 june 1963/london/maida vale srudios
bbc symphony   bartok rumanian folkdances/bartok village scenes/bartok
               divertimento/beethoven symphony 7

june 1963/london/maida vale srudios
bbc symphony   *walton programme*
               viola concerto/symphony 1
               schidlof

24 june 1963/london/royal festival hall
london   stravinsky symphony in 3 movements/bartok piano concerto 3/
symphony   prokofiev symphony 3
               frankl

1 july 1963/cheltenham/town hall
london symphony bredell-smith homage to h.g.wells/schubert symphony 8

4 july 1963/london/royal feswtival hall
london symphony schubert symphony 8/schumann piano concerto/brahms symphony 4
schiller

28 july 1963/aix-en-provence
conservatoire orchestra verdi messa da requiem

8 august 1963/monte carlo
monte carlo opera orchestra mendelssohn symphony 4/kodaly dances of galanta/prokofiev scythian suite/bartok violin concerto 1
menuhin

september 1963/concerts in montreux and besancon
orchestre national *programmes included*
tchaikovsky piano concerto 1/bruch violin concerto 1/bartok concerto for orchestra/wagner tristan prelude and liebestod
janis/milstein

21 september 1963/london/maida vale studios
bbc symphony haydn symphony 91/bartok miraculous mandarin suite/beethoven symphony 5

25 september 1963/london/maida vale studios
bbc symphony mozart idomeneo overture and ballet music/prokofiev piano concerto 1/dvorak symphony 7
katz

2 october 1963/london/royal festival hall
bbc symphony *stravinsky programme*
firebird suite/the flood/oedipus rex
sinclair/dowd/mitchinson/remedios/herincx/noble/stalman/ward/bbc chorus

6 november 1963/london/royal festival hall
bbc symphony beethoven weihe des hauses overture/brahms symphony 2/britten spring symphony
harper/procter/young/bbc chorus
concert for royal philharmonic society

13 november 1963/london/royal festival hall
bbc symphony   schoenberg von heute auf morgen/mahler symphony 4
harper/ schmid/ schachtschneider/ olsen

16 november 1963/london/maida vale studios
bbc symphony   bach cantata 21/beethoven symphony 5
harper/ mitchinson/ olsen/ bbc chorus

20 november 1963/nottingham/albert hall
bbc symphony   bach brandenburg concerto 1/brahms violin concerto/
beethoven symphony 7
gotkovsky

21 november 1963/birmingham/town hall
bbc symphony   *programme and soloist as for 20 november*

27 november 1963/london/royal festival hall
bbc symphony   verdi messa da requiem
brouwenstijn/ allister/ mccracken/ ward/ bbc chorus and choral society
performance dedicated to the memory of john f. kennedy

30 november 1963/london/maida vale studios
bbc symphony   haydn symphony 95/messiaen l'ascension/bartok miraculous
mandarin

3 december 1963/paris/théatre des champs-élysées
orchestre   *bartok programme*
national   music for strings percussion and celesta/bluebeard's castle

23 december 1963/london/royal opera house
covent garden   strauss der rosenkavalier
orchestra   *rysanek/ holt/ veasey/ macdonald/ langdon/ lewis*
four further performances of the opera given

26 january 1964/paris/salle pleyel
lamoureux
orchestra

3 february 1964/copenhagen/odd fellow palaet
royal danish
orchestra

6 february 1964/oslo
oslo
philharmonic

13 february 1964/london/royal festival hall
london   *beethoven programme*
symphony   leonore 3 overture/piano concerto 3/symphony 7
                     browning

22 february 1964/london/maida vale studios
bbc symphony   clementi sinfonia in b flat/britten frank bridge variations/
                     dvorak symphony 6

25 february 1964/london/royal festival hall
london   *bartok programme*
symphony   hungarian sketches/violin concerto 2/bluebeard's castle
                     menuhin/szönyi/farago

4-5 march 1964/manchester/free trade hall
hallé   berlioz les francs huges overture/beethoven symphony 6/walton
orchestra   hindemith variations/hindemith weber metamorphoses

7 march 1964/london/maida vale studios
bbc symphony   mozart symphony 36/gerhard dances from don quixote/brahms
                     symphony 4

8 march 1964/london/maida vale studios
bbc symphony   haydn symphony 102/gerhard dances from don quixote/brahms
                     symphony 4

14 march 1964/london/maida vale studios
bbc symphony   haydn symphony 102/gerhard symphony 1/schumann symphony 4

18 march 1964/london/royal festival hall
bbc symphony   bach magnificat/beethoven symphony 9
                     spoorenberg/tinsley/baker/mitchinson/r.nilsson/rehfuss/bbc chorus

21 march 1964/leeds/town hall
bbc symphony   kodaly hary janos suite/elgar falstaff/strauss don quixote
                     gendron

22 march 1964/hull/city hall
bbc symphony   mozart lucio silla overture/strauss don quixote/beethoven
                     symphony 7
                     gendron

28 march 1964/london/maida vale studios
bbc symphony   bach brandenburg concerto 1/partos sinfonia concertante/
                     beethoven symphony 7
                     partos

1 april 1964/london/royal festival hall
bbc symphony gerhard the plague/mahler symphony 9
murray/bbc chorus

april 1964/london/maida vale studios
bbc symphony beethoven triple concerto
crowson/parikian/bunting

14 april 1964/johannesburg/stadsaal
south african wagner tristan prelude and liebestod/strauss till eulenspiegel/
broadcasting beethoven symphony 3
orchestra

21 april 1964/johannesburg/stadsaal
south african mozart march k408/brahms double concerto/stravinsky
broadcasting petrouchka
orchestra *kossmann/rainier*

28 april 1964/johannesburg/stadsaal
south african bartok concerto for orchestra/brahms symphony 4
broadcasting
orchestra

21 may 1964/london/royal festival hall
london rimsky-korsakov russian easter overture/tchaikovsky piano
symphony concerto 1/shostakovich symphony 5
janis

24 may 1964/london/maida vale studios
bbc symphony brahms haydn variations/bartok miraculous mandarin suite/
beethoven symphony 5

25 may 1964/london/maida vale studios
bbc symphony bach cantata 21/mahler symphony 4
harper/minty/mitchinson/olsen/bbc chorus

31 may 1964/london/royal festival hall
london offenbach-dorati gaité parisienne/overtures by offenbach and
symphony dvorak/dances by falla, arnold, skalkottas, brahms and dvorak
lso jubilee concert

6 june 1964/london/maida vale studios
bbc symphony britten cantata academica/gerhard the plague
harwood/proctor/dowd/robinson/bbc chorus

18 and 20 june 1964/florence/teatro communale
maggio musicale schoenberg erwartung/bartok the miraculous mandarin/
orchestra dallapiccola volo di notte
synek

11 july 1964/london/maida vale studios
bbc symphony   mozart serenade k204/wolf italian serenade/brahms serenade 2

12 july 1964/london/maida vale studios
bbc symphony   mozart serenade k204/brahms serenade 2/beethoven symphony 5

17 july 1964/cheltenham/town hall
bbc symphony   strauss don juan/lutyens music for orchestra 3/william schuman violin concerto/elgar symphony 2
druian

15 august 1964/lucerne/kunsthaus
swiss festival   beethoven leonore 3 overture/brahms piano concerto 2/
orchestra   prokofiev symphony 5
cliburn

18 september 1964/berlin/philharmonie
berlin   stravinsky le chant du rossignol/stravinsky symphony in three
philharmonic   movements/bartok cantata profana/bartok miraculous mandarin suite
korda/mcdaniel/saint hedwig's choir

20 september 1964/london/royal festival hall
bbc symphony   bartok diverimento/dvorak serenade for strings/bartok the miraculous mandarin

26 september 1964/london/maida vale studios
bbc symphony   handel concerto grosso op 6 no 8/messiaen chronochomie/brahms symphony 4

30 september 1964/london/maida vale studios
bbc symphony   haydn symphony 93/beethoven choral fantasy/brahms schicksalslied
vogel/bbc chorus

3 october 1964/london/maida vale studios
bbc symphony   haydn symphony 93/debussy la mer/schumann symphony 2

4 october 1964/london/maida vale studios
bbc symphony   tchaikovsky romeo and juliet/debussy la mer/schumann symphony 2

7 october 1964/london/maida vale studios
bbc symphony   schumann cello concerto/beethoven symphony 3
fleming

12 october 1964/london/maida vale studios
bbc symphony   berlioz benvenuto cellini overture/koechlin les bandar-log/
                beethoven symphony 7

14 october 1964/portsmouth/guildhall
bbc symphony   britten frank bridge variations/beethoven piano concerto 4/
                elgar enigma variations
                ogdon

15 october 1964/london/royal albert hall
bbc symphony   beethoven missa solemnis
                harper/ höffgen/ young/ shirley-quirk/ bbc chorus and choral society

21 october 1964/london/royal festival hall
bbc symphony   *programme and soloists as for 15 october*

26 october 1964/basel/casino
bbc symphony   britten frank bridge variations/bartok miraculous mandarin
                suite/brahms symphony 4

27 october 1964/ascona
bbc symphony   schubert symphony 8/schumann cello concerto/mozart
                symphony 41
                fleming

28 october 1964/zürich/tonhalle
bbc symphony   britten frank bridge variations/debussy la mer/beethoven
                symphony 3

30 october 1964/geneva/victoria hall
bbc symphony   tchaikovsky romeo and juliet/beethoven piano concerto 4/
                elgar enigma variations
                ogdon

2-3 november 1964/zürich/tonhalle
bbc symphony   *programme as for 28 october*

13 november 1964/london/royal albert hall
new   kodaly dances of galanta/bartok concerto for orchestra/
philharmonia   stravinsky petrouchka

18 november 1964/london/royal albert hall
bbc symphony   berlioz la damnation de faust
                fretwell/ moulson/ herincx/ stalman/ bbc chorus and choral society

24 november 1964/london/royal albert hall
bbc symphony   jacob fanfare/rossini scala di seta overture/morgan fanfare for
                freedom/elgar violin concerto/prokofiev piano concerto 1/
                strauss till eulenspiegel
                menuhin/ lympany/ kneller hall trumpeters
                royal concert

1-5 december 1964/paris/théatre des champs-élysées
orchestre national *programmes included works by* jolivet/schumann/brahms

7-10 december 1964/hamburg/musikhalle
ndr orchestra berg 3 pieces/bartok violin rhapsody/tchaikovsky symphony 2

14-18 december 1964/geneva/victoria hall
orchestre de la suisse romande mozart 2 marches/mozart sinfonia concertante for violin and viola/berlioz symphonie fantastique
goldberg/golan

3 january 1965/london/maida vale studios
bbc symphony beethoven piano concerto 4/brahms symphony 4
ogdon

9 january 1965/london/maida vale studios
bbc symphony haydn symphony 98/bartok concerto for orchestra

january-february 1965/concerts in israel
israel philharmonic *programmes included*
beethoven missa solemnis
spoorenberg/merriman/lewis/shirley-quirk/tel aviv chorus

haydn symphony 98/stravinsky petrouchka/tchaikovsky symphony 2

22 february 1965/rome/teatro dell' opera
rome opera orchestra stravinsky oedipus rex/strauss elektra
companeez/picchi/trama/carmeli/rome opera chorus
borkh/ericsdotter/mödl
further performances given

25 february 1965/london/royal festival hall
london symphony *bartok programme*
hungarian sketches/violin concerto 2/bluebeard's castle
menuhin/szönyi/farago

24 march 1965/bristol/colston hall
bbc symphony *beethoven programme*
prometheus overture/piano concerto 1/symphony 7
bishop

27 march 1965/london/maida vale studios
bbc symphony britten frank bridge variations/berlioz symphonie fantastique

31 march 1965/london/maida vale studios
bbc symphony berlioz benvenuto cellini overture/bartok piano concerto 2
anda
concert recorded for television

7 april 1965/manchester/free trade hall
bbc symphony handel concerto grosso 19/beethoven piano concerto 5/
stravinsky chant du rossignol/dvorak 3 slavonic dances
bishop

8 april 1965/manchester/free trade hall
bbc symphony haydn symphony 93/beethoven piano concerto 4/bartok
concerto for orchestra
bishop

9 april 1965/bradford
bbc symphony *programme and soloist as for 8 april*

14 april 1965/london/royal festival hall
bbc symphony haydn symphony 93/berg violin concerto/stravinsky le roi des
étoiles/stravinsky le sacre du printemps
marschner

30 april 1965/new york/carnegie hall
bbc symphony stravinsky chant du rossignol/gerhard concerto for orchestra/
britten our hunting fathers/bartok miraculous mandarin suite
harper

6 may 1965/philadelphia/academy of music
bbc symphony blacher concertante musik/tippett piano concerto/
shostakovich symphony 10
ogdon

8 may 1965/new york/carnegie hall
bbc symphony *programme and soloist as for 6 may*

11 may 1965/syracuse new york
bbc symphony copland music for a great city/elgar cello concerto/
vaughan williams symphony 4
du pré

14 may 1965/new york/carnegie hall
bbc symphony schuller dramatic overture/elgar cello concerto/mahler
symphony 4
du pré/harper

15 may 1965/new york/carnegie hall
bbc symphony copland music for a great city/vaughan williams symphony 4/
stravinsky le sacre du printemps
other concerts on this american tour by bbc symphony orchestra were conducted by pierre boulez

26 september 1965/montreux
orchestre national *francescatti*

1 december 1965/london/royal festival hall
bbc symphony   britten sinfonia da requiem/beethoven piano concerto 5/
prokofiev symphony 2
barenboim

25-26 january 1966/washington/constitution hall
national symphony   beethoven prometheus overture/beethoven symphony 3/
strauss don juan/kodaly hary janos suite

2 february 1966/london/royal albert hall
bbc symphony   beethoven missa solemnis
söderström/ höffgen/ young/ wiemann/ bbc chorus and choral society

16 february 1966/london/royal festival hall
london philharmonic   haydn die schöpfung
harwood/ holden/ wakefield/ shirley-quirk/ london philharmonic choir

21 february 1966/barry/memorial hall
new philharmonia   beethoven symphony 2/stravinsky firebird suite/tchaikovsky symphony 4

22 february 1966/swansea/brangwyn hall
new philharmonia   *programme as foe 21 february*

23 february 1966/fishguard/county secondary school
new philharmonia   *programme as for 21 february*

24 february 1966/aberystwyth/kings hall
new philharmonia   *programme as for 21 february*

25 february 1966/wrexham/aston hall
new philharmonia   *programme as for 21 february*

26 february 1966/llangelli/county secondary school
new philharmonia   *programme as for 21 february*

27 february 1966/rhyl/pavilion theatre
new *programme as for 21 february*
philharmonia

20 march 1966/london/royal festival hall
london mozart piano concerto 21/bruckner symphony 5
philharmonic *katin*

24 march 1966/london/royal festival hall
new beethoven symphony 2/mozart piano concerto 25/rachmaninov
philharmonia paganini rhapsody/bartok dance suite

8 april 1966/london/maida vale studios
bbc symphony *works by antal dorati*
madrigal suite/octet/symphony 1

13 april 1966/london/royal festival hall
bbc symphony britten saint nicholas/berlioz te deum
young/ bbc chorus

27-28 april 1966/stockholm/konserthuset
stockholm haydn symphony 93/strauss 4 letzte lieder/schubert symphony 9
philharmonic *söderström*

11-12 may 1966/stockholm/konserthuset
stockholm beethoven weihe des hauses overture/mozart symphony 41/
philharmonic kodaly peacock variations/ravel daphnis et chloé second suite

14 may 1966/london/westminster abbey
bbc symphony berlioz te deum/vaughan williams tallis fantasia/stravinsky
symphony of psalms
young/ bbc chorus

29 may 1966/london/royal festival hall
new smetana moldau/tchaikovsky piano concerto 1/dvorak
philharmonia symphony 9
anda

26 june 1966/london/royal festival hall
new bartok dance suite/beethoven piano concerto 3/beethoven
philharmonia symphony 2
katchen

28 june 1966/london/royal festival hall
new bartok music for strings percussion and celesta/beethoven
philharmonia german dances/beethoven violin concerto
grumiaux
dorati replaced otto klemperer for the concerts on 26 and 28 june

15 august 1966/london/royal albert hall
bbc symphony   mozart maurerische trauermusik/mozart ave verum corpus/
                     mozart kyrie k341/beethoven missa solemnis
                     harper/höffgen/young/wiemann/bbc chorus and choral society

1 september 1966/auckland/town hall
israel   berlioz carnaval romain overture/ravel la valse/bartok
philharmonic   miraculous mandarin suite/tchaikovsky symphony 5

6 september 1966/wellington/town hall
israel   brahms symphony 4/stravinsky violin concerto/stravinsky
philharmonic   firebird suite
                     zeitlin

8 september 1966/dunedin/town hall
israel   *programme as for 1 september*
philharmonic

10 september 1966/christchurch/civic theatre
israel   *programme and soloist as for 6 september*
philharmonic
other concerts on this tour by israel philharmonic orchestra were conducted by zubin mehta

1 october 1966/montreux
bamberg   *programme included*
symphony   mozart operatic and concert arias/strauss orchestral songs
                     schwarzkopf

5, 7 and 9 ocrober 1966/stockholm/konserthuset
stockholm   verdi messa da requiem
philharmonic   *hallin/finnilä/jehrlander/tyren/philharmonic chorus*

12-13 october 1966/stockholm/konserthuset
stockholm   bartok miraculous mandarin suite/mozart piano concerto 27/
philharmonic   hindemith weber metamorphoses/ravel daphnis et chloé
                     second suite
                     a.fischer

15 october 1966/stockholm/konserthuset
stockholm   haydn symphony 93/mozart piano concerto 27/berlioz
philharmonic   benvenuto cellini overture/blomdahl sysiphos suite/
                     hindemith weber metamorphoses
                     leygraf

19-20 october 1966/stockholm/konserthuset
stockholm   blomdahl sysiphos suite/blomdahl resan i denna nat/brahms
philharmonic   symphony 1
söderström

21 october 1966/stockholm/konserthuset
stockholm   bartok miraculous mandarin suite/prokofiev piano concerto 1/
philharmonic   hindemith weber metamorphoses/ravel daphnis et chloé
second suite
vlassenko

24 october 1966/paris/théatre des champs-élysées
stockholm   *programme as for 21 october*
philharmonic

25 october 1966/colmar
stockholm
philharmonic

26 october 1966/mulhouse
stockholm
philharmonic

27 october 1966/cologne
stockholm
philharmonic

29 october 1966/ulm
stockholm
philharmonic

30 october 1966/nürnberg
stockholm
philharmonic

31 october 1966/frankfurt-hoechst
stockholm
philharmonic

1 november 1966/kassel
stockholm
philharmonic

2 november 1966/hannover
stockholm
philharmonic

3 november 1966/bielefeld
stockholm
philharmonic

4 november 1966/rheydt
stockholm
philharmonic

6 november 1966/hamburg/musikhalle
stockholm   blomdahl sisyphos suite/beethoven leonore 3 overture/strauss
philharmonic   4 letzte lieder/brahms symphony 1
söderström

7 november 1966/lübeck
stockholm
philharmonic

4 december 1966/london/royal festival hall
london   kodaly concerto for orchestra/elgar cello concerto/beethoven
philharmonic   symphony 6
tortelier

11 december 1966/london/royal festival hall
london   mozart symphony 34/beethoven violin concerto/brahms
philharmonic   symphony 4
szeryng

11-12 january 1967/stockholm/konserthuset
stockholm   vivaldi concerto/bartok music for strings percussion and celesta/
philharmonic   messiaen et exspecto resurrectionem mortuorum

20-21 january 1967/stockholm/konserthuset
stockholm   bäck roller per orchestra/berwald symphonie capricieuse/
philharmonic   brahms symphony 1

26 january 1967/washington/constitution hall
national   *programme included*
symphony   dorati largo concertato

28 january 1967/dallas/memorial auditorium theatre
dallas   brahms schicksalslied/dorati madrigal suite/beethoven
symphony   symphony 3
north texas university choir

2 april 1967/london/royal festival hall
london   bach brandenburg concerto 3/brahms double concerto/
philharmonic   dvorak symphony 9
suk/gendron

6 april 1967/watford/town hall
london   wagner faust overture/wagner siegfried idyll/mendelssohn
philharmonic   violin concerto/dvorak symphony 9
holmes

8 april 1967/eastbourne/congress theatre
london   wagner faust overture/wagner siegfried idyll/schumann
philharmonic   piano concerto/dvorak symphony 9
binns

11 april 1967/london/royal festival hall
london   wagner faust overture/wagner siegfried idyll/bruckner
philharmonic   symphony 9

19-21 april 1967/stockholm/konserthuset
stockholm   bach brandenburg concerto 4/mozart sinfonia concertante
philharmonic   for wind/beethoven symphony 5
orchestral soloists

22 april 1967/stockholm/konserthuset
stockholm   bach brandenburg concerto 4/mozart sinfonia concertante
philharmonic   for wind
orchestral soloists

23 april 1967/stockholm/konserthuset
stockholm   bach brandenburg concerto 4/bartok violin rhapsody/
philharmonic   beethoven symphony 5

26-27 april 1967/stockholm/konserthuset
stockholm   mahler symphony 2
philharmonic   *nordin/rujtvedt/philharmonic chorus*

3-5 may 1967/stockholm/konserthuset
stockholm   schuller paul klee studies/nyström sinfonia espressiva/brahms
philharmonic   piano concerto 2
richter-haaser

7 may 1967/stockholm/konserthuset
stockholm   mozart symphony 41/schuller paul klee studies/nyström
philharmonic   sinfonia espressiva

10-11 may 1967/stockholm/konserthuset
stockholm philharmonic webern 6 pieces/prokofiev violin concerto 1/stravinsky the firebird
i.oistrakh

17-19 may 1967/stockholm/konserthuset
stockholm philharmonic haydn die schöpfung
söderström/ r.björlimg/ borg/ philharmonic chorus

22 june 1967/london/royal festival hall
london symphony mozart lucio silla overture/mozart piano concerto 27/ beethoven symphony 3
curzon

25 june 1967/london/royal albert hall
new philharmonia tchaikovsky romeo and juliet/rachmaninov piano concerto 2/ dvorak symphony 9
katin

7 september 1967/trier/trevirissaal
philharmonia hungarica haydn symphony 101/bartok miraculous mandarin suite/ beethoven symphony 7

20-21 september 1967/stockholm/konserthuset
stockholm philharmonic wagner meistersinger overture/tchaikovsky piano concerto 1/ sibelius symphony 2
gilels

27-29 september 1967/stockholm/konserthuset
stockholm philharmonic strauss closing scene from capriccio/mahler symphony 10
söderström

4-5 october 1967/stockhom/konserthuset
stockholm philharmonic berwald symphonie capricieuse/prokofiev violin concerto 1/ bartok 2 portraits/debussy la mer
odnoposoff

8 october 1967/stockholm/konserthuset
stockholm philharmonic rosenberg journey to america/schumann violin concerto/ sibelius symphony 2
thauer

14 october 1967/stockholm/konserthuset
stockholm philharmonic wagner meistersinger overture/sibelius pan and echo/bartok divertimento/blomdahl sisyphos suite

13-15 december 1967/stockholm/konserthuset
stockholm kodaly psalmus hungaricus/beethoven symphony 9
philharmonic *malmborg/hamari/simandy/s.björling/philharmonic chorus*

16 december 1967/stockholm/konserthuset
stockholm kodaly hary janos suite/kodaly psalmus hungaricus/
philharmonic beethoven symphony 9
malmborg/hamari/simandy/s.björling/philharmonic chorus

4-5 january 1968/chicago/orchestra hall
chicago mozart violin concerto 5/mahler symphony 6
symphony *weiss*

12 january 1968/schloss elmau bavaria
london mozart *mozart programme*
players march k335 no 1/diverimento 11/symphony 29/eine kleine nachtmusik

14 january 1968/schloss elmau bavaria
london mozart mozart march k248/handel concerto grosso op 3 no 4/mozart
players flute concerto 1/haydn symphony 89
shaffer

16 january 1968/schloss elmau bavaria
london mozart mozart march k290/purcell chaconne/telemann suite/dvorak
players pastorale, polka and notturno/mozart symphony 33

17 january 1968/schloss elmau bavaria
london mozart mozart march k445/dorati octet/mozart violin concerto 5/
players schubert symphony 5
menuhin

31 january-2 february 1968/stockholm/konserthuset
stockholm *brahms programme*
philharmonic academic festival overture/violin concerto/symphony 1
menuhin

4 february 1968/stockholm/konserthuset
stockholm mozart symphony 14/honegger concerto da camera/tchaikovsky
philharmonic symphony 4

7-8 february 1968/stockholm/konserthuset
stockholm mozart symphony 41/beethoven piano concerto 4/blomdahl
philharmonic sisyphos suite
bishop

10 february 1968/stockholm/konserthuset
stockholm alfven vallflickans dans/rosenberg journey to america/
philharmonic prokofiev peter and the wolf

18 february 1968/stockholm/konserthuset
stockholm philharmonic — beethoven leonore 3 overture/mozart symphony 41/berlioz symphonie fantastique

27 february 1968/harrisburg pennsylvania
stockholm philharmonic

29 february 1968/fort wayne indiana
stockholm philharmonic — beethoven leonore 3 overture/berwald symphonie capricieuse/berlioz symphonie fantastique

1 march 1968/detroit
stockholm philharmonic — rosenberg journey to america/bartok miraculous mandarin suite/berlioz benvenuto cellini overture/sibelius symphony 2

2 march 1968/toledo ohio/museum of art
stockholm philharmonic — rosenberg journey to america/bartok miraculous mandarin suite/berlioz symphonie fantastique

3 march 1968/indianapolis indiana
stockholm philharmonic

4 march 1968/evansville kentucky
stockholm philharmonic

6 march 1968/east lansing michigan
stockholm philharmonic

8 march 1968/ann arbor michigan
stockholm philharmonic

10 march 1968/chicago/orchestra hall
stockholm philharmonic

11 march 1968/oshkosh wisconsin
stockholm philharmonic

12 march 1968/fond du lac wisconsin
stockholm
philharmonic

13 march 1968/minneapolis/northrop auditorium
stockholm
philharmonic

16 march 1968/green bay wisconsin
stockholm
philharmonic

17 march 1968/madison wisconsin
stockholm
philharmonic

18 march 1968/evansville ohio
stockholm
philharmonic

20 march 1968/roanoke virginia
stockholm
philharmonic

21-22 march 1968/raleigh north carolina
stockholm
philharmonic

23 march 1968/washington/constitution hall
stockholm
philharmonic

24 march 1968/stamford connecticut
stockholm
philharmonic

28 march 1968/red bank new york
stockholm
philharmomic

29 march 1968/huntington west virginia
stockholm
philharmonic

30 march 1968/brooklyn new york
stockholm
philharmonic

31 march 1968/new york/carnegie hall
stockholm philharmonic berlioz benvenuto cellini overture/bartok 2 portraits/blomdahl sisyphos suite/sibelius symphony 2

3 april 1968/stockholm/konserthuset
stockholm philharmonic beethoven leonore 3 overture/bartok miraculous mandarin suite/rosenberg journey to america

30 april 1968/zürich/tonhalle
tonhalle-orchester brahms academic festival overture/brahms violin concerto/bartok concerto for orchestra
ferras

9 may 1968/frankfurt-am-main
orchester des hessischen rundfunks

15-17 may 1968/stockholm/konserthuset
stockholm philharmonic beethoven missa solemnis
janowitz/höffgen/jehrlander/tyren/philharmonic chorus

13 july 1968/new york/carnegie hall
royal philharmonic schubert symphony 8/schumann piano concerto/brahms symphony 1
pressler

14 july 1968/new york/carnegie hall
royal philharmonic *programme included works by* elgar/liszt/beethoven
darre

12 september 1968/stockholm/konserthuset
stockholm philharmonic blomdahl resan i denna natt/beethoven choral fantasy/beethoven symphony 9
leygraf/söderström/finnilä/jehrlander/robinson/philharmonic chorus

19-20 september 1968/aarhus/radiohuset
danish radio orchestra berlioz benvenuto cellini overture/ravel shéhérazade/schoenberg erwartung/beethoven symphony 3
collier

9-11 october 1968/stockholm/konserthuset
stockholm philharmonic valen sonetto di michelangelo/rosenberg symphony for wind and percussion/sibelius violin concerto/nielsen symphony 4
kagan

16-17 october 1968/stockholm/konserthuset
stockholm philharmonic dvorak requiem
lindholm/meyer/eliasson/tyren/philharmonic chorus

20 october 1968/london/royal festival hall
london symphony haydn symphony 82/mozart piano concerto 17/nielsen symphony 4
p.serkin

31 october 1968/uppsala
stockholm philharmonic brahms serenade 1/nielsen symphony 4

1 november 1968/stockholm/konserthuset
stockholm philharmonic *brahms programme*
serenade 1/piano concerto 1
barenboim

4 november 1968/portsmouth/guildhall
bournemouth symphony weber oberon overture/brahms symphony 3/britten sinfonia da requiem/kodaly peacock variations

5 november 1968/southampton/guildhall
bournemouth symphony *programme as for 4 november*

7 november 1968/bournemouth/winter gardens
bournemouth symphony *programme as for 4 november*

8 november 1968/weymouth/pavilion
bournemouth symphony *programme as for 4 november*

13 november 1968/tel aviv/mann auditorium
israel philharmonic *stravinsky programme*
pulcinella/oedipus rex
guy/mitchinson/english/angas/stalman/rapoport/chorus

26 january 1969/washington/constitution hall
national symphony tchaikovsky romeo and juliet/liszt piano concerto 1/mussorgsky-ravel pictures from an exhibition
darre

28-29 january 1969/washington/constitution hall
national symphony mozart symphony 33/haydn cello concerto in c/strauss don quixote
fournier

7 february 1969/minneapolis/northrop auditorium
minneapolis symphony
smetana bartered bride overture/dvorak symphony 6/
beethoven symphony 6

19 february 1969/stockholm/konserhuset
stockholm philharmonic
bach brandenburg concerto 3/bach cantata 35/bartok
concerto for orchestra
finnilä

22 february 1969/stockholm/konserthuset
stockholm philharmonic
berlioz benvenuto cellini overture/bartok concerto for orchestra

24 february 1969/prague/rudolfinum
stockholm philharmonic

25 february 1969/berlin ddr
stockholm philharmonic

26 february 1969/dresden/kulturpalast
stockholm philharmonic
berlioz benvenuto cellini overture/strauss don juan/bartok
concerto for orchestra

27 february 1969/dresden/kulturpalast
stockholm philharmonic
blomdahl sisyphos suite/petterson symphony 7/brahms
symphony 1

28 february 1969/leipzig/kongresshalle
stockholm philharmonic
berlioz benvenuto cellini overture/strauss don juan/
blomdahl sisyphos suite/brahms symphony 1

5-6 march 1969/munich/herkulessaal
munich philharmonic
mozart symphony 14/mendelssohn violin concerto/stravinsky
le sacre du printemps
guntner

20-22 march 1969/detroit
detroit symphony
haydn symphony 12/mozart symphony 14/shostakovich
symphony 10

28 march 1969/cincinnati/music hall
cincinnati beethoven leonore 3 overture/bartok concerto for orchestra/
symphony dvorak symphony 8

23-24 april 1969/stockholm/konserthuset
stockholm verdi la traviata preludes/arias from macbeth and forza del
philharmonic destino/wagner dich teure halle/rhine journey, funeral
  march and immolation scene
  nilsson

17 june 1969/london/royal festival hall
london *brahms programme*
symphony symphony 1/piano concerto 2
  arrau

21 june 1969/croydon/fairfield halls
london beethoven leonore
symphony *lindholm/harwood/alexander/english/shirley-quirk/langdon/lso chorus*
  concert performance of the opera

22 june 1969/london/royal festival hall
london *programme and soloists as for 21 june*
symphony

23 june 1969/london/royal festival hall
london skalkottas greek dances/prokofiev piano concerto 2/
symphony skalkottas il ritorno d'ulisse
  béroff

24 june 1969/cheltenham/town hall
london skalkottas symphony/prokofiev piano concerto 2/operatic
symphony arias by mozart and rossini
  béroff/paskalis

16 august 1969/lucerne/kunsthaus
swiss festival strauss oboe concerto/mahler symphony 6
orchestra *holliger*

4 september 1969/london/royal albert hall
london haydn symphony 82/beethoven violin concerto/nielsen
symphony symphony 4
  perlman

25 october 1969/croydon/fairfield halls
london berlioz carnaval romain overture/rachmaninov piano
symphony concerto 2/bartok concerto for orchestra
  entremont

26 october 1969/london/royal festival hall
london *programme and soloist as for 25 october*
symphony

3 november 1969/lausanne/théatre de beaulieu
orchestre de la   mozart symphony 36/mozart concert arias/strauss till
suisse romande   eulenspiegel/hindemith sinfonia serena
                  girones

10 november 1969/swansea/brangwyn hall
london   strauss till eulenspiegel/mozart sinfonia concertante for wind/
symphony   bartok concerto for orchestra
                  orchestral soloists

february-march 1970/concerts with stockholm philharmonic orchestra

22 april 1970/paris/théatre des champs-élysées
orchestre   *programme inccluded works by*
national   beethovem/gerhard
                  vasary

15 may 1970/copenhagen/tivoli concert hall
danish radio   vivaldi concerto in c/mendelssohn piano concerto in a minor/
orchestra   bartok concerto for orchestra
                  alpenheim

27 may 1970/monmouth/monmouth school
london chamber   bach brandenburg concerto 3/bartok diverimento/stravinsky
orchestra   concerto in d/dvorak serenade for strings

28 may 1970/harlech/ysgol a rdudwuy
london chamber   *programme as for 27 may*
orchestra

29 may 1970/saint asaph/cathedral
london chamber   *programme as for 27 may*
orchestra

2 august 1970/tanglewood
boston   *beethoven programme*
symphony   egmont overture/piano concerto 3/symphony 7
                  ashkenazy

6 august 1970/detroit/ford auditorium
detroit   *beethoven programme*
symphony   leonore 3 overture/violin concerto/symphony 5
                  perlman

8 august 1970/detroit/ford auditorium
detroit *tchaikovsky programme*
symphony romeo and juliet/violin concerto/symphony 4
　　　　　perlman

9 august 1970/detroit/ford auditorium
detroit stravinsky scherzo a la russe/stravinsky circus polka/rachmaninov
symphony piano concerto 2/shostakovich symphony 5
　　　　　sandor

13 august 1970/berkeley california/bovard auditorium
string bartok rumanian dances
orchestra *concert organised by university of southern california in which other conductors also participated*

3 september 1970/edinburgh/usher hall
stockholm blomdahl sisyphos suite/beethoven piano concerto 2/sibelius
philharmonic symphony 2
　　　　　bishop

5 september 1970/edinburgh/usher hall
stockholm dvorak requiem
philharmonic *söderström/finnilä/elliason/tyrem/philharmonic chorus*

16-17 september 1970/stockholm/konserthuset
stockholm beethoven leonore 3 overture/peterson barefoot songs/
philharmonic stravinsky le sacre du printemps
　　　　　hagegard

23 september 1970/bristol/colston hall
bournemouth weber euryanthe overture/mozart symphony 41/sibelius
symphony symphony 2

24 september 1970/bournemouth/winter gardens
bournemouth *programme as for 23 september*
symphony

25 september 1970/scunthorpe/essoldo theatre
bournemouth *programme as for 23 september*
symphony

30 september-2 october 1970/stockholm/konserhuset
stockholm schubert rosamunde overture/schumann piano concerto/
philharmonic stenhammar symphony 2
　　　　　gelber

13-14 october 1970/washington/constitution hall
national　　　　*beethoven programme*
symphony　　　symphony 8/symphony 9
　　　　　　　　harper/winden/lewis/estes/university of maryland chorus

16 october 1970/fairfax virginia/woodson high school
national　　　　william schuman crededendum/beethoven symphony 8/
symphony　　　mussorgsky-ravel pictures from an exhibition

17 october 1970/washington/constitution hall
national　　　　william schuman credendum/wagner tristam prelude and
symphony　　　liebestod/verdi forza del destino overture/verdi ritorna
　　　　　　　　vincitor/mussorgsky-ravel pictures from an exhibition
　　　　　　　　farrell/concert for the united nations

20 october 1970/washington/constitution hall
national　　　　bartok miraculous mandarin suite/haydn symphony 12/martin
symphony　　　concerto for woodwind

october 1970/new york/carnegie hall
national　　　　bartok miracolous mandarin suite/martin concerto for
symphony　　　woodwind/haydn symphony 12/tchaikovsky piano concero 1
　　　　　　　　krainev

27-28 october 1970/washington/constitution hall
national　　　　*brahms programme*
symphony　　　haydn variations/violin concerto/symphony 1
　　　　　　　　milstein
one of these october 1970 concerts with national symphony orchestra also included dorati's american serenade

11, 13, 16 and 17 december 1970/stockholm/konserthuset
stockholm　　　schubert symphony 8/beethoven symphony 9
philharmonic　*söderström/ericson/johannson/estes/philharmonic chorus*

19 december 1970/stockholm/konserthuset
stockholm　　　smetana bartered bride overture/stenhammar serenade/prokofiev
philharmonic　peter and the wolf

16 january 1971/stockholm/konserthuset
stockholm　　　purcell trumpet voluntary/haydn piano concerto in d/dorati
philharmonic　night music
　　　　　　　　alpenheim

17 january 1971/stockholm/konserthuset
stockholm   dorati might music/haydn piano concerto in d/brahms symphony 1
philharmonic   *alpenheim*

20-21 january 1971/stockholm/konserthuset
stockholm   bartok bliebeard's castle
philharmonic   *szőnyi/farago*
                   concert also included kodaly choral works conducted by norby

24 january 1971/washington/constitution hall
national   bach brandenburg concerto 3/prokofiev piano concerto 3/
symphony   mozart sinfonia concertante for violin and viola
                   turini/kojian/parnas

26-27 january 1971/washington/constitution hall
national   mozart march k335/mozart notturno for 4 orchestras/
symphony   strauss 4 letzte lieder/strauss also sprach zarathustra
                   schwarzkopf

31 january 1971/washington/constitution hall
national   roussel suite in f/franck variations symphoniques/beethoven
symphony   piano concerto 4
                   rubinstein

2-3 february 1971/washington/constitution hall
national   kodaly dances of galanta/rachmaninov piano concerto 3/
symphony   dvorak symphony 6
                   watts

13 march 1971/stockholm/konserthuset
stockholm   rossini overture/haydn trumpet concerto/sibelius swan of
philharmonic   tuonela/berlioz damnation de faust suite
                   strömblad

17-19 march 1971/stockholm/konserthuset
stockholm   dvorak stabat mater
philharmonic   *harwood/soukupova/shirley-quirk/philharmonic chorus*

10 may 1971/tel aviv/mann auditorium
israel   mozart symphony 39/dvorak biblical songs/vivaldi gloria
philharmonic   *armstrong/finnilä/goldenthal*

29 may 1971/bern
berner sinfonie-   haydn symphony 104/bartok 2 portraits/beethoven symphony 7
orchester

10 june 1971/london/royal festival hall
royal brahms symphony 3/beethoven symphony 3
philharmonic

12 june 1971/york/minster
royal verdi messa da requiem
philharmonic *hunter/guy/mitchinson/estes/york celebration chorus*

13 june 1971/london/royal festival hall
royal *programme and soloists as for 12 june*
philharmonic

29-30 september and 2 october 1971/stockholm/konserthuset
stockholm penderecki utrenja
philharmonic *söderström/meyer/pribyl/borg/lagger/choirs*

19-21 october 1971/washington/kennedy centre
national handel concerto grosso op 6 no 7/bartok violin concerto 2/
symphony mozart sinfonia concertante for wind/kodaly concerto for
 orchestra
 druian/orchestral soloists

26-28 october 1971/washington/kennedy centre
national mozart symphony 36/beethoven piano concerto 3/nielsen
symphony symphony 4
 graffman

31 october 1971/new york/philharmonic hall
national *programme and soloist as for 26-28 october*
symphony

2-4 november 1971/washington/kennedy centre
national haydn die schöpfung
symphony *neblett/winden/mccoy/paul/mayland university chorus and glee club*

9-11 november 1971/washington/kennedy centre
national schubert symphony 8/schumann piano concerto/delius
symphony appalachia
 istomin/howard university choir

25 november 1971/copenhagen/radiohuset
danish radio beethoven symphony 1/mahler symphony 1
orchestra

28 november 1971/copenhagen/radiohuset
danish radio   *beethoven programme*
orchestra   german dances/piano concerto 1/symphony 1
               alpenheim

8 january 1972/stockholm/konserthuset
stockholm   prokofiev symphony 5/brahms piano concerto 1
philharmonic   *bishop*

12-13 january 1972/stockholm/konserthuset
stockholm   schubert symphony 8/dvorak biblical songs/dorati symphony 1
philharmonic   *finnilä*

20 january 1972/stuttgart/liederhalle
sdr orchestra

12 february 1972/stockholm/konserthuset
stockholm   *tchaikovsky programme*
philharmonic   piano concerto 1/symphony 4
               solyom

16-17 february 1972/stockholm/konserthuset
stockholm   mozart symphony 14/mozart oboe concerto/strauss
philharmonic   ein heldenleben
               a.nilsson

23 february 1972/stockholm/konserthuset
stockholm   verdi 4 pezzi sacri/petterson symphony 8
philharmonic   *philharmonic chorus*

27 february 1972/stockholm/konserthuset
stockholm   webern 6 pieces/berg altenberg-lieder/petterson symphony 8
philharmonic   *söderström*

1-2 march 1972/uppsala
stockholm   webern 6 pieces/schoenberg violin concerto/berwald
philharmonic   sinfonie singuliere
               zeitlin

8-9 march 1972/stockholm/konserthuset
stockholm   mahler symphony 7
philharmonic

6 april 1972/new york/carnegie hall
national   messiaen turangalila symphony
symphony   *loriod/westminster choir*

16 april 1972/new york/philharmonic hall
national symphony haydn symphony 3/mozart piano concerto 9/tchaikovsky symphony 4
alpenheim

18-20 april 1972/washington/kennedy centre
national symphony purcell trumpet voluntary/beethoven violin concerto/verdi 4 pezzi sacri
stern/ cathedral choral society

25-27 april 1972/washington/kennedy centre
national symphony strauss elektra
borkh/ schauler/ resnik/ stark/ ludgin/ choral arts society
concert performance of scenes from the opera

9 may 1972/zürich/tonhalle
tonhalle-orchester mahler lieder eines fahrenden gesellen/bruckner symphony 6
widmer

may 1972/geneva/victoria hall
orchestre de la suisse romande *programme included*
bartok concerto for orchestra

15-17 may 1972/cologne/wdr grosser saal
gürzenich-orchester liszt mephisto waltz/bartok concerto for orchestra/mahler symphony 4

21-22 may 1972/rome/auditorio di via della conciliazione
santa cecilia orchestra bach-schoenberg 2 chorale preludes/schoenberg psalm 130/ schoenberg survivor from warsaw/beethoven symphony 6
sbragia/ santa cecilia chorus

4 june 1972/lausanne/théatre de beaulieu
orchestre national mozart lucio silla overture/mendelssohn violin concerto/ berlioz symphonie fantastique
francescatti

21 june 1972/paris/salle pleyel
orchestre   dorati night music/beethoven piano concerto 2/brahms
national   symphony 1
                 rampal/eschenbach

4 july 1972/interlaken/konzerthalle
philharmonia   haydn symphony 92/strauss 4 letzte lieder/mozart symphony 39
hungarica   *della casa*

28 august 1972/amsterdam/concertgebouw
philharmonia   *programme included*
hungarica   fishbach adagio/haydn symphony 45

20 september 1972/stockholm/konserthuset
stockholm   bartok piano concerto 3/mahler symphony 5
philharmonic   *alpenheim*

23 september 1972/stockholm/konserthuset
stockholm   berlioz caranaval romain overture/rangström symphony 2/
philharminic   prokofiev symphony 5

5 november 1972/new york/philharmonic hall
national   handel oboe concerto/brahms violin concerto/strauss also
symphony   sprach zarathustra
                 weiss/pauk

14-16 november 1972/washington/kennedy centre
national   debussy clarinet rhapsody/tchaikovsky violin concerto/
symphony   lees concerto for orchestra/ravel boléro
                 kitt/zukerman

18 november 1972/brookville pennsylvania/post centre auditorium
national   *programme and soloists as for 14-16 november*
symphony

19 november 1972/new york/philharmonic hall
national   *programme and soloists as for 14-16 november*
symphony

12-13 december 1972/stockholm/konserthuset
stockholm   mendelssohn midsummer night's dream overture/mendelssohn
philharmonic   violin concerto/shostakovich symphony 13
                 lagger/rosenberg

17 december 1972/stockholm/konserthuset
stockholm　　　albinoni christmas concerto/bartok concerto for orchestra/
philharmonic　　tchaikovsky casse noisette excerpts

9-11 january 1973/washington/kennedy centre
national　　　　janacek taras bulba/bloch schelomo/strauss don quixote
symphony　　　*starker*

26-28 january 1973/stockholm/konserthuset
stockholm　　　mahler symphony 8
philharmonic　　*valjakka/lövaas/van bork/thallaug/meyer/cathcart/skram/estes/*
　　　　　　　　philharmonic, academic and uppsala choirs

6-7 february 1973/stockholm/konserthuset
stockholm　　　bäck intrada/berwald sinfonie singuliere/bartok concerto for
philharmonic　　orchestra

12 february 1973/heidelberg
stockholm
philharmonic

15 february 1973/frankfurt-hoechst/jahrhunderthalle
stockholm　　　roman drottningholm music/mahler symphony 5
philharmonic

17 february 1973/ludwigshafen/pfalzbau
stockholm　　　berlioz carnaval romain overture/bartok concerto for
philharmonic　　orchestra/tchaikovsky symphony 4

19 february 1973/munich/deutsches museum
stockholm　　　strauss don juan/mahler symphony 5
philharmonic

21 february 1973/stuttgart/liederhalle
stockholm　　　*programme as for 15 february*
philharmonic

23 february 1973/heilbronn/kulturring
stockholm　　　berlioz carnaval romain overture/sibelius symphony 2/
philharmonic　　tchaikovsky symphony 4

24-25 february 1973/vienna/musikvereinssaal
stockholm　　　berlioz carnaval romain overture/bartok concerto for orchestra/
philharmonic　　sibelius symphony 2

13 march 1973/helsinki/finlandia hall
finnish radio orchestra dorati 4 pieces/kodaly psalmus hungaricus/sibelius symphony 7
kozma/finnish radio chorus

17 march 1973/nürnberg/meistersingerhalle
nürnberger sinfoniker strauss serenade for wind/bartok divertimento/beethoven symphony 3

12 may 1973/washington/kennedy centre
national symphony *bach programme*
orchestral suite 2/concerto for 2 violins/cantata 21
kirkpatrick/odiaga/yockey/grillo/kness/beattie/madison choir

24-25 may 1973/frankfurt-am-main/grosser sendersaal
orchester des hessischen rundfunks haydn symphony 52/hindemith cello concerto/dvorak symphony 9
kanngiesser

29 may 1973/hilversum
netherlands radio philharmonic haydn symphony 60/prokofiev lieutenant kijé suite

3 june 1973/hilversum
netherlands radio philharmonic kodaly hary janos suite/prokofiev lieutenant kijé suite

7 july 1973/wellington/town hall
new zealand symphony handel concerto grosso op 6 no 7/mozart piano concerto 9/brahms symphony 1
alpenheim

10 july 1973/palmerston north/opera house
new zealand symphony *programme and soloist as for 7 july*

14 july 1973/wellington/town hall
new zealand symphony berlioz benvenuto cellini overture/bartok concerto for orchestra/tchaikovsky symphony 4

18 july 1973/hamilton/founders theatre
new zealand symphony *programme and soloist as for 7 july*

19 july 1973/auckland/town hall
new zealand symphony *programme and soloist as for 7 july*

20 july 1973/auckland/town hall
new zealand symphony *programme as for 14 july*

21 july 1973/auckland/town hall
new zealand symphony — bach brandenburg concerto 3/beethoven piano concerto 2/haydn symphony 90/kodaly peacock variations
alpenheim

23 july 1973/auckland/town hall
new zealand symphony — *programme and soloist as for 7 july*

28 july 1973/wellington/town hall
new zealand symphony — beethoven piano concerto 1/shostakovich symphony 10
alpenheim

30 july 1973/christchurch/town hall
new zealand symphony — *programme as for 14 july*

31 july 1973/dunedin/town hall
new zealand symphony — *programme and soloist as for 7 july*

1 august 1973/christchurch/town hall
new zealand symphony — *programme and soloist as for 21 july*

10 september 1973/london/royal albert hall
bbc symphony — haydn symphony 60/bartok 2 portraits/bartok piano concerto 3/haydn symphony 83
alpenheim

12 september 1973/stockholm/konserthuset
stockholm philharmonic — petterson barefoot songs/mahler symphony 5
saeden

16 september 1973/stockholm/konserthuset
swedish radio orchestra — petterson symphony 10

19-20 september 1973/stockholm/konserthuset
stockholm philharmonic — strauss also sprach zarathustra/beethoven piano concerto 5
gelber

22 september 1973/stockholm/konserthuset
stockholm philharmonic — strauss also sprach zarathustra/beethoven symphony 7

1 october 1973/washington/kennedy centre
national symphony — purcell trumpet voluntary/william schuman new england triptych/tchaikovsky francesca da rimini/schubert symphony 8/ravel daphnis et chloé second suite

22 october 1973/new york/philharmonic hall
national burton dithyramb for large orchestra/lamontaine wilderness
symphony journal/beethoven piano concerto 4
firkusny/callaway/gramm

16-17 november 1973/cleveland/severance hall
cleveland haydn symphony 60/prokofiev piano concerto 2/bartok
orchestra concerto for orchestra
gutierrez

24 november 1973/berlin/rias studios
rias-orchester haydn symphony 12
workshop concert: rehearsal and performance

5 december 1973/stockholm/konserthuset
stockholm vivaldi piccolo concerto/poulenc la voix humaine/dvorak
philharmonic symphony 6
kaufeldt/söderström

12-15 december 1973/stockholm/konserthuset
stockholm beethoven symphony 9
philharmonic *harper/finnilä/kozma/lagger/philharmonic chorus*

8-11 january 1974/washington/kennedy centre
national martin petite symphonie concertante/bruckner symphony 4
symphony

9 february 1974/amsterdam/concertgebouw
philharmonia haydn symphony 85/bartok dance suite/dvorak symphony 6
hungarica

13 february 1974/stockholm/konserthuset
stockholm dorati pictures for orchestra/brahms piano concerto 2
philharmonic *curzon*

20-21 february 1974/stockholm/konserthuset
stockholm mozart piano concerto 9/mahler symphony 9
philharmonic *alpenheim*

23 february 1974/stockholm/konserthuset
stockholm *programme of works by antal dorati*
philharmonic octet/solo piano pieces/bartok variations/missa brevis
alpenheim/philharmonic chorus

27 february 1974/stockholm/konserthuset
stockholm dorati lo-tay-pe/berg violin concerto/stenhammar symphony 2
philharmonic *spierer/saeden*

3 march 1974/stockholm/konserthuset
stockholm *haydn programme*
philharmonic symphony 49/nelson mass
langebo/thallaug/jehrlander/tyren/philharmonic chorus

24 march 1974/new york/philharmonic hall
national   *brahms programme*
symphony   symphony 3/piano concerto 2
                  gelber

2-4 april 1974/washington/kennedy centre
national   makris efthymia/mendelssohn violin concerto/berlioz harold
symphony   en italie
                  perlman/parnas

may 1974/washington/kennedy centre
national   frid toccata/bartok violin concerto 2/haydn symphony 45
symphony   *menuhin*

12-13 june 1974/stockholm/konserthuset
stockholm   beethoven fidelio
philharmonic   *bjoner/donath/mitchinson/lindroos/tyren/robinson/skram/chorus*
                  concert performances of the opera

23 august 1974/saratoga/performing arts centre
philadelphia   handel concerto grosso op 6 no 8/mozart sinfonia concertante
orchestra   for wind/bartok concerto for orchestra
                  orchestral soloists

4 september 1974/athens/herodes atticus theatre
tonhalle-   weber euryanthe overture/strauss also sprach zarathustra/
orchester   beethoven symphony 3

5 september 1974/athens/herodes atticus theatre
tonhalle-   schubert symphony 8/schumann piano concerto/brahms
orchester   symphony 1
                  alpenheim

6 september 1974/athens/herodes atticus theatre
tonhalle-   tchaikovsky symphony 4/dvorak symphony 8
orchester

10-11 september 1974/zürich/tonhalle
tonhalle-   weber euryanthe overture/schumann piano concerto/dvorak
orchester   symphony 8
                  buchbinder

14 october 1974/washington/kennedy centre
national   gould spirituals/tchaikovsky romeo and juliet/beethoven
symphony   symphony 7

27 october 1974/new york/philharmonic hall
national   mahler symphony 6
symphony

29 october-1 november 1974/washington/kennedy centre
national symphony kodaly old hungarian soldiers' tunes/ginastera harp concerto/ berlioz symphonie fantastique
zabaleta

10 november 1974/new york/philharmonic hall
national symphony dvorak requiem
gibbs/finnilä/vaas/shirley-quirk/chorus

21-23 and 26 november 1974/philadelphia/academy of music
philadelphia orchestra haydn symphony 12/mahler symphony 6

9 december 1974/washington/kennedy centre
national symphony wagner die walküre
kovacs/ruk-focic/killebrew/brilioth/tyl/lagger
performance staged by george london

11 december 1974/washington/kennedy centre
national symphony wagner die walküre *sung in english*
green/haywood/killebrew/rue/garrard/lagger
performance staged by george london

13 december 1974/washington/kennedy centre
national symphony *programme and soloists as for 9 december*

15 december 1974/washington/kennedy centre
national symphony *programme and soloists as for 11 december*

12-13 january 1975/hamburg/musikhalle
ndr orchestra haydn symphony 67/bartok 2 portraits/bloch schelomo/ kodaly hary janos suite
parnas

19 january 1975/zürich/tonhalle
tonhalle-orchester mendelssohn symphony 4/mahler symphony 4
speiser

2 february 1975/new york/philharmonic hall
national symphony ravel introduction and allegro/ravel piano concerto in g/ berlioz symphonie fantastique
béroff

4-7 february 1975/washington/kennedy centre
national symphony stravinsky symphony of psalms/kodaly psalmus hungaricus/ penderecki magnificat
nagy/westminster choir

27 february 1975/detroit/ford auditorium
detroit haydn symphony 30/mahler symphony 6
symphony

12 march 1975/stockholm/konserthuset
stockholm petterson barefoot songs/beethoven symphony 3
philharmonic

21 march 1975/stockholm/konserthuset
stockholm messiaen la transfiguration de notre seigneur
philharmonic *loriod*

2 april 1975/minneapolis/orchestra hall
minnesota haydn symphony 90/dorati night music/bartok concerto
orchestra for orchestra
  s. zeitlin

3 april 1975/minneapolis/o'shaughnessy hall
minnesota *programme and soloist as for 2 april*
orchestra

4 april 1975/minneapolis/orchestra hall
minnesota *programme and soloist as for 2 april*
orchestra

20 april 1975/new york/philharmonic hall
national lees concerto for orchestra/beethoven piano concerto 4/
symphony bartok concerto for orchestra
  istomin

11 july 1975/london/royal albert hall
royal *beethoven cycle*
philharmonic symphony 1/piano concerto 2/symphony 5
  perahia

13 july 1975/london/royal albert hall
royal *beethoven cycle*
philharmonic coriolan overture/piano concerto 1/symphony 3
  lill

15 july 1975/london/royal albert hall
royal *beethoven cycle*
philharmonic egmont overture/piano concerto 3/symphony 7
  vasary

17 july 1975/london/royal albert hall
royal philharmonic
beethoven cycle
prometheus overture/piano concerto 4/symphony 6
lympany

19 july 1975/london/royal albert hall
royal philharmonic
beethoven cycle
weihe des hauses overture/symphony 4/violin concerto
menuhin

20 july 1975/london/royal albert hall
royal philharmonic
beethoven cycle
leonore 3 overture/piano concerto 5/symphony 2
bachauer

23 july 1975/london/royal albert hall
royal philharmonic
beethoven cycle
symphony 8/symphony 9
farley/hodgson/burrows/bailey/brighton festival chorus

21 january 1976/stockholm/konserthuset
stockholm philharmonic
kodaly 2 songs/haydn 7 last words
saeden/straal

26 january 1976/cardiff/capitol theatre
royal philharmonic
beethoven programme
leonore 3 overture/symphony 4/symphony 5

27 january 1976/aberystwyth/great hall
royal philharmonic
programme as for 26 january

28 january 1976/swansea/brangwyn hall
royal philharmonic
beethoven programme
leonore 3 overture/symphony 6/symphony 5

1 february 1976/london/royal festival hall
royal philharmonic
berlioz carnaval romain overture/franck variations symphoniques/orff carmina burana
alpenheim/burrowes/devos/shirley-quirk/brighton festival chorus

2 march 1976/london/royal festival hall
royal philharmonic
haydn symphony 92/mozart violin concerto 5/prokofiev violin concerto 1/stravinsky firebird suite
stern

9 march 1976/london/royal festival hall
royal philharmonic	haydn english overture/haydn symphony 99/brahms piano concerto 2
gelber

11 march 1976/london/royal festival hall
royal philharmonic	*beethoven programme*
egmont overture and incidental music/symphony 3
palmer/lidell

9 may 1976/bristol/colston hall
royal philharmonic	*beethoven programme*
leonore 3 overture/piano concerto 5/symphony 5
frankl

11 may 1976/london/royal festival hall
royal philharmonic	bartok concerto for orchestra
other works in this royal festival hall silver jubilee concert were conducted by sir charles groves with artur rubinstein as soloist

12-13 june 1976/lausanne/théatre de beaulieu
orchestre national	berlioz carnaval romain overture/beethoven piano concerto 5/tchaikovsky symphony 4
gilels

27 august 1976/london/royal albert hall
royal philharmonic	bennett zodiac/brahms double concerto/beethoven symphony 5
parikian/bengtsson

23 september 1976/london/royal festival hall
royal philharmonic	berlioz benvenuto cellini overture/bartok concerto for orchestra/walton belshazzar's feast
luxon/brighton festival chorus

3 october 1976/london/royal festival hall
royal philharmonic	*strauss programme*
don juan/4 letzte lieder/closing scene from capriccio/also sprach zarathustra
söderström

15 october 1976/new york/philharmonic hall
national symphony	*programme included*
beethoven symphony 8

24 october 1976/new york/general assembly hall
national symphony	beethoven egmont overture/tchaikovsky piano concerto 1/copland lincoln portrait/ravel daphnis et chloé second suite
berman/anderson
televised concert for united nations day

2 november 1976/washington/kennedy centre
national *programme included*
symphony beethoven symphony 5

5 december 1976/hamburg/musikhalle
ndr orchestra bartok concerto for orchestra/haydn sinfonia concertante/
brahms symphony 3
orchestral soloists

16 december 1976/london/royal festival hall
royal haydn die schöpfung
philharmonic *popp/doese/roden/luxon/howell/brighton festival chorus*

19-20 january 1977/stockholm/konserthuset
stockholm haydn symphony 99/stravinsky sacre du printemps
philharmonic

1-2 march 1977/washington/kennedy centre
national *strauss programme*
symphony wind serenade/burleske/closing scene from capriccio/
ein heldenleben
alpenheim/lear

8-10 march 1977/washington/kennedy centre
national haydn die jahreszeiten
symphony *zoghby/rolfe-johnson/krause/choral arts society*

13 march 1977/new york/carnegie hall
national *programme and soloists as for 1-2 march*
symphony

17-19 and 22 march 1977/philadelphia/academy of music
philadelphia haydn symphony 85/mozart piano concerto 9/kodaly hungarian
orchestra rondo/ives central park in the dark/strauss till eulenspiegel
alpenheim

31 march and 1-3 april 1977/cleveland/severance hall
cleveland mendelssohn violin concerto/mahler symphony 6
orchestra *majeske*

7-9 april 1977/cleveland/severance hall
cleveland haydn symphony 85/bartok 2 portraits/mozart piano concerto 12/
orchestra bartok hungarian sketches/kodaly hary janos suite
lupu

12-15 april 1977/washington/kennedy centre
national   *brahms programme*
symphony   piano concerto 2/symphony 1
                    dichter

19-20 april 1977/washington/kennedy centre
national   beethoven missa solemnis
symphony   *armstrong/killebrew/tear/gramm/maryland university chorus*

24-25 april 1977/tel aviv/mann auditorium
israel   stravinsky firebird suite/mahler 6 songs from knaben wunderhorn/
philharmonic   vivaldi gloria
                    armstrong/finnilä/goldenthal

17 may 1977/london/royal festival hall
royal   *brahms programme*
philharmonic   haydn vatiations/double concerto/symphony 1
                    k.chung/m.chung

26 may 1977/munich/herkulessaal
munich   berlioz benvenuto cellini overture/bartok 2 portraits/beethoven
philharmonic   symphony 3

12 july 1977/london/royal festival hall
royal   liadov 8 russian folksongs/tchaikovsky violin concerto/shostakovich
philharmonic   symphony 5
                    ricci

14 july 1977/london/royal festival hall
royal   *beethoven programme*
philharmonic   prometheus overture/piano concerto 5/symphony 7
                    bishop

20 august 1977/lucerne/kunsthaus
swiss festival   haydn symphony 85/brahms violin concerto/blomdahl sisyphos
orchestra   suite/strauss till eulenspiegel
                    milstein

10 september 1977/edinburgh/usher hall
royal   haydn symphony 3/beethoven violin concerto/bartok concerto
philharmonic   for orchestra
                    menuhin

9 october 1977/london/royal festival hall
royal *brahms programme*
philharmonic haydn variations/symphony 3/piano concerto 1
gelber

28 october 1977/detroit/grosse pointe concert hall
detroit
symphony

2 november 1977/detroit/ford auditorium
detroit *beethoven cycle*
symphony symphony 1/symphony 4/symphony 5

4 november 1977/detroit/ford auditorium
detroit *beethoven cycle*
symphony symphony 2/symphony 3

10 november 1977/detroit/ford auditorium
detroit *beethoven cycle*
symphony symphony 6/symphony 7

12 november 1977/detroit/ford auditorium
detroit *beethoven cycle*
symphony symphony 8/symphony 9
beatty/carlson/shirley/flagello/wayne university choir
these 4 beethoven concerts were recorded for television and transmitted on 28 december 1977 and 4, 11 and 18 january 1978 respectively

17-19 november 1977/detroit/ford auditorium
detroit william schuman the young dead soldiers/mendelssohn violin
symphony concerto/shostakovich symphony 5
perlman/wade/rees

25 november 1977/detroit/ford auditorium
detroit ives holidays symphony/dvorak symphony 9
symphony *rackham symphonic choir*

27 november 1977/detroit/ford auditorium
detroit *dvorak programme*
symphony cello concerto/symphony 9
rostropovich

10-11 and 20 january 1978/zürich/tonhalle
tonhalle- haydn symphony 67/haydn cello concerto in d/dvorak
orchester symphony 9
walewska

2-4 march 1978/detroit/ford auditorium
detroit durko hungarian rhapsody/prokofiev sinfonia concertante/
symphony strauss don juan/strauss till eulenspiegel
starker

3-5 march 1978/detroit/ford auditorium
detroit dvorak slavonic rhapsody 3/ravel rapsodie espagnole/weber
symphony clarinet concerto 1/enescu rumanian rhapsody 1/liszt
hungarian rhapsody 2
goodman

9-10 march 1978/detroit/ford auditorium
detroit bartok 2 portraits/dorati piano concerto/brahms symphony 1
symphony *alpenheim*

30-31 march and 1 april 1978/detroit/ford auditorium
detroit mozart march k249/mozart piano concerto 26/mahler
symphony symphony 1
curzon

2 april 1978/detroit/ford auditorium
detroit *tchaikovsky programme*
symphony marche slave/piano concerto 1/capriccio italien/1812 overture
kottler

5 april 1978/detroit/united artists theatre
detroit dvorak slavonic rhapsody 3/ravel rapsodie espagnole/enescu
symphony rumanian rhapsody 1/liszt hungarian rhapsody 2/bartok 2 portraits/
tchaikovsky marche slave/tachaikovsky capriccio italien/
tchaikovsky 1812 overture

6-8 april 1978/detroit/ford auditorium
detroit clarke prince of denmark's march/beethoven violin concerto/
symphony bartok suite 1
szeryng

13-15 april 1978/detroit/ford auditorium
detroit haydn die schöpfung
symphony *harper/alexander/lagger/jewell, brazeal and cantata academy choirs*

25-26 april 1978/washington/kennedy centre
national beethoven prometheus overture/beethoven piano concerto 5/
symphony schubert symphony 9
istomin

2-5 may 1978/washington/kennedy centre
national   haydn symphony 97/dorati cello concerto/wagner tannhäuser
symphony   overture and venusberg music/wagner meistersinger overture
starker/ choral arts society

14 may 1978/london/royal festival hall
royal   *beethoven cycle*
philharmonic   leonore 1 overture/symphony 1/symphony 9
harper/ watts/ davies/ howell/ brighton festival chorus

18 may 1978/london/royal festival hall
royal   *beethoven cycle*
philharmonic   leonore 2 overture/triple concerto/symphony 7
frankl/ pauk/ kirschbaum

23 may 1978/london/royal festival hall
royal   *beethoven cycle*
philharmonic   leonore 3 overture/piano concerto 3/symphony 3
gelber

28 may 1978/london/royal festival hall
royal   *beethoven cycle*
philharmonic   egmont overture/piano concerto 5/christus am ölberge
curzon/ armstrong/ tear/ howell/ brighton festival chorus

8 july 1978/lausanne/théatre de beaulieu
orchestre   beethoven leonore 3 overture/beethoven violin concerto/
national   brahms symphony 3
milstein

24 september 1978/london/royal festival hall
royal   *mahler programme*
philharmonic   lieder eines fahrenden gesellen/symphony 6
luxon

25 september 1978/windsor/waterloo chamber
royal   *beethoven programme*
philharmonic   leonore 3 overture/symphony 4/symphony 5

29 september 1978/chichester/festival theatre
royal   *programme as for 25 september*
philharmonic

30 september 1978/windsor/saint george's chapel
royal   haydn symphony 3/mahler symphony 6
philharmonic

11-12 october 1978/stockholm/konserthuset
stockholm   dorati die stimmen/berlioz symphonie fantastique
philharmonic   *lagger*

24 october 1978/geneva/victoria hall
orchestre de la suisse romande	haydn symphony 96/ravel shéhérazade/beethoven symphony 5 *norman* *concert for united nations day*

25 october 1978/geneva/victoria hall
orchestre de la suisse romande	haydn symphony 96/wagner wesendonk-lieder/beethoven symphony 5 *norman*

29 october 1978/london/royal festival hall
royal philharmonic	*dvorak programme* carnival overture/cello concerto/symphony 7 *starker*

2 november 1978/detroit/ford auditorium
detroit symphony	*schubert festival* symphony 1/symphony 8/symphony 9

4, 7 and 8 november 1978/detroit/ford auditorium
schubert festival
chamber concerts in which dorati participates as piano accompanist in lieder and instrumental works

11 november 1978/detroit/ford auditorium
detroit symphony	*schubert festival* alfonso und estrella *söderström/ rayam/ kimborough/ parker/ lagger*

15 november 1978/detroit/ford auditorium
detroit symphony	*schubert festival* works by schubert/schubert-liszt/lanner and j.strauss

18 november 1978/detroit/ford auditorium
detroit symphony	mozart eine kleine nachtmusik/schumann cello concerto/ dvorak symphony 8 *rose*

24-25 november 1978/detroit/ford auditorium
detroit symphony	rachmaninov piano concerto 3/stravinsky sacre du printemps *katsaris*

26 november 1978/detroit/ford auditorium
detroit   mozart concerto for 3 pianos/beethoven symphony 7
symphony   *katsaris/alpenheim/dorati*

30 november-2 december 1978/detroit/ford auditorium
detroit   brahms piano concerto 1/bartok concerto for orchestra
symphony   *arrau*

11 january 1979/utrecht/muziekcentrum vredenburg
concertgebouw   webern 6 pieces/mozart sinfonia concertante for wind/bartok
orchestra   concerto for orchestra
                    orchestral soloists

12 and 14 january 1979/amsterdam/concertgebouw
concertgebouw   *programme and soloists as for 11 january*
orchestra

21 january 1979/london/royal festival hall
royal   beethoven missa solemnis
philharmonic   *harper/watts/davies/howell/brighton festival chorus*

7 february 1979/paris/théatre des champs-élysées
orchestre   bartok dance suite/dorati piano concerto/kodaly hary janos suite
national   *alpenheim*

20-23 february 1979/washington/kennedy centre
national   *brahms programme*
symphony   tragic overture/alto rhapsody/symphony 1
                 forrester/choral arts society

15-17 march 1979/detroit/ford auditorium
detroit   strauss elektra
symphony   *j.mcintyre/de francesca/varnay/shirley/dooley*
                 concert performances of the opera

22-23 march 1979/detroit/ford auditorium
detroit   *strauss programme*
symphony   don juan/burleske/tod und verklärung/till eulenspiegel
                 alpenheim

10-13 april 1979/washington/kennedy centre
national   dorati die stimmen/mozart requiem
symphony   *harper/carlson/rolfe-johnson/lagger/maryland university choir*

17 april 1979/detroit/ford auditorium
detroit   bartok piano concerto 2/beethoven symphony 5
symphony   *ashkenazy*

25 april 1979/detroit/ford auditorium
detroit symphony	*strauss die ägyptische helena* *jones/hendricks/finnilä/kastu/white/jewell chorale* *concert performance of the opera*

27 april 1979/new york/carnegie hall
detroit symphony	*programme and soloists as for 25 april*

3-6 may 1979/detroit/ford auditorium
detroit symphony	*beethoven programme* symphony 4/piano concerto 4 *serkin*

9 may 1979/detroit/united artists theatre/*morning concert*
detroit symphony	*strauss programme* don juan/till eulenspiegel/tod und verklärung

9 may 1979/detroit/ford auditorium
detroit symphony	*programme as for 9 may morning*

10-11 may 1979/detroit/ford auditorium
detroit symphony	mozart symphony 40/mahler symphony 5

24 may 1979/london/royal festival hall
royal philharmonic	*bartok programme* miraculous mandarin suite/violin concerto 2/concerto for orchestra *menuhin*

15 june 1979/amsterdam/rai-gebouw
concertgebouw orchestra	*tchaikovsky programme* piano concerto 1/symphony 4 *egorov*

16 june 1979/utrecht/muziekcentrum vredenburg
concertgebouw orchestra	*programme and soloist as for 15 june*

8 july 1979/london/royal festival hall
royal philharmonic	*strauss programme* till eulenspiegel/burleske/dance of the 7 veils/don quixote *alpenheim/strange*

20-23 september 1979/detroit/ford auditorium
detroit   berlioz benvenuto cellini overture/scriabin poeme de l'extase/
symphony   dvorak symphony 7

27 september 1979/detroit/ford auditorium
detroit   *beethoven programme*
symphony   leonore 3 overture/symphony 8/piano concerto 5
                          gelber

28 september 1979/albion michigan/goodrich chapel
detroit   berlioz benvenuto cellini overture/strauss don juan/brahms
symphony   symphony 1

4-6 october 1979/detroit/ford auditorium
detroit   *tchaikovsky programme*
symphony   piano concerto 1/symphony 4
                          watts

11 october 1979/detroit/ford auditorium
detroit   haydn isola disabitata overture/barber medea's dance of
symphony   vengeance/stravinsky violin concerto/sibelius symphony 2
                          chung

12 october 1979/ann arbor michigan/hill auditorium
detroit   haydn isola disabitata overture/barber medea's dance of
symphony   vengeance/ravel rapsodie espagnole/dvorak symphony 7

18 october 1979/detroit/ford auditorium
detroit   mozart piano concerto 21/mahler symphony 1
symphony   *tocco*

23 october 1979/detroit/ford auditorium
detroit   haydn isola disabitata overture/beethoven symphony 7/
symphony   brahms symphony 1

25-26 october 1979/detroit/ford auditorium
detroit   strauss don juan/ravel rapsodie espagnole/bartok concerto
symphony   for orchestra

30 october 1979/barcelona/palau de la musica
detroit   haydn isola disabitata overture/strauss don juan/barber
symphony   medea's dance of vengeance/bartok concerto for orchestra

31 october 1979/barcelona/palau de la musica
detroit   berlioz benvenuto cellini overture/ravel rapsodie espagnole/
symphony   mahler symphony 1

1 november 1979/madrid/teatro real
detroit symphony berlioz benvenuto cellini overture/strauss don juan/ravel rapsodie espagnole/beethoven symphony 7

3 november 1979/ludwigshafen/feierabendhaus
detroit symphony beethoven leonore 3 overture/ravel rapsodie espagnole/barber medea's dance of vengeance/dvorak symphony 7

4 november 1979/stuttgart/liederhalle
detroit symphony haydn isola disabitata overture/bartok concerto for orchestra/brahms symphony 1

6 november 1979/brussels/palais des beaux-arts
detroit symphony strauss don juan/ravel rapsodie espagnole/dvorak symphony 7

7 november 1979/bonn/beethovenhalle
detroit symphony beethoven leonore 3 overture/strauss don juan/strauss burleske/dvorak symphony 7
alpenheim

8 november 1979/hannover/stadthalle
detroit symphony haydn isola disabitata overture/ravel rapsodie espagnole/strauss burleske/bartok concerto for orchestra
alpenheim

9 november 1979/frankfurt-am-main/jahrhunderthalle
detroit symphony *programme as for 3 november*

12 november 1979/paris/salle pleyel
detroit symphony haydn isola disabitata overture/brahms violin concerto/mahler symphony 1
menuhin

13 november 1979/munich/deutsches museum
detroit symphony beethoven leonore 3 overture/bartok concerto for orchestra/brahms symphony 1

14 november 1979/berlin/philharmonie
detroit symphony berlioz benvenuto cellini overture/barber medea's dance of vengeance/mendelssohn violin concerto/beethoven symphony 7
menuhin

15 november 1979/braunschweig/stadthalle
detroit symphony — beethoven leonore 3 overture/ravel rapsodie espagnole/mahler symphony 1

16 november 1979/düsseldorf/tonhalle
detroit symphony — ravel rapsodie espagnole/bartok concerto for orchestra/beethoven symphony 7

19 november 1979/london/royal festival hall
detroit symphony — barber medea's dance of vengeance/mendelssohn violin concerto/mahler symphony 1
menuhin

20 november 1979/stockholm/konserthuset
detroit symphony — beethoven leonore 3 overture/barber medea's dance of vengeance/mahler symphony 1

22 november 1979/uppsala/universitätssaulen
detroit symphony — *programme as for 20 november*

23 november 1979/oslo/konserthuset
detroit symphony — dvorak symphony 7/mahler symphony 1

24 november 1979/sandefjord/hejrtneshallen
detroit symphony — beethoven symphony 7/dvorak symphony 7

25 november 1979/bergen/grieghalle
detroit symphony — strauss don juan/barber medea's dance of vengeance/mahler symphony 1

27 november 1979/geneva/victoria hall
detroit symphony — *programme as for 6 november*

28 november 1979/zürich/tonhalle
detroit symphony — *programme as for 25-26 october*

29 november 1979/lausanne/théatre de beaulieu
detroit symphony — beethoven symphony 7/bartok concerto for orchestra

30 november 1979/basel/steineberg casino
detroit symphony — *programme as for 6 november*

18 december 1979/london/royal festival hall
royal | *beethoven programme*
philharmonic | egmont overture/symphony 6/symphony 7

3 february 1980/london/royal festival hall
royal | *tchaikovsky programme*
philharmonic | violin concerto/symphony 6
| *mintz*

25-28 march 1980/washington/kennedy centre
national | mozart piano concerto 27/bruckner symphony 7
symphony | *alpenheim*

10 april 1980/detroit/ford auditorium
detroit | *brahms festival*
symphony | academic festival overture/piano concerto 1/symphony 1
| *ashkenazy*

15 april 1980/detroit/ford auditorium
detroit | *brahms festival*
symphony | haydn variations/violin concerto/symphony 2
| *stern*

16 april 1980/detroit/ford auditorium
| *brahms festival*
| chamber concert in which dorati participated as pianist with other artists

19 april 1980/detroit/ford auditorium
detroit | *brahms festival*
symphony | liebeslieder-walzer/symphony 3/double concerto
| *stern/rose/university chamber choit*

23 april 1980/detroit/ford auditorium
detroit | *brahms festival*
symphony | alto rhapsody/piano concerto 2/symphony 4
| *istomin/forrester/wayne state glee club*

26 april 1980/detroit/ford auditorium
detroit | *brahms festival*
symphony | tragic overture/ein deutsches requiem
| *varady/fischer-dieskau/wayne state choir*

1-3 may 1980/detroit/ford auditorium
detroit mendelssohn hebrides overture/mendelssohn violin concerto/
symphony dvorak czech suite/dvorak prague waltzes
perlman

8-10 may 1980/detroit/ford auditorium
detroit prokofiev piano concerto 3/shostakovich symphony 5
symphony *guttierez*

12 may 1980/new york/carnegie hall
detroit tchaikovsky piano concerto 1/stravinsky petrouchka
symphony *watts*

13 may 1980/hempstead new york/calderone theatre
detroit dvorak czech suite/mahler symphony 1
symphony

14 may 1980/new york/carnegie hall
detroit mendelssohn violin concerto/mahler symphony 1
symphony *perlman*

15 may 1980/harrisburg philadelphia/state education forum
detroit brahms haydn variations/dvorak prague waltzes/stravinsky
symphony petrouchka

16 may 1980/new york/carnegie hall
detroit haydn te deum/brahms ein deutsches requiem
symphony *varady/fischer-dieskau/wayne state choir*

17 may 1980/washington/kennedy centre
detroit *programme and soloists as for 16 may*
symphony

29 may 1980/detroit/ford auditorium
detroit haydn symphony 104/mozart symphony 41/beethoven
symphony symphony 5

30 may 1980/detroit/united artists theatre
detroit strauss tod und verklärung/strauss don juan/dvorak
symphony notturno, furiant, polka and polonaise

31 may 1980/detroit/ford auditorium
detroit *programme as for 29 may*
symphony

24 june 1980/london/royal festival hall
royal *brahms cycle*
philharmonic schicksalslied/ein deutsches requiem
  hendricks/brendel/maryland university choir

29 june 1980/london/royal festival hall

royal philharmonic	*brahms cycle* tragic overture/piano concerto 1/symphony 1 *gelber*

1 july 1980/london/royal festival hall

royal philharmonic	*brahms cycle* academic festival overture/piano concerto 2/symphony 2 *istomin*

6 july 1980/london/royal festival hall

royal philharmonic	*brahms cycle* haydn variations/symphony 3/double concerto *stern/tortelier*

4 september 1980/stresa/teatro del palazzo dei congressi

royal philharmonic	beethoven egmont overture/beethoven violin concerto/brahms symphony 4 *szeryng*

5 september 1980/montreux/maison des congres

royal philharmonic	*programme and soloist as for 4 september*

6 september 1980/lucerne/kunsthaus

royal philharmonic	haydn symphony 3/szymanowski violin concerto 2/brahms symphony 1 *szeryng*

7 september 1980/lucerne/kunsthaus

royal philharmonic	clarke trumpet voluntary/mozart sinfonia concertante for wind/beethoven symphony 7 *orchestral soloists*

10 september 1980/snape/maltings

royal philharmonic	*programme included* haydn symphony 3/mozart sinfonia concertante for wind *orchestral soloists*

18 september 1980/besancon/palais des sports

orchestre national	roussel suite in f/debussy la mer/sibelius swan of tuonela/ravel daphnis et chloé second suite

25-27 september 1980/detroit/ford auditorium
detroit haydn symphony 30/wagner meistersinger suite/copland dance
symphony symphony/copland el salon mexico/copland rodeo

2-4 october 1980/detroit/ford auditorium
detroit barber medea's meditation and dance of vengeance/barber
symphony cello concerto/strauss ein heldenleben
babini

10-11 october 1980/detroit/ford auditorium
detroit bach cantata 29/william schuman casey at the bat
symphony *segar/ britton/ jewell chorale*

12 october 1980/detroit/ford auditorium
detroit wagner tannhäuser overture/wagner meistersinger suite/
symphony william schuman casey at the bat
rees/ gramm/ jewell chorale

16-18 october 1980/detroit/ford auditorium
detroit *beethoven programme*
symphony prometheus overture/piano concerto 4/symphony 6
curzon

23-25 october 1980/detroit/ford auditorium
detroit *beethoven programme*
symphony egmont overture and incidental music/symphony 5
w.klemperer/ quilling

27 november 1980/paris/salle pleyel
orchestre bach brandenburg concerto 4/bartok sonata for 2 pianos and
national percussion/debussy images
labeque sisters

29 november 1980/paris/radio france auditorium
orchestre *bartok programme*
national music for strings percussion and celesta/cantata profana/
miraculous mandarin suite
gulyas/ solyom-nagy/ choir

4 december 1980/london/royal festival hall
royal mahler symphony 3
philharmonic *minton/ brighton festival and southend boys choirs*

26 january 1981/lausanne/théatre de beaulieu
lausanne chamber bartok-dorati 3 rondos/schoenberg verklärte nacht/haydn
orchestra symphony 54

4 february 1981/paris/théatre des champs-élysées
orchestre national
mozart symphony 36/mozart flute concerto 1/dutilleux métaboles/messiaen l'ascension
rampal

19-21 february 1981/stockholm/konserthuset
stockholm philharmonic
verdi messa da requiem
söderström/walker/de cesare/talvela/stockholm and uppsala choirs

25 february 1981/stockholm/konserthuset
stockholm philharmonic
bartok programme
piano concerto 3/bluebeard's castle
alpenheim/marton/kovacs

5-7 march 1981/detroit/ford auditorium
detroit symphony
beethoven programme
symphony 1/symphony 9
zoghby/myers/ryam/van halem/jewell chorale

12-13 march 1981/detroit/ford auditorium
detroit symphony
bartok programme
piano concerto 3/bluebeard's castle
sandor/kasza/kovacs

19 march 1981/detroit/ford auditorium
detroit symphony
bartok programme
miraculous mandarin suite/violin concerto 2/concerto for orchestra
menuhin

25 march 1981/new york/carnegie hall
detroit symphony
programme and soloist as for 19 march

26 march 1981/new york/rutgers college gymnasium
detroit symphony
beethoven egmont overture/beethoven symphony 1/ bartok concerto for orchestra

27 march 1981/new york/carnegie hall
detroit symphony
beethoven programme
symphony 1/symphony 9
zoghby/myers/ryam/van halem/maryland university chorus

28 march 1981/washington/kennedy centre
detroit *programme and soloists as for 27 march*
symphony

31 march 1981/detroit/ford auditorium
detroit wagner tannhäuser overture/strauss till eulenspiegel/brahms
symphony symphony 4

30 april-1 may 1981/detroit/ford auditorium
detroit mozart symphony 36/mozart oboe concerto/debussy images
symphony *baker*

3 may 1981/detroit/ford auditorium
detroit copland fanfare for the common man/copland dance symphony/
symphony copland el salon mexico/copland rodeo/beethoven symphony 7

7 may 1981/detroit/ford auditorium
detroit stravinsky le sacre du printemps/schubert symphony 9
symphony

11 may 1981/detroit/united artists theatre
detroit copland fanfare for the common man/copland dance symphony/
symphony copland el salon mexico/copland rodeo/stravinsky le sacre
  du printemps

28 may 1981/london/royal festival hall
royal haydn symphony 104/dorati cello concerto/brahms double
philharmonic concerto
  menuhin/starker

31 may 1981/london/royal festival hall
royal haydn symphony 104/bartok violin concerto 2/brahms
philharmonic symphony 1
  menuhin

2 june 1981/london/royal festival hall
royal *schubert programme*
philharmonic rosamunde excerpts/alfonso und estrella excerpts/symphony 9
  söderström

16-18 june 1981/amsterdam/theater carré
concertgebouw *programme of staged works by bartok*
orchestra miraculous mandarin/bluebeard's castle
  kasza/kovacs/habbema/tanzforum köln

23 june 1981/zürich/tonhalle
tonhalle-orchester   bartok 2 portraits/dvorak cello concerto/beethoven symphony 6
gutman

28 june 1981/amsterdam/concertgebouw
concergebouw orchestra   beethoven violin concerto/bartok concerto for orchestra
verhey

29 june 1981/paris/théatre des champs-élysées
concergebouw orchestra   *bartok programme*
miraculous mandarin suite/2 portraits/concerto for orchestra

2 july 1981/london/royal albert hall
royal philharmonic   *beethoven cycle*
symphony 1/piano concerto 4/symphony 5
curzon

4 july 1981/london/royal albert hall
royal philharmonic   *beethoven cycle*
coriolan overture/violin concerto/symphony 6
sarbu

6 july 1981/london/royal albert hall
royal philharmonic   *beethoven cycle*
symphony 2/ah perfido!/symphony 3
behrens

8 july 1981/london/royal albert hall
royal philharmonic   *beethoven cycle*
egmont overture/symphony 4/piano concerto 5
gelber

10 july 1981/london/royal albert hall
royal philharmonic   *beethoven cycle*
leonore 3 overture/triple concerto/symphony 7
de la pau/y-p tortelier/p tortelier

12 july 1981/london/royal albert hall
royal philharmonic   *beethoven cycle*
symphony 8/symphony 9
harper/hodgson/tear/luxon/brighton festival chorus

14 september 1981/lyon/auditorium maurice ravel
paris opéra *berlioz programme*
orchestra carnaval romain overture/la mort de cléopatre/symphonie
fantastique
norman

17 september 1981/lyon/auditorium maurice ravel
paris opéra *berlioz programme*
orchestra carnaval romain overture/les nuits d'été/symphonie fantastique
hendricks

15-17 october 1981/rome/teatro dell' opera
rome opera beethoven egmont overture/mozart piano concerto 9/
orchestra respighi fontane di roma/stravinsky firebird suite
alpenheim

24-25 october 1981/florence/teatro communale
maggio musicale haydn symphony 3/bartok music for strings percussion and
orchestra celesta/mussorgsky choruses/mussorgsky-ravel pictures
from an exhibition
maggio musicale chorus

27 october 1981/florence/teatro manzoni
maggio musicale *programme as for 24-25 october*
orchestra

28-29 october 1981/florence/teatro communale
maggio musicale *programme as for 24-25 october*
orchestra

23 november 1981/budapest/erkel theatre
hungarian state bartok concerto for orchestra/beethoven symphony 7
orchestra

3-5 december 1981/paris/salle pleyel
orchestre haydn symphony 52/bartok bluebeard's castle
de paris *varady/fischer-dieskau*

13-14 january 1982/amsterdam/concertgebouw
concertgebouw mozart 2 marches/mozart violin concerto 2/liszt a faust
orchestra symphony
spivakov/kozma/chorus

15 january 1982/amsterdam/concertgebouw
concertgebouw wagner faust overture/berlioz damnation de faust suite/
orchestra liszt a faust symphony
kozma/chorus

16 january 1982/den haag/congresgebouw
concertgebouw orchestra   *programme as for 15 january*

23-24 january 1982/amsterdam/concertgebouw
concertgebouw orchestra   bartok divertimento/martin petite symphonie concertante/beethoven symphony 4

28 january 1982/london/royal festival hall
royal philharmonic   *beethoven programme*
german dances/piano concerto 5/symphony 6
firkusny

31 january 1982/london/royal festival hall
royal philharmonic   *beethoven programme*
symphony 1/symphony 9
armstrong/ watts/ tear/ bailey/ brighton festival chorus

11-12 february 1982/rotterdam/de doelen
rotterdam philharmonic   kodaly psalmus hungaricus/beethoven symphony 9
j.price/finnilä/ korondy/ halem/ toonkunstkoor

16-18 february 1982/rotterdam/de doelen
rotterdam philharmonic   haydn symphony 3/mozart piano concerto 9/brahms symphony 2
alpenheim

20-21 february 1982/rotterdam/de doelen
rotterdam philharmonic   dukas apprenti sorcier/sibelius swan of tuonela/strauss till eulenspiegel/ravel la valse/dohnanyi wedding waltz/tchaikovsky waltz from evgeny onegin/j.strauss kaiserwalzer

24-25 february 1982/basel/stadtkasino
basler sinfonie-orchester   brahms symphony 3/beethoven symphony 3

13 march 1982/tokyo
yomyuri symphony   haydn isola disabitata overture/brahms haydn variations/bartok miraculous mandarin suite/haydn symphony 104

31 march-3 april 1982/boston/symphony hall
boston symphony   *haydn programme*
ritorno di tobia overture/symphony 26/7 last words
zoghby/ walker/ ahnsjö/ lenz/ new england conservatory choir

8-10 april 1982/boston/symphony hall
boston *haydn programme*
symphony isola disabitata overture/symphony 83/piano concerto in d/
symphony 82
alpenheim

15-17 april 1982/detroit/ford auditorium
detroit mozart serenata notturna/mozart symphony 35/strauss also
symphony sprach zarathustra/strauss macbeth

22-24 april 1982/detroit/ford auditorium
detroit haydn symphony 31/haydn piano concerto in d/stravinsky
symphony the firebird
alpenheim

15-16 may 1982/vienna/musikvereinssaal
vienna haydn die schöpfung
philharmonic *mathis/araiza/van dam/wiener singverein*
dorati replaced herbert von karajan for these concerts

31 may 1982/budapest/erkel theatre
hungarian state *kodaly programme including*
orchestra te deum/symphony
toth/takacs/korondi/polgar/hungarian state chorus

4 june 1982/budapest/state academy
hungarian state *programme included*
orchestra mozart maurerische trauermusik/dorati cello concerto
starker

5 june 1982/budapest/state academy
hungarian state haydn die jahreszeiten
orchestra *kincses/andor/solyom-nagy/polgar/hungarian state chorus*

6 july 1982/valencia/sala de concertos
royal beethoven symphony 5/brahms symphony 2
philharmonic

7 july 1982/barcelona/palau de la musica
royal haydn brahms variations/schubert symphony 8/dvorak
philharmonic symphony 9

9 july 1982/london/royal festival hall
royal haydn symphony 94/mozart piano concerto 27/schubert
philharmonic symphony 8/j.strauss seid umschlungen waltz
alpenheim

17 october 1982/detroit/ford auditorium
detroit copland hoedown/grofe grand canyon suite/dorati american
symphony symphony/gershwin porgy and bess suite

31 october 1982/indiana indianapolis/musical arts center
orchestra of indiana university strauss till eulenspiegel/bartok dance suite/brahms symphony 3

11 november 1982/london/royal festival hall
royal philharmonic brahms academic festival overture/brahms piano concerto 2/beethoven symphony 5
istomin

12 november 1982/london/whitehall banqueting house
royal philharmonic elgar serenade for strings/mozart musikalischer spass
gala concert with additional works and other conductors

15 november 1982/london/royal festival hall
royal philharmonic mozart 3 german dances/mozart piano concerto 22/mahler symphony 4
holtman/ buchanan

19 november 1982/amsterdam/concertgebouw
concertgebouw orchestra penderecki threnos/haydn die schöpfung
blegen/ kozma/ hölle/ chorus

20 november 1982/den haag/congresgebouw
concertgebouw orchestra *programme and soloists as for 19 november*

24-26 november 1982/amsterdam/concertgebouw
concertgebouw orchestra *programme and soloists as for 19 november*

3 december 1982/birmingham alabama/masonic temple
detroit symphony wagner meistersinger overture/strauss don juan/berlioz damnation de faust suite/copland rodeo/dvorak slavonic dance

8-10 december 1982/paris/salle pleyel
orchestre de paris haydn symphony 104/kodaly psalmus hungaricus/stravinsky firebird suite
kozma/ chorus

15 december 1982/london/royal festival hall
royal philharmonic *kodaly programme*
te deum/psalmus hungaricus/hary janos
kincses/ takacs/ molnar/ melis/ brighton festival chorus

21 january 1983/london/royal festival hall
royal philharmonic dvorak 3 slavonic dances/tchaikovsky violin concerto/tchaikovsky symphony 6
milstein

25 january 1983/london/royal festival hall
royal philharmonic debussy prélude a l'apres-midi/ravel piano concerto in g/ stravinsky le sacre du printemps
collard

1 february 1983/barcelona/palau de la musica
royal philharmonic walton facade/stravinsky le sacre du printemps

17-18 march 1983/rotterdam/de doelen
rotterdam philharmonic frid toccata/dorati cello concerto/dvorak symphony 6
cohen

22-24 march 1983/rotterdam/de doelen
rotterdam philharmonic vivaldi concerto for 4 violins/haydn symphony 100/beethoven symphony 6
orchestral soloists

25 march 1983/leiden/stadgehoorzaal
rotterdam philharmonic haydn symphony 100/mendelssohn violin concerto/beethoven symphony 6
verhey

7 may 1983/den bosch/casino
concertgebouw orchestra schubert symphony 8/haydn sinfonia concertante/tchaikovsky symphony 4
orchestral soloists

9 may 1983/amsterdam/concertgebouw
concertgebouw orchestra haydn sinfonia concertante/tchaikovsky symphony 5
orchestral solists

11 may 1983/utrecht/muziekcentrum vredenburg
concertgebouw orchestra bartok 2 portraits/haydn sinfonia concertante/tchaikovsky symphony 5
orchestral soloists

14 may 1983/amsterdam/concertgebouw
concertgebouw orchestra beethoven leonore 3 overture/bartok divertimento/ tchaikovsky symphony 6

15 may 1983/amsterdam/concertgebouw
concertgebouw orchestra beethoven leonore 3 overture/haydn sinfonia concertante/ tchaikovsky symphony 5
orchestral soloists

18 may 1983/barcelona/palau de la musica
concertgebouw orchestra — bartok divertimento/haydn sinfonia concertante/tchaikovsky symphony 4
orchestral soloists

19 may 1983/barcelona/palau de la musica
concertgebouw orchestra — bartok 2 portraits/schubert symphony 8/tchaikovsky symphony 5

20 may 1983/barcelona/palau de la musica
concertgebouw orchestra — beethoven leonore 3 overture/bartok concerto for orchestra/tchaikovsky symphony 6

23 may 1983/madrid
concertgebouw orchestra — *programme and soloists as for 18 may*

24 may 1983/madrid
concertgebouw orchestra — *programme as for 19 may*

25 may 1983/madrid
concertgebouw orchestra — *programme as for 20 may*

1 june 1983/stockholm/konserthuset
stockholm philharmonic — *beethoven cycle*
symphony 1/symphony 4/symphony 5

4 june 1983/stockholm/konserthuset
stockholm philharmonic — *beethoven cycle*
symphony 2/symphony 3

8 june 1983/stockholm/konserthuset
stockholm philharmonic — *beethoven cycle*
symphony 6/symphony 7

11 june 1983/stockholm/konserthuset
stockholm philharmonic — *beethoven cycle*
symphony 8/symphony 9
murphey/otter/westi/van halem/philharmonic chorus

24 and 26 june 1983/london/royal festival hall
royal philharmonic — beethoven missa solemnis
eathorne/watts/burrows/howell/brighton festival chorus

1983/tokyo
yomyuri symphony — haydn piano concerto in d/mahler symphony 1
alpenheim

19 november 1983/detroit/ford auditorium
detroit symphony — copland rodeo/strauss also sprach zarathustra/stravinsky firebird suite

29-30 january 1984/berlin/philharmonie
rso berlin — mahler symphony 9

13 february 1984/brussels/palais des beaux-arts
royal philharmonic — tippett ritual dances/beethoven piano concerto 2/tchaikovsky symphony 6
alpenheim

14 february 1984/berlin/philharmonie
royal philharmonic — haydn symphony 104/tippett ritual dances/beethoven symphony 6

15 february 1984/bonn/beethovenhalle
royal philharmonic — *programme as for 14 febtuary*

14-15 march 1984/amsterdam/concertgebouw
concertgebouw orchestra — haydn symphony 93/debussy prélude a l'apres-midi/scriabin poeme de l'extase

16-17 march 1984/amsterdam/concertgebouw
concertgebouw orchestra — mendelssohn hebrides overture/chopin piano concerto 1/debussy prélude a l'apres-midi/scriabin poeme de l'extase
alpenheim

19 march 1984/den bosch/casino
concertgebouw orchestra — *programme and soloist as for 16-17 march*

23 and 25 march 1984/amsterdam/concertgebouw
concertgebouw orchestra — vivaldi concerto a 2 cori/bartok music for strings percussion and celesta/brahms symphony 3

28-29 march 1984/basel/stadtkasino
basler sinfonie-orchester — strauss also sprach zarathustra/beethoven symphony 5

20 april 1984/budapest/state academy
hungarian state orchestra — haydn symphony 67/mozart piano concerto 27/beethoven symphony 6
alpenheim

20 april 1984/budapest/state academy
hungarian state orchestra — schubert symphony 8/mozart piano concerto 9/dorati symphony
alpenheim

26 april 1984/budapest/state academy
hungarian radio orchestra — mahler symphony 2
takacs/temesi/hungarian radio chorus

1-3 may 1984/rotterdam/de doelen
rotterdam philharmonic — mozart symphony 40/strauss ein heldenleben

5-6 may 1984/rotterdam/de doelen
rotterdam philharmonic — rossini gazza ladra overture/casella la giara/puccini manon lescaut intermezzo/verdi la traviata preludes/wolf-ferrari gioielli della madonna intermezzo/respighi pini di roma

july 1984/budapest/erkel theatre
hungarian state orchestra — haydn symphony 45/mozart piano concerto 27/beethoven symphony 6
alpenheim

8 august 1984/bolzano/duomo
european community youth orchestra — strauss till eulenspiegel/dvorak cello concerto/bartok concerto for orchestra
cohen

9 august 1984/roveretto/teatro zandonai
european community youth orchestra — *programme and soloist as for 8 august*

11 august 1984/feldbach/schwabenlandhalle
european community youth orchestra — dvorak cello concerto/bartok concerto for orchestra
cohen

17 august 1984/lucerne/kunsthaus
european community youth orchestra — *programme and soloist as for 8 august*

3 october 1984/london/royal festival hall
royal philharmonic debussy prélude a l'apres-midi/bartok violin concerto 2/berlioz symphonie fantastique
menuhin

10-12 october 1984/milan/teatro alla scala
la scala orchestra haydn symphony 55/mozart piano concerto 27/bartok concerto for orchestra
alpenheim

18-20 october 1984/detroit/ford auditorium
detroit symphony *stravinsky programme*
scherzo fantastique/apollon musagete/symphony in e flat

23-24 october 1984/washington/cathedral
smithsonian orchestra handel messiah
mathis/bown/ahnsjö/krause/maryland and cathedral choirs

25-27 october 1984/detroit/ford auditorium
detroit symphony copland appalachian spring/mendelssohn violin concerto/brahms symphony 2
milstein

30 october 1984/detroit/ford auditorium
detroit symphony stravinsky apollon musagete/copland appalachian spring/stravinsky scherzo fantastique/stravinsky symphony in e flat

15-17 november 1984/pittsburgh/heinz hall
pittsburgh symphony beethoven symphony 1/brahms symphony 1

23-25 november 1984/pittsburgh/heinz hall
pittsburgh symphony haydn piano concerto in d/mahler symphony 5
alpenheim

5 december 1984/basel/stadtkasino
basler sinfonie-orchester haydn symphony 85/mozart piano concerto 27/beethoven symphony 6
alpenheim

9-10 december 1984/washington/cathedral
smithsonian orchestra *programme and soloists as for 23-24 october*

9-10 january 1985/basel/stadtkasino
basler sinfonie-orchester kodaly peacock variations/debussy la mer/stravinsky firebird suite

27-29 january 1985/berlin/philharmonie
rso berlin	beethoven missa solemnis
	varady/finnilä/laubenthal/sotin/saint hedwig's choir

17-19 february 1985/hamburg/musikhalle
philharmonisches	haydn symphony 101/haydn piano concerto in d/bartok
staatsorchester	miraculous mandarin suite
	alpenheim

27-29 march 1985/budapest/opera house
budapest opera	beethoven fidelio
orchestra	*kasza/zempleni/molnar/solyom-nagy/bandi/gati/polgar/opera chorus*

17-18 april 1985/amsterdam/concertgebouw
concertgebouw	schubert rosamunde excerpts/schumann piano concerto/brahms
orchestra	symphony 4
	schiff

20 april 1985/den haag/congresgebouw
concertgebouw	*programme and soloist as for 17-18 april*
orchestra

27-28 april 1985/amsterdam/concertgebouw
concertgebouw	haydn symphony 104/beethoven symphony 9
orchestra	*alexander/van nes/laubenthal/mroz/toonkunst choir*

2-4 may 1985/stockholm/konserthuset
stockholm	kodaly hungarian rondo/dorati cello concerto/tchaikovsky
philharmonic	symphony 6
	cohen

25 may 1985/bergen/grieghallen
concertgebouw	bartok concerto for orchestra/tchaikovsky symphony 6
orchestra

26 may 1985/bergen/grieghallen
concertgebouw	haydn symphony 104/brahms symphony 4
orchestra

28 may 1985/london/royal festival hall
royal	barber adagio/dorati night music/bach brandenburg concerto 4/
philharmonic	william schuman new england triptych
	rampal

4 june 1985/london/royal festival hall
royal　　　　　　　bach suite 3/brahms violin concerto/brahms symphony 2
philharmonic　　　　*milstein*

11 june 1985/vaduz/theater am kirchplatz
basler sinfonie-　　　verdi messa da requiem
orchester　　　　　　*kincses/ takacs/ nagy/ kovacs/ american university choirs*

14 june 1985/basel/stadtkasino
basler sinfonie-　　　*programme and soloists as for 11 june*
orchester

5 july 1985/amsterdam/concertgebouw
concertgebouw　　　beethoven symphony 9
orchestra　　　　　　*alexander/ van nes/ laubenthal/ mrozs/ toonkunst choir*

6 july 1985/kerkrade/rodahal
concertgebouw　　　*programme and soloists as for 27-28 april*
orchestra

25 september 1985/budapest/state academy
hungarian state　　　*bartok programme*
orchestra　　　　　　psalmus hungaricus/concerto for orchestra
　　　　　　　　　　nagy/ hungarian state chorus

8 october 1985/london/royal festival hall
royal　　　　　　　*beethoven programme*
philharmonic　　　　egmont overture/violin concerto/symphony 6
　　　　　　　　　　stern

10 october 1985/london/royal festival hall
royal　　　　　　　*beethoven programme*
philharmonic　　　　symphony 1/triple concerto/symphony 5
　　　　　　　　　　de la pau/ y-p tortelier/ p tortelier

31 october-2 november 1985/detroit/ford auditorium
detroit　　　　　　　mozart 2 marches/mozart piano concerto 27/mahler symphony 1
symphony　　　　　　*alpenheim*

7-9 november 1985/detroit/ford auditorium
detroit　　　　　　　berger concerto manuale/tchaikovsky symphony 6
symphony

14-16 november 1985/detroit/ford auditorium
detroit　　　　　　　brahms symphony 3/beethoven symphony 6
symphony

23 november 1985/washington/constitution hall
national symphony   bartok concerto for orchestra/brahms symphony 1

5 december 1985/london/royal festival hall
royal philharmonic   *beethoven programme*
coriolan overture/piano concerto 3/symphony 3
ashkenazy

9 december 1985/london/royal festival hall
royal philharmonic   *beethoven programme*
symphony 2/piano concerto 4/symphony 8
ashkenazy

12 december 1985/brussels/palais des beaux-arts
orchestre national de belgique   haydn symphony 3/mozart piano concerto 27/brahms symphony 4
alpenheim

18-19 december 1985/basel/stadtkasino
basler sinfonie-orchester   bartok concerto for orchestra/tchaikovsky symphony 6

15-16 january 1986/basel/stadtkasino
basler sinfonie-orchester   strauss wind serenade/puccini crisantemi/dorati trittico/haydn symphony 101
holliger

12-13 february 1986/basel/stadtkasino
basler sinfonie-orchester   *brahms programme*
piano concerto 2/symphony 2
gelber

5-7 march 1986/amsterdam/concertgebouw
concertgebouw orchestra   mozart symphony 38/mahler symphony 4
valente

9 march 1986/den haag/congresgebouw
concertgebouw orchestra   *programme and soloist as for 5-7 march*

17 march 1986/budapest/erkel theatre
hungarian radio beethoven missa solemnis
orchestra *soloists/ hungarian radio chorus*

20 march 1986/budapest/congress theatre
hungarian state dorati piano concerto/liszt dante symphony
orchestra *alpenheim*

9 april 1986/london/royal festival hall
royal *beethoven programme to mark dorati's eightieth birthday*
philharmonic piano concerto 2/symphony 9
 alpenheim/ csavlek/ komlosi/ fülop/ kovacs/ brighton festival chorus

2 may 1986/stuttgart/staatstheater
orchester der janacek jenufa
württembergischen *schmeizer/ randova/ jung*
staatsoper *further performances may have been given*

14 may 1986/amsterdam/concertgebouw
concertgebouw dorati symphony 2/mozart piano concerto 9/beethoven
orchestra symphony 7
 alpenheim

15-16 may 1986/den haag/congresgebouw
concertgebouw *programme as for 14 may*
orchestra

22 may 1986/stockholm/konserthuset
stockholm mozart symphony 33/mozart piano concerto 17/stravinsky
philharmonic firebird suite
 alpenheim

28-31 may 1986/stockholm/konserthuset
stockholm beethoven missa solemnis
philharmonic *aruhn/ svenden/ s.dalberg/ scharinger/ philharmonic chorus*

16 june 1986/london/royal festival hall
royal haydn symphony 104/bruch violin concerto 1/franck symphony
philharmonic *stern*

12 august 1986/gstaad/saanen church
english chamber bach suite 1/bach oboe and violin concerto/dorati trittico/
orchestra dvorak serenade for strings
 menuhin/ holliger

3 september 1986/torino/chiesa san filipo
royal *beethoven programme*
philharmonic symphony 6/symphony 7

10 november 1986/lausanne/théatre de beaulieu
lausanne chamber orchestra kodaly-dorati variations/mozart piano concerto 17/dorati american serenade/haydn symphony 85
alpenheim

18 november 1986/berlin/sfb sendessaal
rso berlin brahms ein deutsches requiem
mathis/schmidt/philharmonisches chor berlin

19 november 1986/london/royal festival hall
royal philharmonic handel-beecham the gods go a'begging/haydn symphony 3/bach double violin concerto/chausson poeme/delius walk to the paradise garden
menuhin/chen

27 november 1986/london/royal festival hall
royal philharmonic *brahms programme*
academic festival overture/piano concerto 2/symphony 2
bolet

4-5 december 1986/bern/kasino
berner sinfonie-orchester beethoven symphony 6/bartok concerto for orchestra

7-8 january 1987/basel/stadtkasino
basler sinfonie-orchester *bartok programme*
2 portraits/bluebeard's castle
tacacs/kovacs/olsen

21-22 january 1987/basel/stadtkasino
basler sinfonie-orchester liszt a faust symphony
laubenthal/basler liedertafel

29 january 1987/lausanne/théatre de beaulieu
orchestre de la suisse romande mozart symphony 14/bruckner symphony 9

4-6 february 1987/basel/stadtkasino
basler sinfonie-orchester *schubert programme*
symphony 8/rosamunde excerpts/song arrangements by brahms and webern/alfonso und estella excerpts
mathis/basel radio choir

18-19 february 1987/basel/stadtkasino
basler sinfonie-orchester *schumann programme*
braut von messina overture/piano concerto/symphony 3
alpenheim

14-15 march 1987/florence/teatro communale
maggio musicale   mozart piano concerto 17/beethoven symphony 3
orchestra   *alpenheim*

17 march 1987/pistoia/auditorio
maggio musicale   *programme and soloist as for 14-15 march*
orchestra

18-19 march 1987/florence/teatro communale
maggio musicale   *programme and soloist as for 14-15 march*
orchestra

26-29 march 1987/florence/teatro communale
maggio musicale   *bartok programme*
orchestra   hary janos suite/bluebeard's castle
                         budai/polgar/moroguidelli

3 april 1987/amsterdam/concertgebouw
concertgebouw   debussy images/brahms symphony 2
orchestra

4 april 1987/utrecht/muziekcentrum vredenburg
concertgebouw   *programme as for 3 april*
orchestra

5 april 1987/amsterdam/concertgebouw
concertgebouw   *programme as for 3 april*
orchestra

21 april 1987/berlin/schauspielhaus
junge deutsche   beethoven symphony 7/bartok bluebeard's castle
philharmonie   *tacacs/kovacs/misske/dorati*

22 april 1987/frankfurt-am-main/alte oper
junge deutsche   *programme and soloists as for 21 april*
philharmonie

24 april 1987/hamburg-farmsen/rudolf-steiner-schule
junge deutsche   *programme and soloists as for 21 april*
philharmonie

25 april 1987/hamburg/musikhalle
junge deutsche   *programme and soloists as for 21 april*
philharmonie

26 april 1987/cologne/philharmonie
junge deutsche   *programme and soloists as for 21 april*
philharmonie

5 may 1987/london/royal festival hall
royal　　　　　　*brahms programme*
philharmonic　　haydn variations/violin concerto/symphony 3
　　　　　　　　mutter

6 may 1987/newbury/saint nicholas church
royal　　　　　　*brahms programme*
philharmonic　　haydn variations/violin concerto/symphony 3
　　　　　　　　pauk

7 may 1987/cardiff/saint david's hall
royal　　　　　　*programme and soloist as for 6 may*
philharmonic

12 may 1987/berlin/schauspielhaus
royal　　　　　　beethoven leonore 3 overture/mozart piano concerto 27/
philharmonic　　brahms symphony 4
　　　　　　　　alpenheim

26 june 1987/thun/stadthalle
english chamber　*mozart programme*
orchestra　　　　flute and harp concerto/piano concerto 9/symphony 33
　　　　　　　　studer/holliger/graf

27 june 1987/thun/stadthalle
english chamber　*mozart programme*
orchestra　　　　flute and harp concerto/piano concerto 14/symphony 33
　　　　　　　　dähler/holliger/graf

14-15 october 1987/basel/stadtkasino
basler sinfonie-　haydn symphony 1/haydn symphony 104/mozart symphony 1/
orchester　　　　mozart symphony 41

28-30 october 1987/basel/stadtkasino
basler sinfonie-　haydn symphony 67/brahms piano concerto 1
otchester　　　　*schiff*

12 november 1987/london/royal festival hall
royal　　　　　　*tchaikovsky programme*
philharmonic　　romeo and juliet/violin concerto/symphony 6
　　　　　　　　bell

15 november 1987/london/royal festival hall
royal　　　　　　*tchaikovsky programme*
philharmonic　　romeo and juliet/piano concerto 1/symphony 6
　　　　　　　　virsaldze

18-21 november 1987/amsterdam/concertgebouw
concertgebouw debussy l'enfant prodigue/mozart symphony 41
orchestra *greenawald/van der meel/smit*

25-27 november 1987/amsterdam/concertgebouw
concertgebouw kodaly peacock variations/liszt piano concerto 1/bartok
orchestra concerto for orchestra
  kocsis

16-17 december 1987/basel/stadtkasino
basler sinfonie- haydn symphony 99/bruckner symphony 9
orchester

1987/stockholm/konserthuset
stockholm bruckner symphony 7
philharmonic

18-19 february 1988/bern/kasino
berner sinfonie- *beethoven programme*
orchester triple concerto/symphony 3
  alpenheim/ozim/grimmer

26 february 1988/leverkusen/forum
orchester der berlioz symphonie fantastique
beethovenhalle *concert also included beethoven king srephen overture and dorati symphony 2 conducted by dennis russell-davies*

15 april 1988/lugano/palazzo dei congressi
royal haydn symphony 104/tchaikovsky symphony 6
philharmonic

25 april 1988/amsterdam/concertgebouw
royal haydn symphony 104/bruckner symphony 4
philharmonic

29 april 1988/london/royal festival hall
royal   beethoven missa solemnis
philharmonic   *pickens/van nes/tear/dean/brighton festival chorus*

6 may 1988/brighton/dome
royal   beethoven missa solemnis
philharmonic   *falcon/van nes/tear/dean/brighton festival chorus*

18 may 1988/stockholm/konserthuset
stockholm   mahler symphony 4
philharmonic   *söderström*

25-26 may 1988/stockholm/konserthuset
stockholm   dorati symphony 2/brahms schicksalslied/kodaly psalmus hungaricus
philharmonic   *gulyas/philharmonic chorus*

16 june 1988/basel/volkshaus
basel radio   haydn symphony 99/debussy clarinet rhapsody/bartok concerto
orchestra   for orchestra
                 melchior-maurer

3 july 1988/berlin/philharmonie
european   beethoven missa solemnis
symphony   *kiberg/lang/cochran/krutikov/maryland university choir*

4 july 1988/moscow/tchaikovsky hall
european   beethoven missa solemnis
symphony   *martig-tüller/lang/cochran/krutikov/maryland university choir*

6 july 1988/dresden/semperoper
european   *programme and soloists as for 4 july*
symphony

7 july 1988/london/royal albert hall
european   *programme and soloists as for 4 july*
symphony

these 4 performances of missa solemnis were promoted by world peace organisation and were dorati's final public conducting appearances

late additions to the dorati concert register: concerts with the netherlands radio philharmonic orchestra 1951-1957
these were radio concerts unless otherwise stated; research by roderick krüsemann
works are not necessarily listed in order of performance

6 september 1951
ravel la valse/rossini cenerentola overture/haydn symphony 96

7 september 1951
piston toccata/dvorak symphony 8

11 september 1951
mozart symphony 34/stravinsky orpheus/mozart idomeneo overture and ballet music

13 september 1951
brahms programme haydn variations/symphony 2

16 september 1951
beethoven programme leonore 3 overture/violin concerto *krebbers*

17 september 1951
beethoven symphony 5/william schuman prayer in time of war/schoenberg survivor from warsaw *nierop/groot omroepkoor*

20 september 1951
casella paganiniana/bizet symphony 1/strauss don juan

21 september 1951
kodaly psalmus hungaricus/mussorgsky-ravel pictures from an exhibition
draayer/groot omroepkooe

23 september 1951
debussy ibéria/berlioz benvenuto cellini overture/chausson poeme de l'amour et de la mer *vincent*

7 september 1952
ravel rapsodie espagnole/roussel suite in f/debussy 3 nocturnes *omroepvrouwenkoor*

10 september 1952
stravinsky programme mass/symphony in c *omroepkoor*

13 september 1952
mahler das klagende lied *lindeman/boelsma/draayer/groot omroepkoor*

15 september 1952
respighi pini di roma/rossini cenerentola overture/clementi symphony 1

late additions to the concert register/continued
18 september 1952
bach orchestral suite 3/bartok orchestral suite no 2

22 september 1952
badings symphonic prologue/hindemith harmonie der welt

25 september 1952
ravel daphnis et chloé *groot omroepkoor*

15 august 1956
tchaikovsky piano concerto 1/mozart symphony 35/stravinsky firebird suite/rossini italiana in algeri overture/barber medea's meditation and dance of vengeance

17 august 1956
schubert symphony 9/badings largo and allegro/grieg piano concerto

22 august 1956/scheveningen/kurhaus
beethoven programme symphony 5/symphony 8/piano concerto 3 *del pueyo*

24 august 1956
ravel piano concerto in g/dvorak symphony 5/berlioz benvenuto cellini overture/ravel rapsodie espagnole *haas*

29 august 1956
strauss don juan/strauss burleske/mahler symphony 4 *bijster/arrau*

31 august 1956
brahms programme symphony 1/academic festival overture/piano concerto 2 *arrau*

19 august 1957
tchaikovsky symphony 6/andriessen kuhnau variations/mozart flute and harp concerto *ragetli/bonsel*

21 august 1957/scheveningen/kurhaus
bach violin concerto 1/mahler symphony 1/vivaldi concerto/bach brandenburg concerto 3 *krebbers*

23 august 1957
tchaikovsky symphony 6/badings symphonic prologue/dvorak piano concerto *firkusny*

30 august 1957/scheveningen/kurhaus
bartok concerto for orchestra/schubert symphony 8/mozart piano concerto 27 *askenase*

late additions to the dorati concert register: concerts with the residentie orkest
research by roderick krüsemann

8 june 1949/scheveningen/kurzaal
mozart zauberflöte overture/mendelssohn symphony 4/weber wie nahte mir der schlummer/negro spirituals/tchaikovsky romeo and juliet/kodaly hary janos suite
e.davis

10 june 1949/scheveningen/kurzaal
brahms programme haydn variations/violin concerto/symphony 4 *neveu*

6 september 1950/scheveningen/kurzaal
brahms symphony 1/ravel piano concerto in g/ravel daphnis et chloé second suite
henriot-schweitzer

8 september 1950/scheveningen/kurzaal
tchaikovsky programme romeo and juliet/piano concerto 1/symphony 5
henriot-schweitzer

15 september 1950/scheveningen/kurzaal
andriessen kuhnau variations/beethoven piano concerto 5/kodaly hary suite/strauss till eulenspiegel *de groot*

15 june 1951/scheveningen/kurzaal
orthel sinfonia piccola/beethoven piano concerto 4/bartok music for strings percussion and celesta/strauss till eulenspiegel *casadesus*

16 june 1951/den haag/houtrusthallen
beethoven egmont overture/franck symphony in d minor/frid paradou/tchaikovsky romeo and juliet

19 june 1951/amsterdam/concertgebouw
schubert symphony 5/bartok violin concerto 2/frid paradou/kodaly hary janos suite
olof

21 june 1951/scheveningen/kurzaal
programme and soloist as for 19 june

15 august 1951/scheveningen/kurzaal
beethoven programme egmont complete incidental music/ah perfido!/symphony 3
brouwenstijn

17 august 1951/scheveningen/kurzaal
piston toccata/rachmaninov paganini rhapsody/berlioz symphonie fantastique
simon

22 august 1951/scheveningen/kurzaal
brahms programme academic festival overture/piano concerto 1/symphony 4 *cherkassky*

24 august 1951/scheveningen/kurzaal
smetana moldau/brahms violin concerto/bartok concerto for orchestra *stern*

1 march 1961/den haag/gebouw voor kunsten en wetenschappen
mahler symphony 7

2 march 1961/leiden/stadsgehoorzaal
programme as for 1 march

3 march 1961/den haag/gebouw voor kunsten en wetenschappen
clementi symphony in d/falla homenajes/falla sombrero de 3 picos/vocal works by vivaldi, mozart and falla *rubio*

6 march 1961/hilversum/grand theatre gooiland
programme and soloist as for 3 march

8 march 1961/gouda/nieuwe schouwburg
clementi symphony in d/handel harp concerto/hindemith mathis der maler/falla sombrero de 3 picos *witsenburg*

11 march 1961/den haag/gebouw voor kunsten en wetenschappen
beethoven weihe des hauses/mozart violin concerto 5/mozart violin concerto 3/ beethoven symphony 4 *d. and i.oistrakh*

15 march 1961/den haag/gebouw voor kunsten en wetenschappen
pijper 6 epigrams/ravel piano concerto in g/hindemith mathis der maler/falla sombrero de 3 picos *francois*

17 march 1961/dordrecht/kunstmin
pijper 6 epigrams/ravel piano concerto in g/beethoven symphony 4 *francois*

20 march 1961/delft/stadsdoelen
pijper 6 epigrams/mozart violin concerto 4/beethoven symphony 4 *hagen*

22 march 1961/den haag/gebouw voor kunsten en wetenschappen
bartok piano concerto 2/bruckner symphony 7 *richter-haaser*

23 march 1961/leiden/stadsgehoorzaal
programme and soloist as for 22 march

25 march 1961/den haag/gebouw voor kunsten en wetenschappen
mozart symphony 1/mozart symphony 41/beethoven symphony 3

27 february 1963/den haag/gebouw voor kunsten en wetenschappen
boyce symphony 5/britten young person's guide/bartok piano concerto 3/brahms symphony 2 *anda*

28 february 1963/leiden/stadsgehoorzaal
britten young person's guide/paganini violin concerto 1/brahms symphony 2 *ricci*

4 march 1963/delft stadsdoelen
britten young person's guide/dvorak violin concerto/brahms symphony 2 *ricci*

6 march 1963/den haag/gebouw voor kunsten en wetenschappen
berg three pieces op 6/dvorak violin concerto/beethoven symphony 5 *ricci*

8 march 1963/den haag/gebouw voor kunsten en wetenschappen
mozart symphony 31/mozart piano concerto 26/berg three pieces op 6/ravel daphnis et chloé second suite *casadesus*

9 march 1963/den haag/gebouw voor kunsten en wetenschappen
mozart symphony 31/schumann cello concerto/berg three pieces op 6/ravel daphnis et chloé second suite *gendron*

11 march 1963/hilversum/grand theatre gooiland
schubert symphony 8/dvorak violin concerto/brahms symphony 2 *ricci*

13 march 1963/den haag/gebouw voor kunsten en wetenschappen
schubert symphony 8/mahler das lied von der erde *ludwig/lewis*

14 march 1963/leiden/stadsgehoorzaal
programme and soloists as for 13 march

programmes listed as late additions should be read in conjunction with the main concert register

Discographies by Travis & Emery:
Discographies by John Hunt.

1987: 978-1-906857-14-1: From Adam to Webern: the Recordings of von Karajan.
1991: 978-0-951026-83-0: 3 Italian Conductors and 7 Viennese Sopranos: 10 Discographies: Arturo Toscanini, Guido Cantelli, Carlo Maria Giulini, Elisabeth Schwarzkopf, Irmgard Seefried, Elisabeth Gruemmer, Sena Jurinac, Hilde Gueden, Lisa Della Casa, Rita Streich.
1992: 978-0-951026-85-4: Mid-Century Conductors and More Viennese Singers: 10 Discographies: Karl Boehm, Victor De Sabata, Hans Knappertsbusch, Tullio Serafin, Clemens Krauss, Anton Dermota, Leonie Rysanek, Eberhard Waechter, Maria Reining, Erich Kunz.
1993: 978-0-951026-87-8: More 20th Century Conductors: 7 Discographies: Eugen Jochum, Ferenc Fricsay, Carl Schuricht, Felix Weingartner, Josef Krips, Otto Klemperer, Erich Kleiber.
1994: 978-0-951026-88-5: Giants of the Keyboard: 6 Discographies: Wilhelm Kempff, Walter Gieseking, Edwin Fischer, Clara Haskil, Wilhelm Backhaus, Artur Schnabel.
1994: 978-0-951026-89-2: Six Wagnerian Sopranos: 6 Discographies: Frieda Leider, Kirsten Flagstad, Astrid Varnay, Martha Moedl, Birgit Nilsson, Gwyneth Jones.
1995: 978-0-952582-70-0: Musical Knights: 6 Discographies: Henry Wood, Thomas Beecham, Adrian Boult, John Barbirolli, Reginald Goodall, Malcolm Sargent.
1995: 978-0-952582-71-7: A Notable Quartet: 4 Discographies: Gundula Janowitz, Christa Ludwig, Nicolai Gedda, Dietrich Fischer-Dieskau.
1996: 978-0-952582-72-4: The Post-War German Tradition: 5 Discographies: Rudolf Kempe, Joseph Keilberth, Wolfgang Sawallisch, Rafael Kubelik, Andre Cluytens.
1996: 978-0-952582-73-1: Teachers and Pupils: 7 Discographies: Elisabeth Schwarzkopf, Maria Ivoguen, Maria Cebotari, Meta Seinemeyer, Ljuba Welitsch, Rita Streich, Erna Berger.
1996: 978-0-952582-77-9: Tenors in a Lyric Tradition: 3 Discographies: Peter Anders, Walther Ludwig, Fritz Wunderlich.
1997: 978-0-952582-78-6: The Lyric Baritone: 5 Discographies: Hans Reinmar, Gerhard Huesch, Josef Metternich, Hermann Uhde, Eberhard Waechter.
1997: 978-0-952582-79-3: Hungarians in Exile: 3 Discographies: Fritz Reiner, Antal Dorati, George Szell.
1997: 978-1-901395-00-6: The Art of the Diva: 3 Discographies: Claudia Muzio, Maria Callas, Magda Olivero.
1997: 978-1-901395-01-3: Metropolitan Sopranos: 4 Discographies: Rosa Ponselle, Eleanor Steber, Zinka Milanov, Leontyne Price.
1997: 978-1-901395-02-0: Back From The Shadows: 4 Discographies: Willem Mengelberg, Dimitri Mitropoulos, Hermann Abendroth, Eduard Van Beinum.
1997: 978-1-901395-03-7: More Musical Knights: 4 Discographies: Hamilton Harty, Charles Mackerras, Simon Rattle, John Pritchard.
1998: 978-1-901395-94-5: Conductors On The Yellow Label: 8 Discographies: Fritz Lehmann, Ferdinand Leitner, Ferenc Fricsay, Eugen Jochum, Leopold Ludwig, Artur Rother, Franz Konwitschny, Igor Markevitch.
1998: 978-1-901395-95-2: More Giants of the Keyboard: 5 Discographies: Claudio Arrau, Gyorgy Cziffra, Vladimir Horowitz, Dinu Lipatti, Artur Rubinstein.
1998: 978-1-901395-96-9: Mezzo and Contraltos: 5 Discographies: Janet Baker, Margarete Klose, Kathleen Ferrier, Giulietta Simionato, Elisabeth Hoengen.

1999: 978-1-901395-97-6: The Furtwaengler Sound Sixth Edition: Discography and Concert Listing.
1999: 978-1-901395-98-3: The Great Dictators: 3 Discographies: Evgeny Mravinsky, Artur Rodzinski, Sergiu Celibidache.
1999: 978-1-901395-99-0: Sviatoslav Richter: Pianist of the Century: Discography.
2000: 978-1-901395-04-4: Philharmonic Autocrat 1: Discography of: Herbert Von Karajan [Third Edition].
2000: 978-1-901395-05-1: Wiener Philharmoniker 1 - Vienna Philharmonic and Vienna State Opera Orchestras: Discography Part 1 1905-1954.
2000: 978-1-901395-06-8: Wiener Philharmoniker 2 - Vienna Philharmonic and Vienna State Opera Orchestras: Discography Part 2 1954-1989.
2001: 978-1-901395-07-5: Gramophone Stalwarts: 3 Separate Discographies: Bruno Walter, Erich Leinsdorf, Georg Solti.
2001: 978-1-901395-08-2: Singers of the Third Reich: 5 Discographies: Helge Roswaenge, Tiana Lemnitz, Franz Voelker, Maria Mueller, Max Lorenz.
2001: 978-1-901395-09-9: Philharmonic Autocrat 2: Concert Register of Herbert Von Karajan Second Edition.
2002: 978-1-901395-10-5: Sächsische Staatskapelle Dresden: Complete Discography.
2002: 978-1-901395-11-2: Carlo Maria Giulini: Discography and Concert Register.
2002: 978-1-901395-12-9: Pianists For The Connoisseur: 6 Discographies: Arturo Benedetti Michelangeli, Alfred Cortot, Alexis Weissenberg, Clifford Curzon, Solomon, Elly Ney.
2003: 978-1-901395-14-3: Singers on the Yellow Label: 7 Discographies: Maria Stader, Elfriede Troetschel, Annelies Kupper, Wolfgang Windgassen, Ernst Haefliger, Josef Greindl, Kim Borg.
2003: 978-1-901395-15-0: A Gallic Trio: 3 Discographies: Charles Muench, Paul Paray, Pierre Monteux.
2004: 978-1-901395-16-7: Antal Dorati 1906-1988: Discography and Concert Register.
2004: 978-1-901395-17-4: Columbia 33CX Label Discography.
2004: 978-1-901395-18-1: Great Violinists: 3 Discographies: David Oistrakh, Wolfgang Schneiderhan, Arthur Grumiaux.
2006: 978-1-901395-19-8: Leopold Stokowski: Second Edition of the Discography.
2006: 978-1-901395-20-4: Wagner Im Festspielhaus: Discography of the Bayreuth Festival.
2006: 978-1-901395-21-1: Her Master's Voice: Concert Register and Discography of Dame Elisabeth Schwarzkopf [Third Edition].
2007: 978-1-901395-22-8: Hans Knappertsbusch: Kna: Concert Register and Discography of Hans Knappertsbusch, 1888-1965. Second Edition.
2008: 978-1-901395-23-5: Philips Minigroove: Second Extended Version of the European Discography.
2009: 978-1-901395--24-2: American Classics: The Discographies of Leonard Bernstein and Eugene Ormandy.

Discography by Stephen J. Pettitt, edited by John Hunt:
1987: 978-1-906857-16-5: Philharmonia Orchestra: Complete Discography 1945-1987

Available from: Travis & Emery at 17 Cecil Court, London, UK. (+44) 20 7 240 2129. email on sales@travis-and-emery.com .

© Travis & Emery 2009

Music and Books published by Travis & Emery Music Bookshop:
Anon.: Hymnarium Sarisburiense, cum Rubricis et Notis Musicis.
Agricola, Johann Friedrich from Tosi: Anleitung zur Singkunst.
Bach, C.P.E.: edited W. Emery: Nekrolog or Obituary Notice of J.S. Bach.
Bateson, Naomi Judith: Alcock of Salisbury
Bathe, William: A Briefe Introduction to the Skill of Song
Bax, Arnold: Symphony #5, Arranged for Piano Four Hands by Walter Emery
Burney, Charles: The Present State of Music in France and Italy
Burney, Charles: The Present State of Music in Germany, The Netherlands ...
Burney, Charles: An Account of the Musical Performances ... Handel
Burney, Karl: Nachricht von Georg Friedrich Handel's Lebensumstanden.
Cobbett, W.W.: Cobbett's Cyclopedic Survey of Chamber Music. (2 vols.)
Corrette, Michel: Le Maitre de Clavecin
Crimp, Bryan: Dear Mr. Rosenthal ... Dear Mr. Gaisberg ...
Crimp, Bryan: Solo: The Biography of Solomon
d'Indy, Vincent: Beethoven: Biographie Critique
d'Indy, Vincent: Beethoven: A Critical Biography
d'Indy, Vincent: César Franck (in French)
Frescobaldi, Girolamo: D'Arie Musicali per Cantarsi. Primo & Secondo Libro.
Geminiani, Francesco: The Art of Playing the Violin.
Handel; Purcell; Boyce; Geene et al: Calliope or English Harmony: Volume First.
Häuser: Musikalisches Lexikon. 2 vols in one.
Hawkins, John: A General History of the Science and Practice of Music (5 vols.)
Herbert-Caesari, Edgar: The Science and Sensations of Vocal Tone
Herbert-Caesari, Edgar: Vocal Truth
Hopkins and Rimboult: The Organ. Its History and Construction.
Hunt, John: Adam to Webern: the recordings of von Karajan
Isaacs, Lewis: Hänsel and Gretel. A Guide to Humperdinck's Opera.
Isaacs, Lewis: Königskinder (Royal Children) A Guide to Humperdinck's Opera.
Kastner: Manuel Général de Musique Militaire
Lacassagne, M. l'Abbé Joseph : Traité Général des élémens du Chant.
Lascelles (née Catley), Anne: The Life of Miss Anne Catley.
Mainwaring, John: Memoirs of the Life of the Late George Frederic Handel
Malcolm, Alexander: A Treaty of Music: Speculative, Practical and Historical
Marx, Adolph Bernhard: Die Kunst des Gesanges, Theoretisch-Practisch
May, Florence: The Life of Brahms
May, Florence: The Girlhood Of Clara Schumann: Clara Wieck And Her Time.
Mellers, Wilfrid: Angels of the Night: Popular Female Singers of Our Time
Mellers, Wilfrid: Bach and the Dance of God
Mellers, Wilfrid: Beethoven and the Voice of God
Mellers, Wilfrid: Caliban Reborn - Renewal in Twentieth Century Music

Music and Books published by Travis & Emery Music Bookshop:
Mellers, Wilfrid: François Couperin and the French Classical Tradition
Mellers, Wilfrid: Harmonious Meeting
Mellers, Wilfrid: Le Jardin Retrouvé, The Music of Frederic Mompou
Mellers, Wilfrid: Music and Society, England and the European Tradition
Mellers, Wilfrid: Music in a New Found Land: ... ... American Music
Mellers, Wilfrid: Romanticism and the Twentieth Century (from 1800)
Mellers, Wilfrid: The Masks of Orpheus: ...... the Story of European Music.
Mellers, Wilfrid: The Sonata Principle (from c. 1750)
Mellers, Wilfrid: Vaughan Williams and the Vision of Albion
Panchianio, Cattuffio: Rutzvanscad Il Giovine
Pearce, Charles: Sims Reeves, Fifty Years of Music in England.
Playford, John: An Introduction to the Skill of Musick.
Purcell, Henry et al: Harmonia Sacra ... The First Book, (1726)
Purcell, Henry et al: Harmonia Sacra ... Book II (1726)
Quantz, Johann: Versuch einer Anweisung die Flöte traversiere zu spielen.
Rameau, Jean-Philippe: Code de Musique Pratique, ou Methodes.
Rastall, Richard: The Notation of Western Music.
Rimbault, Edward: The Pianoforte, Its Origins, Progress, and Construction.
Rousseau, Jean Jacques: Dictionnaire de Musique
Rubinstein, Anton : Guide to the proper use of the Pianoforte Pedals.
Sainsbury, John S.: Dictionary of Musicians. Vol. 1. (1825). 2 vols.
Serré de Rieux, Jean de : Les dons des Enfans de Latone
Simpson, Christopher: A Compendium of Practical Musick in Five Parts
Spohr, Louis: Autobiography
Spohr, Louis: Grand Violin School
Tans'ur, William: A New Musical Grammar; or The Harmonical Spectator
Terry, Charles Sanford: J.S. Bach's Original Hymn-Tunes for Congregational Use.
Terry, Charles Sanford: Four-Part Chorals of J.S. Bach. (German & English)
Terry, Charles Sanford: Joh. Seb. Bach, Cantata Texts, Sacred and Secular.
Terry, Charles Sanford: The Origins of the Family of Bach Musicians.
Tosi, Pierfrancesco: Opinioni de' Cantori Antichi, e Moderni
Van der Straeten, Edmund: History of the Violoncello, The Viol da Gamba ...
Van der Straeten, Edmund: History of the Violin, Its Ancestors... (2 vols.)
Waltern: Musikalisches Lexicon
Walther, J. G.: Musicalisches Lexikon ober Musicalische Bibliothec

Travis & Emery Music Bookshop
17 Cecil Court, London, WC2N 4EZ, United Kingdom.
Tel. (+44) 20 7240 2129

© Travis & Emery 2009

www.ingramcontent.com/pod-product-compliance
Lightning Source LLC
Chambersburg PA
CBHW052053230426
43671CB00011B/1892